Department of Health
Welsh Office
Scottish Office Department of Health
DHSS (Northern Ireland)

1 9 9 6

Immunisation

against

Infectious

Disease

Edited by
Dr David M Salisbury
and Dr Norman T Begg

Edward Jenner
Bicentenary Edition

London: HMSO

Published by HMSO and available from:

HMSO Publications Centre
(Mail, telephone and fax orders only)
PO Box 276, London SW8 5DT
General enquiries 0171 873 0011
Telephone orders 0171 873 9090
Fax orders 0171-873 8200

HMSO Bookshops
49 High Holborn, London, WC1V 6HB
(counter service and fax orders only)
Fax 0171-831 1326
68-69 Bull Street, Birmingham, B4 6AD
0121 236 9696 Fax 0121 236 9699
33 Wine Street, Bristol, BS1 2BQ
0117 9264306 Fax 0117 9294515
9-21 Princess Street, Manchester,M60 8AS
0161 834 7201 Fax 0161 833 0634
16 Arthur Street. Belfast, BT1 4GD
01232 238451 Fax 01232 235401
71 Lothian Road, Edinburgh, EH3 9AZ
0131 479 3141 Fax 0131 479 3142
The Stationery Office Oriel Bookshop
The Friary, Cardiff CF1 4AA
01222 395548 Fax 01222 384347

HMSO's Accredited Agents
(see Yellow Pages)

and through good booksellers

Printed in the UK for HMSO

Dd 303073 9/96 C2000

Preface

This 1996 edition of Immunisation against Infectious Disease (the 'Green Book') almost exactly coincides with the bicentenary of Jenner's remarkable demonstration that an individual could be rendered immune to smallpox by the inoculation of James Phipps with material obtained from a cowpox vesicle. Recent changes in immunity brought about by immunisation have been equally remarkable. The 1992 edition of the 'Green Book' coincided with the introduction of *Haemophilus influenzae* b vaccine (Hib). *Haemophilus influenzae* meningitis, epiglottis and other serious infections from this organism have now virtually disappeared from paediatric wards.

In 1992, the changing age distribution of measles was noted and some modification in immunisation strategy anticipated. Mass measles-rubella immunisation to prevent an epidemic of measles in school-age children was conducted during November 1994. The Measles/Rubella Immunisation Campaign reached over 8 million children and necessitated an enormous exercise in planning and implementation throughout the UK. It also involved a vast number of doctors, nurses and other health personnel, particularly in the school health service, and we are greatly indebted to them for its success. Susceptibility to measles in this target population has dropped dramatically and the few cases of measles since the campaign occur mostly in adults or infants too young to have been protected by immunisation. The inclusion of rubella vaccine has greatly reduced the susceptibility to rubella in males and therefore the risk to susceptible pregnant women. It is logical to follow up this campaign by introducing a two-dose strategy for MMR vaccine to prevent further accumulations of susceptible children which could sustain future epidemics of measles, and to allow the termination of the schoolgirl rubella immunisation programme. Other changes reflect the continuing importance of surveillance and of monitoring the epidemiology of infection not only in this country but world-wide: the outbreaks of diphtheria in eastern Europe and the resurgence of tuberculosis are two problems of particular concern.

The Joint Committee on Vaccination and Immunisation (JCVI) continues to pay close attention to vaccine safety. Particular care was taken to monitor and investigate the apparent adverse reactions that occurred during the Measles/Rubella Immunisation Campaign. In this edition separate chapters are devoted to adverse reactions and to the problem of anaphylaxis; and information is provided on the vaccine damage payments scheme. It is always difficult to distinguish true vaccine reactions from coincidental events in a child's life, but doctors are urged to be meticulous in reporting reactions and in obtaining the details and appropriate specimens that will help in their thorough investigation.

Preface

I should like to record my gratitude and that of my colleagues on the Joint Committee to all those who worked on this Handbook, but particularly to the editors Dr David Salisbury and Dr Norman Begg, their contributors in the Department of Health, and to Mrs Maureen Ambler.

A G M Campbell MB FRCP(Edin) DCH
Chairman, Joint Committee on Vaccination and Immunisation (JCVI)

Acknowledgements

Many people, from the Department of Health and the PHLS in particular, have contributed to this edition. We would like to thank especially Mrs Maureen Ambler for her tireless efforts in creating order out of chaos, Dr Jane Leese, Dr Hugh Nicholas, Ms Helen Campbell (Department of Health), Dr Elizabeth Miller and Ms Joanne White (PHLS) for their technical contributions.

Editors

Dr David Salisbury
Immunisation and Infectious
Disease Group
Department of Health

Dr Norman Begg
Communicable Disease Surveillance
Centre
PHLS

FOR QUERIES PLEASE CONTACT:

Department of Health
Wellington House
133 - 155 Waterloo Road
London SE1 8UG

Professional matters: contact Dr D M Salisbury, room 707
Vaccine supply matters: contact Mr F Coleman, room 716
Pharmaceutical matters: contact Mrs L Gershon, room 708
Nursing matters: contact Ms J McIntyre, room 721

Contents

Contents

Two hundred years ago, Edward Jenner was able to demonstrate that vaccination with material from cowpox provided protection against smallpox, which at that time was one of the most feared infectious diseases. Before then, few people reached adulthood without having caught smallpox and the case fatality rates were often around 10%. At the end of the eighteenth century, smallpox caused one fifth of all deaths in Glasgow and nine out of ten people who died of smallpox were under 5 years of age. One hundred and seventy years later, smallpox virus was extinct. Through that course of events, we have seen all of the key lessons of immunisation, and hopefully learnt from them. Few medical procedures or treatments can compare with the enormous benefit to humanity from immunisation, one of the safest and most cost effective of interventions.

Within a remarkably short time of Jenner's first publication of his observations, thousands of people were being vaccinated. By the beginning of the nineteenth century, vaccination was being undertaken in many European countries. Yet an anti-vaccination lobby was already making its efforts felt. A cartoon by Gillray in 1802 shows vaccine recipients growing cowlike parts, and spurious information about the risks of vaccination was often quoted as if it were true. To overcome such resistance, vaccination was encouraged through the Vaccination Acts of 1840, 1841 and 1853 making vaccination successively universal, free, and finally compulsory. The Acts of 1861, 1867 and 1871 made vaccination enforceable by the appointment of Vaccination Officers and ultimately parents were liable to repeated fines until their children were vaccinated.

Legislation to make immunisation compulsory was widely unpopular and all legislation enforcing compulsion was finally withdrawn in 1948.

The last large epidemic of smallpox (variola major) was in London in 1901-02. After that time, importations continued, notably from Africa and Asia, a pattern that has been repeated with poliomyelitis and measles. By the mid 1970s, it was clear that the risk of death from the complications of smallpox vaccination outweighed the predicted number of deaths that would follow importations, because of the success of the global programme of smallpox eradication. Smallpox vaccination was then abandoned, apart from the requirements for international travel. The world's last naturally occurring case of smallpox was in Somalia in October 1977. In May 1980, the World Health Assembly accepted that smallpox had been eradicated worldwide. The principles of its eradication - the use of an effective vaccine, with a strategy that focused on surveillance, along with a global coalition towards a concerted action, fulfilled a prophecy made by Jenner that "the annihilation of the Small Pox, the most dreadful scourge of the human species, must be the final result of this practice". We are now in a position to expect the global eradication of poliomyelitis within a few years, and hopefully, measles eradication will follow.

Two hundred years after Jenner's first observations, we are seeing a new era beginning for vaccines. With the application of genetic manipulation techniques, better understanding of processes of infection and immunity, and a widespread recognition that investment in disease prevention is one of the best uses of resources, we can expect ever more vaccines, and ever more diseases eradicated.

Sir Kenneth Calman
Chief Medical Officer

Layout of the Memorandum

A number of new chapters have been included in this edition, with more detailed information on contraindications and adverse reactions. A new chapter has been included on immunisation of laboratory staff. The individual vaccine chapters are in alphabetical order. Details of designated yellow fever immunisation centres are available in 'Health Information for Overseas Travel, 1995'. At the end of the memorandum, you will find a list of addresses of local computer centres where immunisation data are managed. In conjunction with existing local arrangements, you may find this helpful for updating information, or for speeding up the transfer of information for children who have moved into, or out of, your locality. England, Scotland, Wales and Northern Ireland have now harmonised their processes for collection and analysis of immunisation coverage data. Future editions will therefore better reflect UK data on coverage, and on surveillance of target diseases.

Diphtheria

A low dose booster for school leavers is recommended as a combined vaccine (Td) in place of single antigen tetanus. This is to improve the immunity of adults, in whom low levels of antibodies had been identified, and counters the threat of the re-emergence of diphtheria as has been seen in Eastern Europe. Td can be used in place of tetanus for the treatment of tetanus prone wounds in Accident and Emergency Departments for young people aged over 13, if the school-leaving booster has not already been given. The local Health Authority, NHS Trust, or Health Board should be informed, by return of an 'unscheduled immunisation' form.

Measles Mumps Rubella (MMR)

From October 1996 a second dose of MMR vaccine is recommended for all children, to be given at the same time as the pre-school boosters. Children who have had their pre-school boosters but who were too young to be included in the measles-rubella immunisation campaign of 1994 should be given a second dose of MMR vaccine. The purpose of this programme is to prevent the re-accumulation of sufficient susceptible children to sustain future epidemics, as happens with a single dose programme. The schoolgirl rubella immunisation programme has been brought to an end.

Hib vaccine

Since the publication of the 1992 edition of 'Immunisation against Infectious Disease', Hib vaccine has become established in the routine immunisation programme. There is now good evidence that a course of Hib vaccine started with one product can be completed with another manufacturer's product without any deleterious effect. Combined products, where Hib is reconstituted with DTP for a single injection, are now being provided.

Splenectomy

Reducing the risk of overwhelming infection in asplenic and hyposplenic patients is addressed in the chapter on pneumococcal vaccine. Guidelines from the British Committee for Standards in Haematology, Clinical Haematology Task Force were published in 1996.

BCG

BCG immunisation policy was reviewed during 1995/96. Immunisation of school children between the ages of 10 and 14 years continues to be part of national policy in addition to selective immunisation of higher risk groups. All health authorities should ensure BCG immunisation is offered to all appropriate children.

The BCG chapter draws attention to the importance of ordering and using the correct preparation of BCG vaccine for the technique being used: 'intradermal' vaccine is for routine intradermal administration using a separate needle and syringe for each recipient; 'percutaneous' BCG should be used when the vaccine is administered by the multiple puncture technique - *this technique is suitable for infants and very young children only*. A new single use disposable Heaf testing device has recently become available.

Travel

Travel vaccines continue to be included in this memorandum, although detailed country by country risks, recommendations and a list of yellow fever centres are now contained in the new companion volume 'Health Information for Overseas Travel'.

Rabies

The recommendations for re-inforcing doses of rabies vaccine have changed: subjects who have received a full three dose primary course of vaccine do not require further reinforcing doses if, as in the UK, post-exposure treatment is readily available, unless they are at continuous risk. The recommendations for post-exposure rabies specific immunoglobulin have also changed and are based on a risk assessment in each individual case.

■ 2.1   Immunity can be induced, either actively (long term) or provided by passive transfer (short term), against a variety of bacterial and viral agents.

■ 2.2   **Active immunity** is induced by using inactivated or attenuated live organisms or their products. Live attenuated vaccines include those for poliomyelitis (OPV), measles, mumps and rubella, and BCG vaccine. Bacterial vaccines such as pertussis, wholecell typhoid, and inactivated poliomyelitis virus (IPV) vaccines contain inactivated organisms. Others such as influenza and pneumococcal vaccine contain immunising components of the organisms; tetanus and diphtheria vaccines contain toxoid - that is, toxins inactivated by treatment with formaldehyde.

■ 2.3   Vaccines produce their protective effect by inducing cell mediated immunity and serum antibodies which can be demonstrated by their detection in the serum. Live vaccines promote cell mediated immunity, which, after BCG immunisation, is demonstrated by a positive tuberculin skin test.

■ 2.4   A first injection of inactivated vaccine or toxoid in a subject without prior exposure to the antigen produces a slow antibody or antitoxin response of predominantly IgM antibody - the primary response. Two injections may be needed to produce such a response. Depending on the potency of the product and time interval, further injections will lead to an accelerated response in which the antibody or antitoxin titre (IgG) rises to a higher level - the secondary response. Following a full course, the antibody or antitoxin levels remain high for months or years, but even if the level of detectable antibody falls, the immune mechanism has been sensitised and a further dose of vaccine reinforces immunity.

■ 2.5   Some inactivated vaccines contain adjuvants (substances which enhance the antibody response). Examples are aluminium phosphate and aluminium hydroxide which are contained in adsorbed diphtheria/tetanus/pertussis vaccine and adsorbed diphtheria/tetanus vaccine.

■ 2.6   In many individuals, live attenuated virus vaccines such as measles, mumps and rubella promote a full, long-lasting antibody response after one dose. Live poliomyelitis vaccine (OPV) requires three doses. An important additional effect of oral poliomyelitis vaccine is the establishment of local immunity in the intestine.

■ 2.7   Viruses that are used for production of vaccines must be grown in cells. A variety of cell types are used for this purpose. Some viruses (measles, mumps, yellow fever, influenza) are grown in chick cells; some polio viruses are grown in monkey kidney cells. Rubella, rabies, hepatitis A and some polio viruses are grown in human diploid cells. This cell line was derived from a single sample of fetal lung tissue obtained following a termination of pregnancy for medical indications 30 years ago. Great care is taken to ensure that there are no extraneous viruses in the cell cultures.

■ 2.8   **Passive immunity** results from the injection of human immunoglobulin (see Chapter 19); the protection afforded is immediate but lasts only a few weeks. There are two types:

(i)   Human normal immunoglobulin (HNIG) derived from the pooled plasma of donors and containing antibody to infectious agents which are currently prevalent in the general population. Examples of the use of HNIG are the protection of immunosuppressed children exposed to measles, and protection of individuals against hepatitis A.

(ii)   Specific immunoglobulins for tetanus, hepatitis B, rabies and varicella-zoster. These are obtained from the pooled blood of convalescent patients, donors recently immunised with the relevant vaccine, or those who on screening are found to have sufficiently high antibody titres. Each specific immunoglobulin therefore contains antibody at a higher titre than that present in normal immunoglobulin.

■ 2.9   Recommendations for the use of normal and specific immunoglobulins are given in the relevant chapters.

3   Consent

■ 3.1   Consent must always be obtained before immunisation. Recent studies, undertaken on behalf of the Health Education Authority and the Department of Health, have shown the importance that parents attach to being involved in the decision making process for immunisation. Care should be taken to ensure that parents feel that their questions have been adequately answered and that their concerns about immunisation have been sensitively considered. For some questions, advice may need to be sought from a Consultant Paediatrician, Consultant in Communicable Disease Control or District (Health Board) Immunisation Co-ordinator.

■ 3.2   Written consent provides a permanent record, but consent - either written or verbal - is required at the time of each immunisation after the child's fitness and suitability have been established (see 3.4).

■ 3.3   Consent obtained **before** the occasion upon which a child is brought for immunisation is only an agreement for the child to be included in the immunisation programme.

■ 3.4   Bringing a child for immunisation after an invitation to attend for this purpose may be viewed as acceptance that the child may be immunised. When a child is brought for this purpose, and fitness and suitability have been established, consent to that immunisation may be implied in the absence of any expressed reservation to the immunisation proceeding at that stage.

■ 3.5   Similarly, the attendance of a child at school on the day that the parent/guardian has been advised that the child will be immunised may also be viewed as acceptance that the child may be immunised, in the absence of any reservation expressed to the contrary. However, because of the parent/guardian's legal responsibilities in respect of the child's attendance at school, the possibility that immunisation will be offered should be made clear to the parent/guardian.

■ 3.6   A child under 16 years of age may give consent for immunisation, provided he or she understands fully the benefits and risks involved. However, the child should be encouraged to involve a parent/guardian, if possible, in the decision.

■ 3.7   Where a child under 16 who fully understands the benefits and risks of the proposed immunisation wishes to refuse the immunisation, that wish should be respected.

■ 3.8   If a child's fitness and suitability cannot be established, immunisation should be deferred. Specialist advice may need to be obtained (see 3.1).

4 Storage, Distribution and Disposal of Vaccines

■ 4.1   Manufacturers' recommendations on storage must be observed and care should be taken to ensure that, on receipt, vaccines are checked against the order, examined for leakage or other damage and immediately placed under the required storage conditions. Vaccines must not be kept at temperatures below 0°C as freezing can cause deterioration of the vaccine and breakage of the container.

■ 4.2   A pharmacist or other suitably trained person should be nominated for each clinic as being responsible for the safe storage of vaccines, and should work to a written procedure developed to meet local needs. This person should have a designated deputy to cover in times of absence. General medical practitioners should make similar arrangements.

■ 4.3   Care should be taken to avoid over-ordering or stockpiling vaccines. Systems should be developed to ensure stock rotation, and regular checks should be made to remove time expired vaccines.

■ 4.4   Vaccines should be stored in the refrigerator, allowing air to circulate around the packages. **They should not be stored on the shelves or in storage compartments of the refrigerator door.**

■ 4.5   Food and drink should not be stored in refrigerators used for vaccines. Door opening should be kept to a minimum.

■ 4.6   Domestic refrigerators are not designed for storage of vaccines and wherever possible should not be used. Refrigerators specifically for storage of medicinal products are available from a number of suppliers (see 4.16).

■ 4.7   Care should be taken to ensure that the electricity supply to the vaccine storage refrigerator cannot be accidentally interrupted e.g. by using a switchless socket or by placing cautionary notices on plugs and sockets.

■ 4.8   A maximum/minimum thermometer should be used in refrigerators where vaccines are stored, irrespective of whether the refrigerator incorporates a temperature indicator dial. Such thermometers may be purchased from reputable laboratory suppliers, some of whom are able to provide a certificate of conformance/calibration (see 4.16). More sophisticated temperature recording devices are available which may be particularly useful for validation and periodic audit of storage and transport facilities.

■ 4.9   The maximum and minimum temperatures reached should be monitored and recorded regularly - preferably daily but at least at the beginning of each immunisation session. Temperature record logs are best kept close to the refrigerator for ease of reference. The written procedure referred to in 4.2 should indicate the action to be taken in the event of the temperature going outside the specified range.

■ 4.10   Refrigerators should be defrosted regularly. Special care should be taken during defrosting to ensure that the temperature of the vaccine does not go outside the specified range. An alternative refrigerator or insulated containers should be used for vaccine storage during defrosting of refrigerators.

■ 4.11   If vaccines have been despatched by post, they should not be accepted by the recipient if more than 48 hours have elapsed since posting. The date and time of dispatch should be clearly marked.

■ 4.12   The use of cool-boxes or insulated containers to transport vaccines should be validated to ensure that the required temperature is maintained throughout the period of transit. Care should be taken to keep frozen ice-packs out of direct contact with the vaccine as this can cause the product to freeze.

■ 4.13   Reconstituted vaccine must be used within the recommended period, varying from one to four hours, according to the manufacturer's instructions. Single dose containers are preferable; once opened, multi-dose vials must not be kept after the end of the session and any vaccine left unused must be discarded.

■ 4.14   Unused vaccine, spent or partly spent vials should be disposed of safely, preferably by heat inactivation or incineration. Contaminated waste and spillage should be dealt with by heat sterilisation, incineration or chemical disinfection as appropriate. Those providing or handling live vaccines should consult their local Consultant in Communicable Disease Control, Consultant in Public Health Medicine (CPHM), Consultant in Communicable Disease and Environmental Health (CD & EH) in Scotland, or Infection Control Committee about suitable procedures.

■ 4.15   The procedures being followed for storage, distribution and disposal of vaccines should be audited regularly to ensure that they comply with the written procedure (see 4.2).

4 Storage, Distribution and Disposal of Vaccines

■ 4.16   Advice on suppliers of refrigeration equipment and accessories is available from:

> Communicable Disease Branch
> Department of Health
> Area 708, Wellington House
> 133-155 Waterloo Road
> London SE1 8UG
> (Tel 0171 972 4472).

> or

> Pharmaceutical Division
> Scottish Office
> Department of Health
> St Andrew's House
> Edinburgh
> EH1 3DE

■ 4.17 Bibliography

> The safe disposal of clinical waste.
> Health and Safety Commission: Health Services Advisory
> Committee, 1992.
> HMSO ISBN 0 11 883641 2.

Consent must be obtained (see Chapter 3), and suitability for immunisation established.

Doctors and nurses providing immunisation should have received training and be proficient in the appropriate techniques.

Preparations must be made for the management of anaphylaxis and other immediate reactions (see 10.6).

■ 5.1   Preliminary points

■ 5.1.1   The recommendations set out in the 'Green Book' are based on the current expert advice available to the Joint Committee on Vaccination and Immunisation (JCVI), although in some circumstances they may differ from that contained in the vaccine manufacturers' data sheets. These recommendations reflect present national immunisation policy.

■ 5.1.2   The leaflets supplied with the product and prepared by the manufacturer in consultation with the Licensing Authority should be read, but see 5.1.1.

■ 5.1.3   The identity of the vaccine must be checked to ensure the right product is used in the appropriate way on every occasion.

■ 5.1.4   The expiry date must be noted. Vaccines should not be used after the expiry date on the label.

■ 5.1.5   The date of immunisation, title of vaccine and batch number must be recorded on the recipient's record. **When two vaccines are given simultaneously, the relevant sites should be recorded** to allow any reactions to be related to the causative vaccine.

■ 5.1.6   The recommended storage conditions must have been observed (see Chapter 4).

Immunisation
Procedures

■ 5.2   Reconstitution of vaccines

■ 5.2.1   Freeze dried vaccines must be reconstituted with the diluent supplied and used within the recommended period after reconstitution (see 4.13).

■ 5.2.2   Before injection the colour of the product must be checked with that stated by the manufacturer in the package insert. The diluent should be added slowly to avoid frothing. A sterile 1ml syringe with a 21G needle should be used for reconstituting the vaccine, and a smaller gauge needle for injection (see 5.5), unless only one needle is supplied with a pre-filled syringe (e.g. Hib/DTP).

■ 5.3   Cleaning of skin

■ 5.3.1   If the skin is to be cleaned, alcohol and other disinfecting agents must be allowed to evaporate before injection of vaccine since they can inactivate live vaccine preparations.

■ 5.4   Route of administration

■ 5.4.1   By mouth

Oral polio vaccine must **never** be injected. OPV should not be allowed to remain at room temperature awaiting or following an immunisation as this may decrease the potency of the vaccine.

■ 5.4.2   Subcutaneous and intramuscular injection

With the exception of BCG, oral typhoid vaccine and OPV, all vaccines should be given by intramuscular or deep subcutaneous injection. In infants, the antero-lateral aspect of the thigh or upper arm are recommended. If the buttock is used, injection into the upper outer quadrant avoids the risk of sciatic nerve damage. Injection into fatty tissue of the buttock has been shown to reduce the efficacy of hepatitis B vaccine.

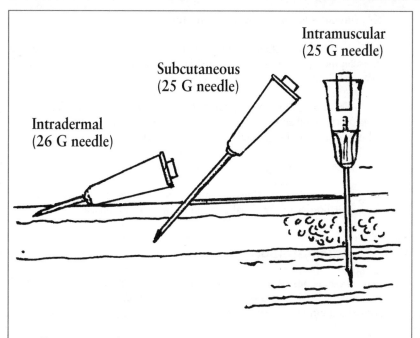

Intramuscular (25 G needle)

Subcutaneous (25 G needle)

Intradermal (26 G needle)

Needle orientation for intradermal, subcutaneous and intramuscular injections.

■ 5.4.3   Intradermal injections

(a) Technique

BCG vaccine is **always** given intradermally; rabies, cholera and typhoid vaccines may also be given this way. When giving an intradermal injection, the operator should stretch the skin between the thumb and forefinger of one hand, and with the other slowly insert the needle (size 25G), bevel upwards, for about 2mm into the superficial layers of the dermis, almost parallel with the surface. A raised, blanched bleb showing the tips of the hair follicles is a sign that the injection has been made correctly and its diameter gives a useful indication of the amount that has been injected. Considerable resistance is felt from a correctly given intradermal injection. If this is not felt, and it is suspected that the needle is too deep, it should be removed and reinserted before more vaccine is given. A bleb of 7mm diameter is approximately equivalent to 0.1ml.

(b) Suitable sites for intradermal injections

- For BCG the site of injection is over the insertion of the left deltoid muscle; the tip of the shoulder must be avoided because of the increased risk of keloid formation at this site (see 32.20.1).

- For tuberculin sensitivity tests (Mantoux or Heaf), intradermal injections are given in the middle of the flexor surface of the forearm. This site should not be used for injecting vaccines.

- The use of jet injectors is **not** recommended.

- For intradermal rabies vaccine, the site of injection is behind the posterior border of the distal portion of the deltoid muscle.

■ 5.5   Administration

For deep subcutaneous or intramuscular immunisation in infants, a 23 or 25G needle should be used. For adults, a 23G needle is recommended. Intradermal immunisations should use a 25G needle.

■ 6.1   A doctor may delegate responsibility for immunisation to a nurse provided the following conditions are fulfilled:

(i)   The nurse is willing to be professionally accountable for this work as defined in the UKCC guidance on the 'Scope of Professional Practice'.

(ii)   The nurse has received training and is competent in all aspects of immunisation, including the contraindications to specific vaccines.

(iii)   Adequate training has been given in the recognition and treatment of anaphylaxis.

■ 6.2   If these conditions are fulfilled and nurses carry out the immunisation in accordance with accepted District Health Authority, NHS Trust or Health Board policy, the Authority/Trust/Board will accept responsibility for immunisation by nurses. Similarly, nurses employed by general practitioners should work to agreed protocols including all the above conditions.

It is every child's right to be protected against infectious diseases. No child should be denied immunisation without serious thought as to the consequences, both for the individual child and for the community. Where there is any doubt, advice should be sought from a Consultant Paediatrician, Consultant in Communicable Disease Control or District (Health Board) Immunisation Co-ordinator.

■ 7.1 Special risk groups

■ 7.1.1   Some conditions increase the risk of complications from infectious diseases and children and adults with such conditions should be immunised **as a matter of priority**. These conditions include the following: asthma, chronic lung and congenital heart diseases, Down's syndrome, Human Immunodeficiency Virus (HIV) infection (see 7.4), small for dates babies and those born prematurely. This last group should be immunised according to the recommended schedule from two months after birth, irrespective of the extent of prematurity. Studies have shown that antibody responses and adverse events are not significantly different in pre-term and term infants immunised 2, 3 and 4 months after birth.

■ 7.1.2   When babies are immunised in Special Care Units, or children are immunised opportunistically in Accident and Emergency Units or in-patient facilities, it is most important that a record of the immunisation is sent to the Health Authority, NHS Trust or Health Board by return of an 'unscheduled immunisation' form.

■ 7.1.3   **Unimmunised children and others with unknown immunisation histories**

Some children, for a variety of reasons, may not have been immunised or their immunisation history may be unknown. If children coming to the UK are not known to have been completely immunised, they should be assumed to be unimmunised and a full course of immunisations should be planned. For children under 10 years of age, this should be the full UK primary immunisation schedule of 3 doses of diphtheria, tetanus, pertussis and oral polio vaccine (Hib only up to 4 years, 3 doses for children under 1 year, only one dose for children aged 1 to 4 years) with boosting for diphtheria, tetanus and polio, 5 and 10 years thereafter. Children of all ages above 12 months should receive two doses of MMR, separated by at least 3 months. For children over 10 years of age,

Td should be used along with MMR and OPV. Boosting with Td and OPV should be given 5 and 10 years later. In the event of a severe adverse reaction, blood should be taken for tetanus antibody titres as these may provide a marker for previous immunisation. No further diphtheria, tetanus and pertussis immunisations are needed in children where there is evidence of previous immunisation including booster doses; immunisation should be completed with OPV and Hib if appropriate.

■ 7.1.4   Children coming to the United Kingdom, part way through their immunisation schedule, should be transferred onto the standard UK schedule, as appropriate for their age.

■ 7.1.5   Children and adults with no spleen, or who have functional hyposplenism, are at increased risk from bacterial infections, most commonly caused by encapsulated organisms. Such infection is most common in the first two years after splenectomy; the risk is greatest amongst children but persists into adult life. The following vaccines are recommended in addition to those in the routine schedule: pneumococcal vaccine (over two years of age, see Chapter 25), Hib vaccine (irrespective of age, see Chapter 16), influenza (Chapter 20), meningococcal A and C vaccine (see Chapter 23). Where possible, immunisation should be given two weeks before splenectomy together with advice about the increased risk of infection.

■ 7.1.6   Adults and children who receive haemodialysis are at increased risk of hepatitis B and hepatitis C although these risks have declined. Haemodialysis patients should be screened for serological evidence of hepatitis B immunity and antibody negative individuals should have three doses of hepatitis B vaccine, ideally before dialysis commences or as soon as possible thereafter. In haemodialysis patients, protection only lasts as long as anti-HBs antibodies remain over 10miu/ml. Patients on haemodialysis should be monitored annually for anti-HBs antibodies and re-immunised if antibodies fall below this level. Recipients of renal transplants and individuals with chronic renal disease are at increased risk of infection and should be considered for annual influenza immunisation, Hib and pneumococcal immunisation.

■ 7.2   General Contraindications

■ 7.2.1   If an individual is suffering from an acute illness, immunisation should be postponed until recovery has occurred. Minor infections without fever or systemic upset are not reasons to postpone immunisation. Antibody responses and incidence of adverse reactions were the same in children with or without acute mild illness, when given MMR vaccine. The acute illnesses were upper respiratory tract infection, diarrhoea or otitis media.

■ 7.2.2   Immunisation should not be carried out in individuals who have a definite history of a severe local or general reaction to a preceding dose. Detailed enquiry may reveal that the reported reaction does not match the specifications below and immunisation can proceed. Appropriate specialist advice should be sought if there is doubt. The following reactions should be regarded as severe:

Local: an extensive area of redness and swelling which becomes indurated and involves most of the antero-lateral surface of the thigh or a major part of the circumference of the upper arm.

General: fever equal to or more than 39.5°F within 48 hours of vaccine; anaphylaxis; bronchospasm; laryngeal oedema; generalised collapse. Prolonged unresponsiveness; prolonged inconsolable or high-pitched screaming for more than 4 hours; convulsions or encephalopathy occurring within 72 hours.

■ 7.2.3 Although there is evidence to suggest that rubella and polio vaccines are not teratogenic (see Chapter 28), live vaccines should not be administered to pregnant women because of the theoretical possibility of harm to the fetus. Where there is a significant risk of exposure to the disease, for example to poliomyelitis or yellow fever, the need for immunisation outweighs any possible risk to the fetus.

■ 7.3   Live Vaccines - special risk groups

■ 7.3.1 There are some individuals for whom there may be risks if they are given live vaccines. Inactivated vaccines are not dangerous to these recipients but may be ineffective. These individuals may not be able to make a normal immune response to live vaccines and could suffer from severe manifestations such as disseminated infection with BCG or paralytic poliomyelitis from vaccine virus. These individuals include:

■ 7.3.2   (a) All patients currently being treated for malignant disease with chemotherapy or generalised radiotherapy, or within 6 months of terminating such treatment.

Indications and Contraindications

(b) All patients who have received an organ transplant and are currently on immunosuppressive treatment.

■ 7.3.3   Patients who within the previous six months have received a bone marrow transplant. Such individuals, irrespective of age, should have their immunity to diphtheria, tetanus, polio, measles, mumps, rubella and Hib checked six months after transplantation and be immunised appropriately. Such tests are difficult to interpret if performed within three months after the receipt of any blood product, including HNIG.

■ 7.3.4   Children who receive prednisolone, orally or rectally, at a daily dose (or its equivalent) of 2 mg/kg/day for at least one week, or 1 mg/kg/day for one month. For adults, an equivalent dose is harder to define but immunosuppression should be considered in those who receive 40 mg prednisolone per day for more than one week. Corticosteroids, administered by other routes, such as aerosols, topically or intra-articularly, are not immunosuppressive. Administration of live vaccines should be postponed for at least three months after immunosuppressive treatment has stopped, or three months after levels have been reached that are not associated with immunosuppression.

■ 7.3.5   Lower doses of steroids, given in combination with cytotoxic drugs (including anti thymocyte globulin or other immunosuppressants) should be considered to cause immunosuppression. The advice of the physician in charge or immunologist should be sought.

■ 7.3.6   Occasionally, there may be individuals on lower doses of steroids or other immunosuppressants for prolonged periods, or who because of their underlying disease, may be immunosuppressed, and are at increased risk of infection. The clinician should ideally discuss their management with a consultant in infectious disease, microbiology, paediatrics or relevant specialist physician.

■ 7.3.7   Patients with evidence of impaired **cell mediated immunity**, for example HIV infection with current symptoms, Severe Combined Immunodeficiency Syndrome, Di George Syndrome and other combined immunodeficiency syndromes. Patients with minor **deficiencies of antibodies** are not at risk; those with major antibody deficiencies will be receiving antibodies in their immunoglobulin treatment preparations and hence are not at risk from receipt of live vaccines.   Because the patient is receiving immunoglobulin preparations, live vaccines are likely to be ineffective, apart from yellow fever vaccine as it is most unlikely that there are significant amounts of anti-yellow fever antibodies in immunoglobulin.

- 7.3.8   For HIV positive individuals, see 7.4

- 7.3.9   After exposure to measles or chickenpox (see Chapters 22 and 34), individuals who fulfil the above criteria, and are susceptible to measles or chickenpox on the grounds of history or antibody titres, should be given an injection of the appropriate preparation of immunoglobulin as soon as possible.

■ 7.4   Immunisation of individuals with antibody to the Human Immunodeficiency Virus (HIV positive)

- 7.4.1   HIV positive individuals **with or without symptoms** should receive the following as appropriate:

Live vaccines: **measles; mumps; rubella; and polio.**

Inactivated vaccines: **pertussis; diphtheria; tetanus; polio; typhoid; cholera; hepatitis B; and Hib.**

- 7.4.2   For HIV positive symptomatic individuals, inactivated polio vaccine (IPV) may be used instead of OPV, at the discretion of the clinician.

- 7.4.3   HIV positive individuals should **not** receive **BCG** vaccine; there have been reports of dissemination of BCG in HIV positive individuals.

- 7.4.4   Yellow fever vaccine should not be given to either symptomatic or asymptomatic HIV positive individuals since there is as yet insufficient evidence as to the safety of its use. Travellers should be told of this uncertainty and advised not to be immunised unless there are compelling reasons. If such travellers still intend to visit countries where a yellow fever certificate is required for entry, then they should obtain a letter of exemption from a medical practitioner.

- 7.4.5   No harmful effects have been reported following live attenuated vaccines for **measles, mumps, rubella and polio** in HIV positive individuals who are at increased risk from these diseases. Immunisation of known measles seronegative HIV positive individuals is advised; a measurable antibody response may occur in only some vaccinees. It should be noted that in HIV positive individuals, polio virus may be excreted for longer periods than in other people. Contacts of a recently immunised HIV positive individual should be warned of this, and of the need for washing their hands after changing an immunised infant's nappies. For HIV positive contacts of an immunised individual (whether that individual is HIV positive or not) the potential risk of infection is greater than that in non-HIV individuals.

■ 7.4.6   Vaccine efficacy may be reduced in HIV positive individuals. Consideration should be given to the use of normal immunoglobulin for HIV positive individuals after exposure to measles (see 22.9).

■ 7.4.7   For HIV positive individuals exposed to **chickenpox or zoster,** see 34.5

■ 7.4.8   HIV positive individuals may also receive: pneumococcal, rabies, hepatitis A and meningococcal A+C vaccines.

NB. **Some of the above advice differs from that for other immunocompromised patients (7.3).**

> Specific contraindications to individual vaccines are given in the relevant chapters and must be observed.

■ 7.5   Immunisation intervals

■ 7.5.1   Live virus vaccines, with the exception of yellow fever vaccine, should not be given during the three months following injection of immunoglobulin because the immune response may be inhibited. Human normal immunoglobulin obtained from UK residents is unlikely to contain antibody to yellow fever virus which would inactivate the vaccine. In travellers, when time is short and there is a significant risk of exposure to polio, vaccine **should** be given even if immunoglobulin has been given at any time in the previous three months.

■ 7.5.2   If it is necessary to administer more than one live vaccine at the same time, they should either be given simultaneously in different sites (unless a combined preparation is used) or in theory be separated by a period of at least three weeks. There are no current data using presently available vaccines to support this recommendation which came from earlier observations about 'take rates' of smallpox vaccination; these may have been reduced if another live vaccine had been given shortly before smallpox vaccination. It probably has little relevance for intervals between oral polio vaccine and other presently used live virus vaccines. It is recommended that a three week interval should be allowed between the administration of live virus vaccines especially measles vaccine, and tuberculin testing; there is experience that shows that measles infection or immunisation can give false negative results in tuberculin positive individuals. No interval needs to be observed between the administration of live and inactivated vaccines.

■ 7.6   The following conditions are NOT contraindications to immunisation:

a.	Family history of any adverse reactions following immunisation.
b.	Previous history of pertussis, measles, rubella or mumps infection.
c.	Prematurity: immunisation should not be postponed.
d.	Stable neurological conditions such as cerebral palsy and Down's syndrome.
e.	Contact with an infectious disease.
f.	Asthma, eczema, hay fever or 'snuffles'.
g.	Treatment with antibiotics or locally-acting (eg topical or inhaled) steroids.
h.	Child's mother is pregnant.
i.	Child being breast fed.
j.	History of jaundice after birth.
k.	Under a certain weight.
l.	Over the age recommended in immunisation schedule.
m.	'Replacement' corticosteroids.

■ 7.7   Other contraindication issues

■ 7.7.1   A history of allergy is **not** a contraindication.
Hypersensitivity to egg contraindicates influenza vaccine; previous
anaphylactic reaction to egg contraindicates influenza and yellow fever
vaccines. There is increasing evidence that MMR vaccine can be safely
given even to children with a history of previous anaphylaxis after egg
ingestion (see 22.7).

■ 7.7.2   A personal or family history of inflammatory bowel disease
(Crohn's or ulcerative colitis) does not contraindicate measles or MMR
immunisation. Evidence for an association between measles vaccine and
inflammatory bowel disease is not convincing.

■ 7.7.3   Family history of convulsions (see 24.4.8). Where there is a
close family history (parents or sibling) of febrile convulsions, there is an
increased chance that a febrile convulsion could follow a fever in a
vaccine recipient. Immunisation should be carried out after advice on the
prevention of pyrexia has been given (see 24.5.2).

■ 7.7.4   Siblings and close contacts of immunosuppressed children
should be immunised against measles, mumps and rubella. There is no
risk of transmission of virus following immunisation.

■ 7.7.5   Oral poliomyelitis vaccine (OPV) should **not** be given to
immunosuppressed children, their siblings or other household contacts.
Inactivated poliomyelitis vaccine should be given instead; this should
also be given to immunosuppressed adults and their contacts (see 26.6.1
and 26.6.3).

■ 7.7.6   Recently immunised children may be taken swimming, even
if they have been given OPV. Similarly, there is no risk of an
unimmunised child contracting vaccine associated poliomyelitis from a
recently immunised child if they are taken swimming. In such public
places, care must be taken to dispose of soiled napkins without
contaminating facilities that others might use.

■ 7.7.7   Surgery is not a contraindication to immunisation, nor is
recent immunisation a contraindication to anaesthesia or surgery. Recent
receipt of OPV does not contraindicate tonsillectomy. In the United
States, where recent OPV administration has never been considered a
contraindication for tonsillectomy, there has been no recorded case of
vaccine associated poliomyelitis following this procedure.

■ 7.7.8   Homoeopathy: the Council of the Faculty of Homoeopathy strongly supports the immunisation programme and has stated that immunisation should be carried out in the normal way using the conventional tested and approved vaccines, in the absence of medical contraindications.

■ 7.8   Bibliography:

Adverse events and antibody response to accelerated immunisation in term and pre-term infants.
Ramsay M E, Miller E, Ashworth L A E, Coleman T J, Rush M, Waight P A.
Arch Dis Childhood 1995; 72: 230-232.

Antibody response to measles/mumps/rubella vaccine of children with mild illness at the time of vaccination.
King G E, Markowitz L E, Heath J, Redd S C, Coleman S, Bellini W J, Sievert A
JAMA 1996; 275(9): 704-7.

Immunisation for the immunosuppressed child.
Campbell A G M.
Arch. Dis. Childhood 1988: 63(2); 113-4.

Human Immunodeficiency Virus infection and routine childhood immunisation.
von Reyn C F, Clements C J, Mann J M.
The Lancet 1987: ii: 669.

Global Programme on AIDS and Expanded Programme on Immunisation.
Joint WHO/UNICEF statement on early immunisation for HIV-infected children.
Weekly Epidem. Rec. 1989 No 7. (Feb.17); 48-49.

Immunization of Children infected with Human Immunodeficiency Virus: supplementary ACIP statement.
MMWR 1988; 37 (12): 181-5.

■ 8.1   Surveillance and reporting of suspected adverse reactions

■ 8.1.1   All vaccines are extensively tested by their manufacturers prior to licensing for quality, safety and efficacy. In addition, manufacturers must submit samples of each batch and results of their own potency, safety and purity tests for independent assessment before that batch can be released into general use. However, careful surveillance must still be maintained.

■ 8.1.2   The Post Licensing Division of the Medicines Control Agency (MCA) has responsibility for monitoring the safety of all marketed medicines including vaccines. Spontaneous reports of adverse drug reactions (ADRs) are received from UK doctors, dentists and coroners under the voluntary 'Yellow Card' scheme, whilst there is a statutory requirement for pharmaceutical companies to report serious adverse reactions to their products on a world-wide basis. Such reports of suspected adverse reactions are classified and entered onto a national computer database operated by the MCA. The number, pattern and severity of reported reactions are regularly reviewed, and appropriate investigation and action initiated if a possible problem is identified. Important information on the safety of vaccines is also collected from other sources, including the medical literature, post-marketing safety studies and an international spontaneous ADR database.

■ 8.1.3   The Joint Committee on Vaccination and Immunisation (JCVI) and Committee on the Safety of Medicines are independent committees which provide expert advice on immunisation policy and the quality, safety and efficacy of vaccines respectively.

■ 8.1.4   The success of the spontaneous reporting system for vaccines depends on early, complete and accurate reporting of suspected ADRs through the yellow cards. For currently marketed vaccines, **serious** suspected reactions, including those which are fatal, life-threatening, disabling, incapacitating or which result in hospitalisation should be reported; this applies to all serious reactions whether or not such reactions have been previously recognised. For new vaccine formulations, which have a black triangle, **all** suspected reactions should be reported. When submitting a yellow card for an adverse reaction, it is most important that the vaccine is correctly identified, so that it is clear which formulation has been used; for example, combined Tetanus and low dose diphtheria vaccine (Td) should be distinguished from Diphtheria/Tetanus vaccine (DT). Wherever possible the batch number should be provided.

It is important to give as much information as possible about the nature, timing and severity of the observed reaction, if the patient was hospitalised, what treatment was given and the final outcome. Information about other factors such as concomitant medication, underlying disease, allergies or family history should be provided whenever possible. The provision of additional information such as test results or relevant hospital correspondence is always helpful.

If further information becomes available after reporting a reaction, this should be sent to the MCA to help in the assessment of a suspected reaction.

■ 8.1.5   Yellow cards are supplied to general practitioners and pharmacists, and are available through the CSM Freefone or by writing to 1 Nine Elms Lane, London SW8 5NQ. They are also available at the back of the British National Formulary, the APBI data sheet compendium and FP10s.

■ 8.1.6   Most of the reports submitted on Yellow Cards are of self-limiting illness, such as fever, rashes or injection site reactions which are associated with a complete recovery. More serious reactions are reported less frequently. Although a reaction might occur in close temporal association with an immunisation, often it can be very difficult to assess whether or not there is a causal link. Most reported reactions can occur independently of immunisation and there are few specific tests that can establish or exclude whether a vaccine caused a reported reaction. The probability that a vaccine has played a causal role in an event is increased if the event has occurred at a time interval after the immunisation which is in accordance with the known incubation periods of live organisms. For example, pyrexial illness occurring 5-10 days after measles immunisation, or parotid swelling three weeks after mumps immunisation, would be consistent with the incubation periods for these particular viruses. Pyrexia occurring less than 3 days after measles vaccine is unlikely to be caused by the immunisation and an intercurrent infection is much more likely.

■ 8.1.7   Assessing the probability of whether a reaction is caused by a vaccine is particularly difficult in young children. Illness such as fever or convulsions occur frequently in the first year of life and almost every child is immunised on 3 separate occasions in this period. Interpretation of the significance of clinical events occurring after immunisation depends on the biological plausibility, an identified excess of events in a specified post-immunisation period compared against background rates, and laboratory evidence that support the association. In general, the risk of serious illness following natural infection far outweighs any possible risk from the relevant vaccine.

■ 8.1.8   From 1 November 1990 to 31 October 1995 there were 5433 reports of suspected adverse reactions to all vaccines given to children under 15 years of age reported through the Yellow Card scheme. The number of reports is based on the date each report was received. Approximately 80 million doses of vaccines were distributed as part of the childhood programme (some of these vaccines are also given to adults) in the UK in those 5 years. Most reports were of mild, self-limiting illness, such as fever, rashes and injection site reactions. During 1995, there were 648 yellow card reports of suspected adverse reactions relating to routinely administered childhood vaccines for the UK as a whole. Again, most reports were of mild, self-limiting illness such as fever, rashes and injection site reactions. There were 152 reports that included reactions classified as 'serious'. To put this in perspective, over 14 million doses of these vaccines were distributed in the UK in 1995. Thus, 'serious' suspected reactions were reported at a rate of approximately one per hundred thousand distributed doses of vaccine.

■ 8.1.9   Immunisation can rarely increase the risk of a specific disease. By linking computer records of hospital admissions for idiopathic thrombocytopenic purpura (ITP) and community computer records of MMR immunisation, a positive association was found with an absolute risk of ITP in one in every 24,000 immunisations.

Within certain groups, the evidence of harm from immunisation is not supported. Whilst natural rubella infection is often associated with arthropathy, especially in adult women, one recent retrospective case control study showed no increase in risk of arthropathy in under-immune women immunised post partum, compared with unimmunised controls. A US study of re-immunisation of college students with MMR vaccine showed no increase in fever or rash in immunised students, compared with unimmunised controls.

Although cases of Sudden Infant Death Syndrome (SIDS) have been reported within a short time of DTP immunisation, there is no evidence that the risk is increased. Indeed there is some evidence that immunised infants are at decreased risk from SIDS.

■ 8.1.10   Serious neurological reactions such as encephalitis may occur very rarely after vaccines. All such cases should be investigated and referred to hospital in the normal way. A final clinical diagnosis of a suspected reaction to a vaccine should only be made once all other causes have been excluded. A suspected serious adverse reaction however, can still be reported on a Yellow Card before other results become available. Further information can always be submitted at a later date (see 8.1.4).

■ 8.1.11   After several reports of severe encephalopathy and permanent brain damage in children who had received pertussis vaccine, the National Childhood Encephalopathy Study was set up to examine the association between pertussis immunisation and encephalopathic disorders. After three years of case finding and follow-up, it was concluded that if there was an increased risk of encephalopathy and permanent brain damage or death after pertussis vaccine, it was too small to be demonstrated statistically.

■ 8.1.12   Serious reactions to vaccine have been reviewed by an expert committee convened by the Institute of Medicine in the United States. For only a few conditions was there enough available information to suggest a possible or probable causal relationship with a vaccine (see table). Furthermore, the American Academy of Paediatrics has recently stated that it concurs with the ad hoc sub-committee of the US National Vaccine Advisory Committee and the US Advisory Committee on Immunisation Practices that whole-cell pertussis vaccine has not been proven to be a cause of brain damage.

	Evidence favours acceptance of a causal relationship	Evidence establishes a causal relationship
DTP	Acute encephalopathy Shock and unusual shock-like state	Anaphylaxis Protracted inconsolable crying
OPV/IPV	Guillain Barré Syndrome Syndrome (OPV)***	Poliomyelitis in vaccine recipient or contact (OPV) Death from polio vaccine strain viral infection*
Hib	-	-
Measles	Anaphylaxis	Thrombocytopenia (MMR) Anaphylaxis (MMR) Death from measles vaccine strain viral infection*
Mumps	-	-
Rubella**	Chronic arthritis	Acute arthritis
T/DT/Td	Guillain Barré Syndrome Brachial neuritis	Anaphylaxis
Hepatitis B	-	Anaphylaxis

*   These data come primarily from individuals proven to be immunocompromised.
**   See 8.1.9 for a counter view.
***   Subsequently retracted

Bibliography:

Farrington P et al.
A new method for active surveillance of adverse events from
diphtheria/tetanus/pertussis and measles/mumps/rubella vaccines.
Lancet 1995; 345: 546-69

'Adverse effects of pertussis and rubella vaccines' ed. Howson C P et al 1991:
National Academy Press, Washington DC

'Adverse events associated with childhood vaccines: evidence bearing on
causality' ed. Stratton K R et al. 1994: National Academy Press, Washington DC.

Slater P E et al.
Absence of an association between rubella vaccination and arthritis in under
immune postpartum women
Vaccine 1995; 13(16):1529-32

Chen R T et al.
Adverse events following measles-mumps-rubella and measles vaccinations in
college students
Vaccine 1991;9:297-9

Committee on Infectious Diseases.
The relationship between pertussis vaccine and central nervous system
sequelae: continuing assessment.
Pediatrics 1996; 97:279-281.

Adverse Reactions

9   Vaccine Damage Payments Scheme

■ 9.1   Introduction

■ 9.1.1   The Vaccine Damage Payments scheme provides a single, tax free payment for people who have suffered severe mental and/or physical disablement of 80% or more, as defined below, as a result of immunisation against one or a group of the following diseases:

diphtheria	tetanus
pertussis	poliomyelitis
measles	rubella
tuberculosis	smallpox
mumps	Haemophilus influenzae type b (Hib)

Claims can be made on the basis of combination vaccines, for instance: diphtheria, tetanus and pertussis (DTP) or measles, mumps and rubella (MMR). Claimants are asked to give details of all the immunisations they have been given.

■ 9.1.2   Claims can also be made if someone is thought to be severely disabled because their mother was immunised against any of the specified diseases while she was pregnant **or** if someone is thought to be severely disabled because they have been in close contact with a person who has been immunised against polio (using orally administered vaccine). The payment **is not compensation** but is designed to ease the present and future burdens of those suffering from vaccine damage and their families. The amount payable is £30,000 for claims made on or after 15 April 1991.

■ 9.2   The 80% disability test

The severity of disablement in individual cases is assessed on the same basis as for the Industrial Injuries Disablement Benefit Scheme - a widely accepted test of severity. In physical terms, 80% disablement equates to, for example, amputation below the hip or below the shoulder, or to deafness so severe that the sufferer cannot hear a shout beyond a distance of 3 feet. Similarly, somebody whose corrected vision was 6/60 in both eyes may be considered as 80% disabled. These levels of disablement are easily described and a doctor who has been given special training required to make such assessments would be able to make a balanced judgement on the overall level of disability.

■ 9.3 Time and age limits

■ 9.3.1   The disabled person must be 2 or more years old and must have been immunised in the UK or the Isle of Man unless they or someone in their family were in the armed forces and the immunisation was given as part of the armed services medical facilities.

■ 9.3.2   They must have been immunised before their 18th birthday, unless the immunisation was against polio or rubella or during an outbreak given within the UK or the Isle of Man.

■ 9.3.3   The claim must be made within 6 years of the date of immunisation or of the child reaching the age of 2 - whichever is the later.

■ 9.4 How to claim

Claimants can get a claim form by writing to:

Vaccine Damage Payments Unit
Department of Social Security
Palatine House
Lancaster Road
Preston
PR1 1HB

■ 9.5 The decision making process

Decisions on claims are made by the Secretary of State for Social Security on the basis of a medical officer's assessment of the percentage level of disablement and whether it is the result of the immunisation. If a claim is medically disallowed the claimant may, at any time, seek a review of the medical officer's assessments by an independent Vaccine Damage Tribunal.

■ 9.6 Further information

The Benefits Agency have produced leaflet HB3 'Payment for people severely disabled by a vaccine' about the Vaccine Damage Payment Scheme. Copies are available from BA Distribution and Storage Centre, Manchester Road, Lancashire, OL10 2PZ or the Vaccine Damage Payments Unit.

10   Anaphylaxis

■ 10.1   Recipients of any vaccine should be observed for an immediate adverse reaction and should remain under observation until they have been seen to be in good health and not to be experiencing an immediate adverse reaction. As vaccines are administered subcutaneously or intramuscularly, the time of onset of anaphylaxis is variable and onset may be delayed for up to 72 hours. Patients should be advised to seek medical attention if they develop early symptoms such as breathlessness, swelling and rash. Parents should be advised to seek medical advice should unexpected symptoms develop after immunisation. All cases of anaphylaxis should be reported using the Yellow Card scheme.

■ 10.2   Clinical Characteristics of anaphylaxis:

Anaphylaxis is typically rapid and unpredictable with variable severity and clinical features. The most serious features include cardiovascular collapse, bronchospasm, angioedema, pulmonary oedema, loss of consciousness and urticaria. Asthmatic patients often develop bronchospasm during anaphylaxis. Anaphylaxis generally responds promptly to parenteral adrenaline.

■ 10.3   **In the three year period from June 1992, there were 87 spontaneous reports in people of all ages through the Yellow Card scheme of all types of anaphylaxis, following immunisation (excluding MR vaccine which is considered separately below) received by the MCA. No deaths were reported. In that time, over 55 million doses of vaccines were supplied to hospitals and GPs.**

■ 10.4   During the national Measles and Rubella Immunisation Campaign in November 1994, approximately 8 million children between the ages of 5 and 16 years (up to 18 years in Scotland) were immunised. 81 cases of anaphylaxis were reported; a reporting rate of approximately one in 100,000 children. There was a slight preponderance in children aged 9 years and older and in females. All children with anaphylaxis, for whom there is information available, appear to have made a full recovery.

■ 10.5   Anaphylactic reactions to vaccines are therefore probably very rare, but they cannot be predicted and have the potential to be fatal. Most anaphylactic reactions occur in individuals who have no known risk factors, making it difficult to advise on special precautions. It is uncertain whether a history of hypersensitivity significantly increases the risk of anaphylaxis.

Anaphylaxis

■ 10.6   Management of anaphylaxis:

■ 10.6.1 Differential Diagnosis:

Findings from the Measles/Rubella Immunisation Campaign of November 1994 suggest that medical and nursing staff can have difficulty distinguishing between anaphylactic reactions, convulsions and fainting. It is important that health professionals involved in immunisation are able to distinguish these conditions. Most convulsions reported after measles and rubella vaccine occurred within one hour of immunisation and had features suggesting syncope rather than epileptic fits. Syncope occurs commonly after any injection such as an immunisation in adults and adolescents. Very young children rarely faint and sudden loss of consciousness at this age should be presumed to be anaphylaxis if a central pulse (such as the carotid) cannot be felt. **A central pulse is maintained during a faint or convulsion.**

■ 10.6.2 Anaphylaxis can occur without warning. Therefore, adrenaline and an appropriate sized oral airway must always be immediately available whenever immunisation is given. All health professionals responsible for immunisation must be familiar with techniques for resuscitation of a patient with anaphylaxis to prevent disability and loss of life.

IDENTIFICATION OF ANAPHYLAXIS, SYNCOPE & PANIC ATTACKS

VACCINE GIVEN

symptoms develop

0 - 72 hours

0 - 1 hour

symptoms suggestive of *anaphylaxis*

general signs:	*pallor, limpness, apnoea*
cardiovascular:	*profound hypotension in association with **tachycardia;** sinus tachycardia*
Upper airway obstruction:	*angioedema – swelling of lips, face, neck, tongue difficulty in breathing, speaking, swallowing; hoarseness, stridor*
Lower airway obstruction:	*subjective feelings of retrosternal tightness and dyspnoea bronchospasm – audible expiratory wheeze*
skin:	*diffuse erythema urticaria – itchy weals with erythematous edges and pale blanched centres peripheral oedema*

TREATMENT: See table at 10.7

symptoms suggestive of *syncope or panic attacks*

general signs:	*sweating, nausea, dizziness, ringing in the ears, dimmed vision, weakness, may precede the event. choking and difficulty breathing may lead to hyperventilation, paraesthesiae and spasms of the hands*
cardiovascular:	*hypotension bradycardia*
neurological:	*transient jerking movements and eye rolling can occur rarely.*

There should be rapid recovery. Although symptoms of malaise may persist, the patient should regain consciousness in 1-2 minutes. Any abnormal cardiovascular signs usually revert within a few minutes.

VERY YOUNG CHILDREN RARELY FAINT AND SUDDEN LOSS OF CONSIOUSNESS AT THIS AGE SHOULD BE PRESUMED TO BE ANAPHYLAXIS IN THE ABSENCE OF A STRONG CENTRAL (CAROTID) PULSE, WHICH PERSISTS DURING A FAINT OR CONVULSION.

TREATMENT: The patient should remain lying down for 10-15 minutes with their feet raised. At any age, if in doubt, treat the patient for anaphylaxis.

Anaphylaxis

■ 10.7   Treatment:

TREATMENT (see 10.8, 10.9 and 10.10 for dosages)

1.   Lie patient in left lateral position. If unconsious, insert airway
2.   Send for professional assistance. Never leave the patient alone.

Mild anaphylaxis/allergic reactions (slowly progressing periphal oedema or changes restricted to the skin eg. urticaria)
oral antihistamines or *subcutaneous adrenaline* with observation and reassurance. Nebulised salbutamol, oral or parenteral steroids, parenteral antihistamine, if necessary and/or available.

Severe anaphylaxis (with cardiovascular collapse)
Administer intramuscular adrenaline immediately. If appropriate, begin cardio-pulmonary resuscitation.

If there is no improvement in the patient's condition in 5/10 minutes, repeat the dose of adrenaline to a maximum of 3 doses.

Chlorpheniramine maleate (piriton) may be given intravenously by appropriately trained individuals. Intravenous hydrocortisone may also be given to prevent further deterioration in severely affected cases.

If available, volume replacement with colloid solutions should be considered.

Bronchospasm
Administer nebulised adrenaline or adrenaline by intramuscular injection immediately.
Steroids may also be administered. Other nebulised bronchodilators, such as ßeta 2 agonist (eg. salbutamol) or parenteral aminophylline should be considered.

Angio-oedema/laryngeal oedema
Administer nebulised adrenaline or adrenaline by intramuscular injection. Antihistamines should be given and intubation may be necessary.

Patients with anaphylaxis should be refered to hospital for assessment and further treatment may be necessary, such as provision of bronchodilators, adrenaline by infusion, colloids and assisted ventilation. NB. patients should be monitored after IV administration of adrenaline as adverse effects may be more common when the drug is given in this way.

All cases of anaphylaxis should be observed for at least 6 hours, in case of any delayed reations

REPORT ALL CASES OF ANAPHYLAXIS TO THE CSM USING YELLOW CARDS.

Anaphylaxis

■ 10.7.1 The reaction should be reported to the Medicines Control Agency using the Yellow Card scheme.

■ 10.8   Adrenaline dosage: Adrenaline 1/1,000 (1mg/ml) by intramuscular or subcutaneous injection.

■ 10.8.1 **Adults:** 0.5 to 1.0ml repeated as necessary up to a maximum of three doses. The lower dose should be used for the elderly or those of slight build.

■ 10.8.2 Infants and children:

Age	Dose of adrenaline
Less than 1 year	0.05ml
1 year	0.1ml
2 years	0.2ml
3-4 years	0.3ml
5 years	0.4ml
6-10 years	0.5ml

■ 10.8.3 **Slow intravenous injection may be considered only in extreme emergency.** Dilute adrenaline (1/10,000) should be used for the intravenous route. Where intramuscular injection might still succeed, time should not be wasted seeking intravenous access. Patients should be monitored after intravenous administration as adverse effects may be more common when the drug is administered in this way.

■ 10.9   Chlorpheniramine maleate

Age	Dose of chlorpheniramine maleate
up to 1 year	200µg/kg body weight
1-5 year	2.5-5mg
6-12 years	5-10mg
over 12 years	10-20mg
By slow intravenous injection over 1 minute	

This table is based on the Alder Hey book of children's doses which provides guidelines on suitable doses of chlorpheniramine maleate for children. Chlorpheniramine maleate is not licensed for injection in children and clinicians take responsibility for its use in this group.

■ 10.10 Hydrocortisone

Age	Dose of hydrocortisone
up to 1 year	25mg
1-5 year	50mg
6-12 years	100mg
adult	100-500mg
By slow intravenous injection	

■ 10.11 Bibliography

Treatment of acute anaphylaxis
Fisher M
BMJ 1995; 311: 731-3

Treatment of acute anaphylaxis
BMJ 1995; 311: 1434-6

Treatment of acute anaphylaxis
Fisher M
BMJ 1995; 312: 637-8

Adverse reactions to Measles/Rubella Vaccine
Current Problems in Pharmacovigilance 1995; 21; 9-10

The use of adrenaline for anaphylactic shock (for ambulance paramedics)
Resuscitation Council (UK) and the Joint Royal Colleges and Ambulance
Liaison Committee
March 1996

Treating anaphylaxis with sympathomimetic drugs
Fisher M
BMJ 1992; 305: 1107-8

Adverse events associated with childhood vaccines : Evidence bearing on causality
Ed. Stratton K R et al
National Academy Press, Washington DC 1994

Anaphylaxis

■ 11.1 The schedule for primary immunisation with DPT and Hib and polio starts at two months, with an interval of one month between each dose[1]. This allows completion of the primary course at an early age, which provides the earliest possible protection against whooping cough and Hib which are most dangerous for the very young. No booster dose of pertussis vaccine or Hib is currently recommended; the fourth DT and polio booster continues to be given before school entry.

■ 11.2 This accelerated schedule was adopted following recognition that one of the most frequent reasons for low vaccine uptake was the mobility of young families who move out of districts before their children had completed primary courses. This problem was compounded by the variation in schedules between Health Authorities. The schedule at two, three and four months removes this problem by providing uniformity; starting the programme early, and having short intervals reduces the opportunities for failing to complete a course.

■ 11.3 Studies comparing the antibody levels of diphtheria, pertussis, tetanus and poliomyelitis one year after the third dose showed adequate levels of antibodies for both accelerated and extended schedules.

■ 11.4 **Studies undertaken to monitor adverse events associated with the accelerated schedule have shown that there are fewer adverse events when compared to the former extended schedule.**

■ 11.5 Every effort should be made to ensure that **all children are immunised even if they are older than the recommended age-range; no opportunity to immunise should be missed.** The number of doses needed for Hib depends on the child's age (see 15.3). Hib vaccine is not recommended for those over four years.

■ 11.6 When such opportunistic immunisation has been carried out, it must be reported to the Health Authority (HA), NHS Trust or Health Board as an unscheduled immunisation.

■ 11.7 **If any course of immunisation is interrupted, it should be resumed and completed as soon as possible.**

■ 11.8 The schedule for routine immunisation is given below. Details of the procedure for each vaccine are given in the relevant chapters and should be consulted.

---

1   *In some parts of Scotland, the schedule is started at two months and should be completed by six months, with intervals between injections of not less than one month.*

Vaccine	Age	Notes
D/T/P and Hib Polio	1st dose 2 months) 2nd dose 3 months) 3rd dose 4 months)	Primary Course
Measles/mumps/ rubella (MMR)	12-15 months	Can be given at any age over 12 months
Booster DT and polio, MMR second dose	3-5 years	Three years after completion of primary course
BCG	10-14 years or infancy	
Booster tetanus diphtheria and polio	13-18 years	

Children should therefore have received the following vaccines:

By 6 months:	3 doses of DTP, Hib and polio.
By 15 months:	measles/mumps/rubella.
By school entry:	4th DT and polio; second dose measles/mumps/rubella.
Between 10 and 14 years:	BCG.
Before leaving school:	5th polio and tetanus diphtheria (Td).

Adults should receive the following vaccines:

Women sero-negative for rubella:	rubella.
Previously unimmunised individuals:	polio, tetanus, diphtheria.
Individuals in high risk groups:	hepatitis B, hepatitis A, influenza, pneumococcal vaccine.

Bibliography:

The efficacy of DPT and oral poliomyelitis immunisation schedules initiated from birth to 12 weeks of age.
Halsey N, Galazka A.
Bulletin of World Health Organisation 1985: 63 (6); 1151-69.

Durability of immunity to diphtheria, tetanus and poliomyelitis after a three dose immunisation schedule completed in the first eight months of life.
Jones A E, Johns A, Magrath D I, Melville-Smith M, Sheffield F.
Vaccine 1989: 7; 300-302.

Immunogenicity of combined diphtheria, tetanus and pertussis vaccine given at 2, 3 and 4 months, versus 3, 5 and 9 months of age.
Booy R, Aitken S J M, Taylor S, Tudor Williams G et al
Lancet 1991: i, 507-510

Diphtheria, pertussis and tetanus vaccination
Cutts F T and Begg N T
The Lancet 1992: 339: 1356

Symptoms following accelerated immunisation schedule with diphtheria, tetanus and pertussis vaccine
Ramsay M E B, Rao M, Begg N T
BMJ 1992; 304: 1534-6

12 Immunisation of Laboratory Staff

■ 12.1 Introduction

■ 12.1.1 The Control of Substances Hazardous to Health (COSHH) Regulations 1994 require that an assessment is made of, among other things, the exposure of workers to biological agents as defined. The Approved Code of Practice entitled 'Control of Biological Agents' gives practical advice on this matter. In particular, the assessment is intended to reveal what control measures are required to prevent or control exposure to infection. Where a risk of infection is recognised and where effective vaccines are available, the employer should make those vaccines available to staff who are not already immune, if they are exposed or liable to be exposed in the course of their work. Staff should be made fully aware of the benefits and drawbacks of immunisation. The Health and Safety at Work etc Act 1974 provides for immunisation to be offered free of charge to workers. An immunisation record should be kept which should be made available to the person in question, on request.

■ 12.1.2 All local laboratory safety policies should include an immunisation policy. Arrangements for the administration of recommended vaccines will vary between laboratories. In most cases the service will be provided by the local Occupational Health Department.

■ 12.1.3 Laboratory Directors should ensure that arrangements are in place so that all staff are aware of the immunisation policy and can be offered all vaccines recommended under the policy. Laboratory Directors should review the immunisation status of their staff. Where a member of staff does not wish to accept the offer of a recommended vaccine, or does not respond to a vaccine, the Director together with the local Occupational Health Physician should carry out a risk assessment to determine the likelihood of infection for the individual member of staff and his/her colleagues. If the risk is unacceptable, efforts should be made to seek alternative employment within the laboratory for the member of staff.

■ 12.2 Risks of infection in laboratory workers

■ 12.2.1 Several surveys of infections in British laboratory workers have been carried out. The risk of occupationally-acquired infection is greatest among medical laboratory scientific officers. Risks are declining among all categories of staff. For example, four cases of pulmonary tuberculosis were reported among Public Health Laboratory Service staff in 1971, at a rate of 97.2 per 100,000 person years, six times the rate for the general population. Three of the four cases were in medical laboratory scientific officers. By comparison, only one case of tuberculosis (probably not occupationally acquired) was reported in any British microbiology laboratory worker between 1988 and 1989. The risk of laboratory-acquired hepatitis B has shown a similar decline. None of the other infections reported in the 1988-89 survey were potentially preventable by immunisation.

■ 12.2.2 Two general categories of occupational risk in laboratory staff may be recognised:

- High risk. Those who regularly handle pathogens or potentially infected specimens, or who have regular patient contact (e.g. medical laboratory scientific officers, laboratory technicians, cleaners, porters, medical and non-medical microbiologists). Secretaries and receptionists in laboratories may be at high risk if they handle specimens).

- Low risk. Those who do not regularly handle pathogens or potentially infected specimens and do not have regular patient contact.

■ 12.3 Indications for immunisation of laboratory staff

■ 12.3.1 The most effective method for preventing laboratory acquired-infections is by adoption of safe working practices. Immunisation should never be regarded as a substitute for good laboratory practice, although it provides additional protection.

■ 12.3.2 Indications for immunisation of laboratory staff are listed below. Guidance on contraindications to immunisation, vaccine schedules, routes of administration, sources of vaccines, vaccine storage and the management of anaphylaxis are contained in this document. Only the nationally recommended schedules should be used when immunising laboratory staff.

■ 12.3.3 COSHH Regulations require that a risk assessment be carried out to determine which pathogens staff may be exposed to. This assessment should take into account the local epidemiology of the disease, the nature of material handled (clinical specimens, cultures of pathogens or both), the frequency of contact with infected or potentially infected material, the laboratory facilities including containment measures and the nature and frequency of any patient contact. Staff considered to be at risk of exposure to pathogens should be offered routine pre-exposure immunisation as appropriate. This decision should also take into account the safety and efficacy of available vaccines. Staff not considered to be at risk need not routinely be offered immunisation, although post-exposure prophylaxis may occasionally be indicated. It should be noted that secretaries and receptionists are likely to be included in the group of staff at risk. The records of risk assessments should be kept by the laboratory director or his/her designated deputy.

■ 12.4   Immunisation of a laboratory employee may be indicated for a number of reasons:

■ 12.4.1   To protect the individual from an occupational risk.

There are several vaccine-preventable infections that staff may be exposed to in the course of their work. Staff who work mainly with clinical specimens or have patient contact may be exposed to a variety of infections, including hepatitis B, typhoid, tuberculosis and vaccine strains of polio virus. Staff who work mainly with pathogens are only likely to be exposed to the specific pathogens handled in their laboratory.

■ 12.4.2   To protect other laboratory staff and any others (eg family members) to whom a laboratory acquired infection may be secondarily transmitted. Transmission of certain infections in the workplace may be associated with significant morbidity. In this situation it is desirable to ensure that all susceptible staff are protected. The most important vaccine-preventable infection in this category is rubella, however other vaccines (e.g. influenza) might occasionally be indicated in certain circumstances, such as an expected severe epidemic.

■ 12.4.3   For staff who have not received generally recommended vaccines.

The workplace provides an opportunity to identify and protect individuals who have not received immunisations such as tetanus and polio that are recommended for the entire population.

Indication for Specific Vaccines

■ 12.5   Anthrax (Chapter 13)

■ 12.5.1 The probability that clinical specimens and environmental samples of UK origin contain *B. anthracis* and present any risk to staff is extremely low, and thus routine immunisation of laboratory workers is not indicated. Staff for whom the vaccine is indicated include:

(i). Those who work with the organism.

(ii). Those who have direct contact with imported animal products likely to contact the organism.

■ 12.5.2 Specific queries about anthrax immunisation and side effects may be addressed to the Centre for Applied Microbiology and Research, Porton Down, (telephone 01980 612429).

■ 12.6   BCG (Chapter 32)

■ 12.6.1 Before starting employment all staff who handle material likely to contain tubercle bacilli such as sputum should be checked for evidence of a BCG scar. If they have a scar, they do not require BCG. If they have no scar, they should have a Heaf or Mantoux test. Those with a negative reaction (Heaf grade 0 or 1) should be offered BCG immunisation and the immunisation site should be checked 6 weeks later. Those with a moderate reaction (Heaf grade 2) do not require BCG. Those with a strong reaction (Heaf grade 3 or 4) should be questioned about symptoms suggestive of TB. If symptoms suggest it, or if the worker comes from a country where tuberculosis is common, they should be referred to the local chest physician, either through the occupational health department or their general practitioner, for full investigation and follow-up. Tuberculin positivity takes up to 12 weeks to develop following BCG immunisation, and recently immunised staff should not be allowed to handle material such as sputum likely to contain tubercle bacilli during this period.

■ 12.6.2 Anyone likely to come in contact with material containing tubercle bacilli who is found to be susceptible and refuses BCG should have the risks explained and both this and the refusal recorded in their occupational health record.

■ 12.6.3 Pre-employment and in-service chest X rays are no longer routinely recommended for health care workers.

12 Immunisation of Laboratory Staff

■ 12.7 Cholera (Chapter 14)

The probability that faecal material will contain *V. cholerae* 01 or 0139 is low, and the infective dose required is high (10^9 organisms). The risk of laboratory-acquired infection is therefore negligible. In addition, the efficacy of the currently available vaccine is low (40-50%). For these reasons, routine immunisation of laboratory staff is not indicated. Staff in reference laboratories who work with the organism may however be at higher risk and a risk assessment should be carried out of the activities in which individuals are involved to determine the need for immunisation.

■ 12.8 Diphtheria (Chapter 15)

■ 12.8.1 Laboratory-acquired diphtheria has been reported in the UK. Staff who handle clinical material that may contain pathogenic corynebacteria, or who work with the organism or who may come into contact with infected patients should be considered for a booster or for primary immunisation following a risk assessment. Staff for whom immunisation is likely to be appropriate include those in reference laboratories or who handle control strains.

■ 12.8.2 Low dose (adult type) vaccine should be used either as a single antigen preparation (d), or in combination with tetanus toxoid (Td). Td is contraindicated in those with a history of a severe reaction to tetanus toxoid. A full primary course should be given (if previously unimmunised) or a booster dose (if previously immunised). If the adult single antigen diphtheria vaccine is not available, one fifth dose of the paediatric vaccine may be used instead. Immunity to diphtheria should be checked at least three months after immunisation is completed by measuring antitoxin levels in serum. Immunity testing should be carried out using the Vero cell toxin neutralisation assay at the Respiratory and Systemic Infection Laboratory. Further booster doses should be offered at ten yearly intervals. Staff considered to require immunisation with a history of a booster dose in the past 10 years should be tested, boosted if non-immune, then tested post immunisation. Staff with no history of a booster dose in the past 10 years should be boosted without pre-immunisation testing, then tested post immunisation. The cut off level for immunity should be 0.01 iu/Ml with the exception of those regularly handling toxigenic strains, in whom it should be 0.1 iu/Ml. Staff considered to require immunisation who have been previously tested by ELISA should now be retested by neutralisation assay.

■ 12.9 Hepatitis A (Chapter 17)

■ 12.9.1 Although it is likely that many laboratory workers are exposed to material that contains hepatitis A virus, there is little evidence of an occupational risk. There are two groups who may be at higher risk, to whom immunisation should be offered:

(i).   Those attempting to culture the virus.

(ii).   Those who travel regularly to endemic areas in the course of their work or who travel for periods greater than three months. For other categories of travellers, human normal immunoglobulin (HNIG) is an inexpensive alternative to vaccine, offering short term protection.

■ 12.9.2 Testing for antibodies (IgG) to hepatitis A virus prior to immunisation may be worthwhile in those aged fifty years or over, those born in areas of high or moderate endemicity and those who have a history of jaundice. There is no evidence that staff performing routine hepatitis A serology tests are at particular risk.

■ 12.10 Hepatitis B (Chapter 18)

■ 12.10.1 Hepatitis B immunisation should be offered to all staff who handle material that may contain the virus (blood, blood-stained body fluids and patients' tissues). Post-immunisation antibody testing should be carried out two to four months after completing the primary course. Poor responders (anti-HBs = 10-100 miu/ml) and non responders (anti-HBs < 10miu/ml) should be offered a further dose of vaccine. Vaccine non-responders should, with their consent, be tested for serological markers of past and current HBV infection. Vaccine non-responders without markers of previous infection may be at risk of acquiring HBV; their practice however need not be restricted provided that occupational exposures are promptly reported and managed according to existing guidance.

■ 12.10.2 Staff at continuing risk of exposure should be offered a booster dose at five-yearly intervals.

■ **12.11 Influenza** (Chapter 20)

There is little evidence that annual influenza immunisation of healthy adults reduces sickness absence from work and it is not indicated for laboratory staff except in those working with the virus. For those in non-occupational risk groups for whom annual immunisation is recommended as part of national policy (e.g. those with chronic diseases), it would normally be offered by the GP. This policy would be reviewed in the event of a major epidemic.

■ **12.12 Japanese encephalitis** (Chapter 21)

Immunisation is indicated for two groups:

(i). Those who work with the virus.

(ii). Those travelling in the course of their work to infected areas of South East Asia and the Far East who will be staying in rural areas for more than one month.

■ **12.13 Meningococcal disease** (Chapter 23)

The majority of strains of *N. meningitidis* encountered in the laboratory will be group B, for which no vaccine is available. Protection against the vaccine-preventable strains (A and C) with the currently-available vaccine is short-lived. For these reasons, routine immunisation of laboratory staff is not indicated. Staff in reference laboratories who work with the organism may however be at higher risk and a risk assessment should be carried out to determine the need for immunisation. Consideration should also be given to the need to protect staff in the field investigating outbreaks where considerable exposure to *N. meningitidis* may be experienced in the course of taking throat swabs.

■ **12.14 Poliomyelitis** (Chapter 26)

No adult should remain unimmunised against polio. All staff should have their polio immunisation history checked on commencing employment and offered a primary course if necessary. Staff likely to be exposed to polio viruses should be offered a booster every ten years. This will include staff who handle material such as faeces that may contain polio viruses. A booster dose should also be given to any member of staff travelling on business to a country where polio still occurs, if more than ten years have elapsed since the last dose.

■ 12.15 Rabies (Chapter 27)

Pre-exposure immunisation is indicated for three groups:

(i).   Those who work with the virus.

(ii).   Those who work with recently imported primates and other animals that may be infected.

(iii).   Those working in rural areas of countries where rabies is endemic.

■ 12.16 Rubella (Chapter 28)

Rubella is a potential risk to pregnant women and currently occurs predominantly in young males. Less than 2 % of females and less than 10 % of males are susceptible. Hence, documented evidence of rubella immunisation should be asked for in all new members of staff. If there are no documents, they should be offered to have their rubella status checked and immunised if found to have inadequate antibody levels.

■ 12.17 Smallpox (Chapter 29)

■ 12.17.1 Although a number of laboratory staff work with recombinant vaccinia virus, vaccination of such laboratory workers is no longer routinely recommended.

■ 12.17.2 Where a Laboratory Director considers that there may be a special case for vaccination of a particular member of staff, the case should be discussed with the Director, Public Health Laboratory Service, Virus Reference Division, 61 Colindale Avenue, Colindale, London NW9 5HT (Tel. 0181-200 4400) or Scottish Centre for Infection and Environmental Health (SCIEH) (Tel. 0141 946 7120).

■ 12.18 Tetanus (Chapter 30)

■ 12.18.1 All staff should have their tetanus immunisation history checked on commencing employment and offered a primary course if found to be unimmunised. In assessing the likelihood that an individual has been previously immunised against tetanus, the following points should be borne in mind:

(i). Routine use of tetanus toxoid in the British army began in 1938.

(ii). Routine tetanus immunisation of infants began in 1961.

(iii). Routine use of tetanus toxoid in wound prophylaxis began in 1970.

■ 12.18.2 Regular booster doses are not indicated, although post-exposure prophylaxis may be necessary at the time of injury. Any adult who has received five doses of vaccine is likely to have lifelong immunity. Further doses may provoke hypersensitivity reactions and are not indicated.

■ 12.19 Tick borne encephalitis (Chapter 31)

Immunisation is indicated for two groups:

(i). Those who work with the virus.

(ii). Those travelling in the course of their work to infected areas of Central and Eastern Europe where prolonged exposure is likely.

■ 12.20 Typhoid (Chapter 33)

■ 12.20.1 Approximately 200 cases of typhoid are reported each year in the UK, thus it is likely that many workers in microbiological laboratories will be exposed to the organism at some time. The risk of exposure may vary in different parts of the country.

■ 12.20.2 Typhoid vaccine offers suboptimal protection (approximately 70%) and regular boosters are required. It is recommended that all staff who may handle faeces, or who work with the organism, should be immunised. The subunit (Typhim Vi) vaccine is likely to cause fewer local and systemic reactions.

■ 12.21 Yellow Fever (Chapter 35)

Immunisation is indicated for two groups:

(i). Those who work with the virus or handle material from suspected cases.

(ii). Those travelling in the course of their work to infected areas of Africa or South America.

■ 12.22 Bibliography

Health and Safety Commission's Health Services Advisory Committee. Safe working and the prevention of infection in clinical laboratories. London: HMS0, 1991 ISBN 0-11-885446-1.
Health and Safety Commission's Health Services Advisory Committee. Safe working and the prevention of infection in the mortuary and post-mortem room. London: HMSO, 1991 ISBN 0-11-885448-8

Safety Precautions: Notes for guidance. Fourth edition. Public Health Laboratory Service, 1992.

Advisory Committee on Dangerous Pathogens and Advisory Committee on Genetic Modification. Vaccination of laboratory workers handling vaccinia and related pox viruses infectious far humans. London: HMSO, 1990.
Reid D D. Incidence of tuberculosis among workers in medical laboratories. Br Med J 1957; 2: 10-14.

Grist NR. Hepatitis in clinical laboratories: a three-year survey. J Clin Pathol 1975; 28 255-259.

Harrington J M Shannon H S. Incidence of tuberculosis, hepatitis, brucellosis and shigellosis in British medical laboratory workers. Br Med J 1976; 1: 759-762.

Grist NR Emslie JAN. Infections in British clinical laboratories, 1982-83. J Clin Pathol 1985; 39: 72 1-725.

Grist NR Emslie JAN. Infections in British clinical laboratories, 1984-85. J Clin Pathol 1987; 40: 826-829.

Grist NR Emslie JAN. Infections in British clinical laboratories, 1986-87. J Clin Pathol 1989; 42: 677-681.

Grist NR Emslie JAN. Infections in British clinical laboratories, 1988-89. J Clin Pathol 1991 ; 44 : 667-669.

Collins CH. Laboratory-acquired infections. Second edition. London: Butterworths, 1988.

Subcommittee of the Joint Tuberculosis Committee of the British Thoracic Society. Control and prevention of tuberculosis in the United Kingdom: Code of Practice 1994. Thorax 1994; 49 : 1193-1200

Protecting health care workers and patients from hepatitis B. Communicable Disease Report 1993; 3: 159.

PHLS Hepatitis Subcommittee. Exposure to hepatitis B virus: guidance on post-exposure prophylaxis. Communicable Disease Report 1992; 2: R97-101.

Association of Clinical Pathologists survey of infections in British clinical laboratories 1970-1989. Grist NR, Emslie JAN J.Clin.Pathol. 1994;47:391-394.

13   Anthrax

■ 13.1 Introduction

Anthrax is an acute bacterial disease affecting the skin (and rarely, the lungs or gastro-intestinal tract) caused by the aerobic bacillus, *Bacillus anthracis* and spread through its spores. Anthrax is primarily a disease of herbivorous animals but all mammals may be susceptible to infection. Spores can be found in animal products such as wool, hair, hides, skins, bones, bonemeal, and in the carcasses of infected animals. The spores can also contaminate soil. Spores may survive for many years. New areas of infection may develop through the use of infected animal feed. In the UK human anthrax is rare, and is almost entirely an occupational disease affecting workers handling infected animals (abattoir workers) or exposed to imported infected animal products. Prevention depends on, for example, controlling anthrax in livestock and on disinfecting imported animal products. Processing of hides, wool and bone by tanning, dyeing, carbonising or acid treatment also provides a means to control the risk of infection. Bonemeal used as horticultural fertiliser may rarely contain anthrax spores if it has not been correctly treated (e.g. by steam sterilisation) in the country of origin; a certificate of sterilisation should accompany any consignment on entry to the UK. Those handling it in bulk should wear impervious gloves which should be destroyed after use.

■ 13.2 Vaccine

Human anthrax vaccine is the alum precipitate of the antigen found in the sterile filtrate from cultures of the Sterne strain of *Bacillus anthracis*, preserved with thiomersal. It creates protective immunity to the toxin produced by the bacillus. The vaccine must be kept at 2-8°C and should be well shaken before being given by intramuscular injection. Freezing must be avoided.

■ 13.3 Recommendations

■ 13.3.1   Immunisation against anthrax is recommended **only for workers at risk of exposure to the disease (13.1).**

■ 13.3.2 Workers at risk should receive information, instruction and training on the nature of anthrax including its mode of transmission and how to recognise early symptoms of the disease. Good hygiene practice, i.e. regular handwashing, avoidance of hand to eye/mouth contact and covering cuts and abrasions before working, should be demonstrated. Suitable protective clothing should be worn. Adequate washing facilities should be provided. Where appropriate, industry/engineering controls, e.g. enclosure of dusty processes and exhaust ventilation, should be employed with procedures for regular workplace cleaning and disinfection.

Anthrax

■ 13.4 Route of administration and dosage

■ 13.4.1   Four injections of 0.5ml should be given intramuscularly, with intervals of three weeks between the first three injections and six months between the third and fourth. Annual reinforcing doses of 0.5ml intramuscularly are advised. The batch number of the vaccine should be recorded in the recipient's records.

■ 13.4.2   Advice on the use of anthrax vaccine can be obtained from the Centre for Applied Microbiology and Research (Tel. 01980 612100).

■ 13.5   Adverse reactions

■ 13.5.1   Reports of adverse reactions to anthrax vaccine are very rare. Mild erythema and swelling lasting up to two days may occur at the site of the injection. Occasionally regional lymphadenopathy, mild fever and urticaria may develop.

■ 13.5.2   Severe reactions should be reported to the Committee on Safety of Medicines through the Medicines Control Agency using the yellow card system.

■ 13.6   Contraindications

There are no specific contraindications. A local or general reaction to the first injection does not necessarily indicate a predisposition to reactions following subsequent injections.

■ 13.7   Management of outbreaks

All cases of anthrax should be notified. An attempt should be made to confirm the diagnosis bacteriologically and the source of infection should be investigated. Penicillin is the treatment of choice. Skin lesions should be covered; any discharge or soiled articles should be disinfected. Anthrax vaccine has no role in the management of a case or outbreak.

■ 13.8   Supplies

Anthrax vaccine is available from:

Public Health Laboratory Service:
Communicable Disease Surveillance Centre, Tel. 0181 200 6868

Cardiff Tel. 01222 755944
Leeds Tel. 0113 264 5011
Liverpool Tel. 0151 525 2323

Scotland:
Perth Royal Infirmary Tel. 01738 23111
Law Hospital Tel. 01698 361100, ext 2785
Borders General Hospital. Tel. 01896 754333

Northern Ireland:
Public Health Laboratory, Belfast City Hospital Tel. 01232 329241, ext 2968
or 2215.

■ 13.9 Bibliography

Vaccine against anthrax
Editorial
BMJ 1965; ii: 717-8.

The epidemiology of anthrax
James D G
J Antimicrob Chemother 1976; 2: 319-20.

Thoroughly modern anthrax
Turnbull PC
Abstracts of Hygiene, Bureau Hyg & Trop Dis 1986; 61(9)

A case of anthrax septicaemia in a London teaching hospital
Comm Dis Rep 1995; 5 : 169

A spot of bother : a report of a case and a review of human anthrax in the UK
1970-1991.
Comm Dis and Env Health in Scotland Weekly Report 1992 : (21); 4-6.

Anthrax

14   Cholera

■ 14.1   Introduction

■ 14.1.1   Cholera is an acute diarrhoeal illness caused by an enterotoxin produced by *Vibrio cholerae* which have colonised the small bowel. The illness is characterised by the sudden onset of profuse, watery stools with occasional vomiting. Dehydration, metabolic acidosis and circulatory collapse may follow rapidly. Untreated, over 50% of the most severe cases die within a few hours of onset; with prompt, correct treatment, mortality is less than 1%. Mild cases with only moderate diarrhoea also occur and asymptomatic infection is common. The incubation period is usually between two and five days but may be only a few hours.

■ 14.1.2   The disease is mainly water-borne and acquired by the ingestion of contaminated water, shellfish or other food, but person-to-person spread may also occur. Even in infected areas the risk to travellers is very small.

■ 14.1.3   Cholera due to the classical biotype of *V. cholerae* was endemic in the Ganges Delta of West Bengal and Bangladesh during the last two centuries and caused epidemics and global pandemics. The seventh global pandemic which started in 1961 is due to the El Tor biotype and is now widespread in the Far East, Africa and central South America. A new type (0139) producing similar symptoms has been identified in India, Bangladesh and Thailand.

■ 14.1.4   The last indigenous case of cholera in England and Wales was reported in 1893. Occasional imported cases occur, but the risk of an outbreak is very small in countries with modern sanitation and water supplies and high standards of food hygiene.

■ 14.1.5   Prevention of cholera depends primarily on improving sanitation and water supplies in endemic areas and on scrupulous personal and food and water hygiene. Cholera vaccine gives only limited personal protection and does not prevent spread of the disease. **The World Health Organisation (WHO) therefore no longer recommends use of the vaccine, and immunisation against cholera is no longer an official requirement for entry into any foreign country.**

■ 14.2 Vaccine

No cholera vaccine is currently available in the UK.

■ 14.3 Recommendations

Cholera vaccine should not be required of any traveller. Officials at a few remote borders may occasionally ask people travelling from infected areas for evidence of immunisation. Travellers who are likely to cross such borders, especially overland, should be advised to carry a signed statement on official paper that cholera vaccine is not indicated (see Health Information for Overseas Travel).

■ 14.4 Managements of outbreaks

Cholera vaccine has **no role** in the management of contacts of any cases, or in controlling the spread of infection. Control of the disease depends on public health measures rather than immunisation. Suspected cases should be notified to the CCDC or CAMO immediately. Sources of infection should be identified and treated appropriately. Contacts should maintain high standards of personal hygiene to avoid becoming infected.

■ 14.5 Bibliography

International Travel and Health 1995.
World Health Organisation, Geneva.

15   Diphtheria

■ 15.1 Introduction

■ 15.1.1   Diphtheria is an acute infectious disease affecting the upper respiratory tract and occasionally the skin. It is characterised by an inflammatory exudate which forms a greyish membrane in the respiratory tract which may cause respiratory obstruction. The incubation period is from two to five days. Patients with disease may be infectious for up to four weeks, but carriers may shed *Corynebacteria diphtheriae* for longer. A toxin is produced by diphtheria bacilli which affects particularly myocardium and nervous and adrenal tissues. Spread is by droplet infection and through contact with articles soiled by infected persons (fomites). In countries where hygiene is poor, cutaneous diphtheria is the predominant source of infection.

■ 15.1.2   Effective protection against the disease is provided by active immunisation. The introduction of immunisation against diphtheria on a national scale in 1940 resulted in a dramatic fall in the number of notified cases and deaths from the disease. In 1940, 46,281 cases with 2,480 deaths were notified, compared with 37 cases and six deaths in 1957. From 1986 to 1995, 38 isolates of toxigenic *C. diphtheriae* were identified by the PHLS Diphtheria Reference Unit. Of these, 19 were carriers and 7 were cutaneous infections. There was one death in 1994: a 14 year old with no record of immunisation who had visited Pakistan.

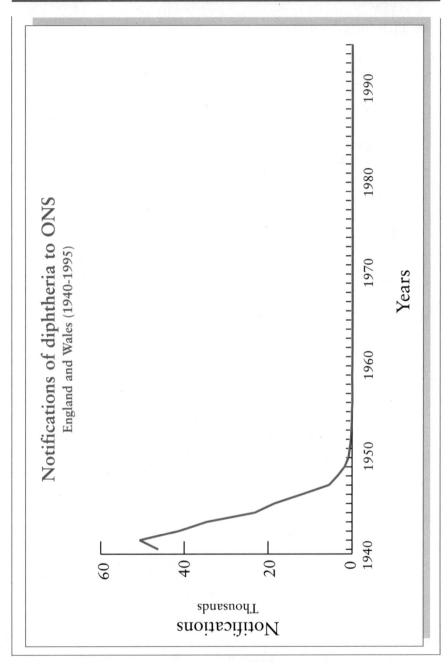

Notifications of diphtheria to ONS
England and Wales (1940-1995)

Years

Notifications
Thousands

Diphtheria

■ 15.1.3   The increase in notifications of diphtheria since 1992 has been due to a rise in isolations of a non-toxigenic C. *diphtheriae var gravis*. Presentation is usually with a sore throat without signs of toxicity.

■ 15.1.4   Since 1991, there has been an epidemic of diphtheria in Russia, now involving other Newly Independent States of the former Soviet Union. In 1995, approximately 52,000 cases of diphtheria and 1,700 deaths were reported. The causes of this epidemic are low immunisation coverage in young children, waning immunity in adults and large scale population movements. There have been some importations from the former Soviet Union countries into neighbouring countries but no evidence of importation into the UK.

■ 15.1.5   The disease and the organism have been virtually eliminated from the United Kingdom; the few cases which have occurred in recent years have nearly all been imported from the Indian subcontinent or from Africa, with minimal spread. There is thus no possibility now of acquiring natural immunisation from sub-clinical infection. High immunisation uptake must be maintained in order to protect the population against the possibility of a resurgence of the disease which could follow the introduction of cases or carriers of toxigenic strains from overseas.

■ 15.1.6   Recent published data indicate that approximately 38% of UK blood donors are susceptible to diphtheria. A significant trend of decreasing immunity with increasing age was apparent: 25% of donors aged 20-29 were susceptible compared with 53% of those aged 50-59.

■ 15.2 Diphtheria vaccine

■ 15.2.1 Diphtheria immunisation protects by stimulating the production of antitoxin which provides immunity to the effects of the toxin. The immunogen is prepared by treating a cell-free purified preparation of toxin with formaldehyde, thereby converting it into the innocuous diphtheria toxoid. This however is a relatively poor immunogen, and for use as a vaccine it is usually adsorbed on to an adjuvant, either aluminium phosphate or aluminium hydroxide. Bordetella pertussis also acts as an effective adjuvant.

Diphtheria

15   Diphtheria

■ 15.2.2   The recommended vaccines for immunisation are:
Adsorbed diphtheria/tetanus/pertussis (**DTP**).
Adsorbed diphtheria/tetanus (**DT**).
Adsorbed diphtheria (**D**).
Adsorbed low dose diphtheria vaccine for adults (**d**).
Adsorbed tetanus/low dose diphtheria vaccine for adults (**Td**).

The dose is 0.5ml given by intramuscular or deep subcutaneous injection.

Plain vaccines are less immunogenic and have no advantage in terms of reaction rates and are no longer available.

Vaccines should be stored at 2-8°C and protected from light. Vaccine which has been frozen should not be used.   Disposal should be by incineration at a temperature not less than 1100°C at a registered waste disposal contractor.

■ 15.3   Recommendations

■ 15.3.1   **For immunisation of infants and children up to ten years of age.**

a. **Primary immunisation**

Diphtheria vaccine as a component of triple vaccine (diphtheria toxoid, tetanus toxoid and Bordetella pertussis toxoid) is recommended for infants from two months of age. Adsorbed vaccine should be used as it has been shown to cause fewer reactions than plain vaccine which is no longer available.   If the pertussis component is contraindicated, adsorbed diphtheria/tetanus vaccine should be used. **A course of primary immunisation consists of three doses starting at two months with an interval of one month between each dose** (see 11.1). If a course is interrupted it may be resumed; there is no need to start again.

b. **Reinforcing immunisation**

Booster doses of vaccine containing diphtheria and tetanus toxoids are recommended for: (i) children before school entry - DT, preferably at least three years after the last dose of the primary course, and (ii) before leaving school at 13 to 18 years of age - Td, both at the same time as OPV.

In approximately 25% of children, a fifth tetanus vaccine dose is said to have been given by the time the school leaving booster (Td) is due. If a child requires a tetanus booster after a tetanus prone wound, **after the fourth dose** has been given (at around 4 years of age) and ten years has elapsed, then Td should be given. The school leaving Td dose is then not necessary.

If there is a documented history of a fifth dose of tetanus vaccine having already been given when the school leaving booster is due, **and** supplies of a low dose diphtheria vaccine product are readily available (either low dose diphtheria vaccine (d) or 0.1 ml of paediatric strength diphtheria vaccine (D)), then one of these latter two products should be used. If neither is available, then Td should be given with an interval of at least one month since the last dose of tetanus vaccine. Recent experience has shown that when Td is given to children who have already had 5 doses of tetanus vaccine, there is some increase in the number who have local reactions and low grade pyrexias, but no increase in the numbers with pyrexias over 38.5°C

■ 15.3.2 **Immunisation of persons aged ten years or over**

a. **Primary immunisation**

Low dose diphtheria vaccine for adults (d) must be used because of the possibility of a reaction in an individual who is already immune. Past experience showed that when full strength diphtheria vaccine preparations (D) were given to adults, there were considerably more localised and generalised reactions, such as high fever. Three doses (0.5ml) of low dose vaccine for adults (d) should be given by deep subcutaneous or intramuscular injection at intervals of one month. When this product is not available, then a 0.1 ml injection of the standard paediatric diphtheria vaccine (D) may be given as an alternative. For adults who have never received either diphtheria or tetanus vaccine previously, three doses of Td should be used, each given one month apart.

b. **Reinforcing immunisation**

A single dose of 0.5ml of low-dose diphtheria vaccine (d) must be used for all persons aged ten years and over. When this product is not available, then a 0.1 ml injection of the standard paediatric diphtheria vaccine (D) may be given as an alternative. When a reinforcing dose of tetanus vaccine is also required, then Td should be used. Prior Schick testing is not necessary and the material is no longer available.

■ 15.3.3   Children given DTP at monthly intervals without a booster dose at 18 months have been shown to have adequate levels of diphtheria and tetanus antibody at school entry. A booster dose at 18 months for such children is therefore not necessary.

■ 15.3.4   **Travel:** Primary or reinforcing doses are recommended for travellers to epidemic or endemic areas (see 'Health Information for Overseas Travel' for more information).

■ 15.3.5   **Contacts of a diphtheria case, or carriers of a toxigenic strain**

Individuals exposed to such a risk should be given a complete course or a reinforcing dose according to their age and immunisation history as follows:

a. **Immunised** children up to ten years.
One injection of diphtheria vaccine (D).

b. **Immunised** children ten years and over, and adults.
One injection of low dose diphtheria vaccine for adults (d or Td).

c. **Unimmunised** children under ten years.
   Three injections of diphtheria (D) vaccine (or DTP and polio vaccines if appropriate) at monthly intervals.

d. **Unimmunised** children ten years and over, and adults.
Three injections of low dose diphtheria vaccine for adults (d) or Td at monthly intervals.

Unimmunised contacts of a case of diphtheria should in addition be given a prophylactic course of erythromycin or penicillin. Symptomatic contacts (including close contacts) of cases of sore throat associated with non-toxigenic C. *diphtheriae* should be swabbed and treated accordingly; asymptomatic contacts do not require swabbing or antibiotic prophylaxis. Contacts of cases of C. *ulcerans* do not require prophylaxis as human to human transmission does not occur.

■ 15.3.6   HIV positive individuals may be immunised against diphtheria in the absence of any contraindications.

■ 15.4 Testing for diphtheria immunity

The material for carrying out the Schick test is no longer available. Individuals who may be exposed to diphtheria in the course of their work should have their immunity checked by antibody testing at least three months after immunisation is completed and boosted at ten year intervals thereafter.

■ 15.5 Adverse reactions

■ 15.5.1 Swelling and redness at the injection site are common. Malaise, transient fever and headache may also occur. A small painless nodule may form at the injection site but usually disappears without sequelae. Severe anaphylactic reactions are rare. Neurological reactions have been reported occasionally.

■ 15.5.2 Severe reactions should be reported to the Committee on Safety of Medicines using the yellow card system.

■ 15.6 Contraindications

■ 15.6.1 a. If a child is suffering from any acute illness, immunisation should be postponed until the child has fully recovered. Minor infections without fever or systemic upset are not reasons to postpone immunisation.

b. Immunisation should not proceed in children who have had a severe local or general reaction to a preceding dose (see 7.2.2), if it is thought that the diphtheria component has caused the preceding reaction. Reactions to the pertussis component of DTP are the most likely and immunisation should proceed with DT; acellular pertussis vaccine can be used if the previous reaction was a local one.

■ 15.6.2 When there is a need to control an outbreak, diphtheria vaccine may have to be given to individuals suffering from acute febrile illness. Low-dose diphtheria vaccine for adults (d or Td) must be used for persons aged ten years and over.

Diphtheria

■ 15.7 Diphtheria antitoxin

Diphtheria antitoxin is now only used in suspected cases of diphtheria. Tests with a trial dose to exclude hypersensitivity should precede its use. It should be given without waiting for bacteriological confirmation since its action is specific for diphtheria. It may be given intramuscularly or intravenously, the dosage depending on the clinical condition of the patient. This is shown in the following table. It is no longer used for diphtheria prophylaxis because of the risk of provoking a hypersensitivity reaction to the horse serum from which it is derived. Unimmunised contacts of a case of diphtheria should be promptly investigated, kept under surveillance and given antibiotic prophylaxis and vaccine, as in 15.3.5.

Table: Dosage of antitoxin recommended for various types of diphtheria

Type of diphtheria	Dosage (units)	Route
Nasal	10,000 - 20,000	Intramuscular
Tonsillar	15,000 - 25,000	Intramuscular or intravenous
Pharyngeal or laryngeal	20,000 - 40,000	Intramuscular or intravenous
Combined types or delayed diagnosis	40,000 - 60,000	Intravenous
Severe diphtheria e.g. with extensive membrane and/or severe oedema (bull-neck diphtheria)	40,000 - 100,000	Intravenous or part intravenous and part intramuscular

If acute anaphylaxis develops, intravenous adrenaline (0.2 to 0.5ml of 1:1000 solution) should be administered immediately by intravenous injection.

Antitoxin is probably of no value for cutaneous disease, although some authorities use 20,000 to 40,000 units of antitoxin because toxic sequelae have been reported.

■ 15.8 Supplies

■ 15.8.1   Adsorbed diphtheria/tetanus/pertussis (DTP) and adsorbed diphtheria/tetanus (DT) vaccines (15.2.2) are manufactured by Evans Medical (Tel. 01372 364000) and Pasteur Merieux MSD Ltd (Tel. 01628 773200). Adsorbed diphtheria vaccine is manufactured by Evans Medical.

■ 15.8.2   Low-dose diphtheria vaccine for adults (d) is manufactured by Swiss Serum and Vaccine Institute, Berne, and distributed in the UK by Farillon (Tel. 01708 379000).

■ 15.8.3   Adsorbed low dose diphtheria vaccine for adults combined with tetanus (Td) is manufactured by Pasteur Merieux MSD Ltd (Tel. 01628 773200).

■ 15.8.4   These vaccines are supplied by Farillon (Tel. 01708 379000) as part of the childhood immunisation programme, except for the syringe presentation of adsorbed low dose diphtheria vaccine for adults combined with tetanus (Td) which is supplied by Pasteur Merieux MSD Ltd (Tel. 01628 773200).

■ 15.8.5   In Scotland these vaccines can be obtained through Scottish Healthcare Supplies Division of Common Service Agency (Tel. 0131 552 6255).

■ 15.8.6   Diphtheria antitoxin is supplied in vials containing 1000 iu per ml. Manufactured by Pasteur Merieux MSD Ltd and distributed in the UK by the Communicable Disease Surveillance Centre (Tel 0181 200 6868). In Northern Ireland the source of diphtheria antitoxin is the Public Health Laboratory, Belfast City Hospital, Lisburn Road, Belfast Tel. 01232 329241.

Diphtheria

■ 15.9 Bibliography

Immunity of children to diphtheria, tetanus and poliomyelitis.
Bainton D, Freeman M, Magrath D, Sheffield F W, Smith J G W.
BMJ 1979; (1), 854-857.

Advantages of aluminium hydroxide adsorbed combined diphtheria, tetanus and pertussis vaccines for the immunisation of infants.
Butler N R, Voyce M A, Burland W M, Hilton M L.
BMJ 1959; (1), 663-666.

Susceptibility to diphtheria.
Report of Ad Hoc Working Group.
Lancet 1978; (i), 428-430.

Immunisation of adults against diphtheria.
Sheffield F W, Ironside A G, Abbott J D.
BMJ 1978; (2), 249-250.

Durability of immunity to diphtheria, tetanus and poliomyelitis after a three dose immunisation schedule completed in the first eight months of life.
Jones E A, Johns A, Magrath D I, Melville-Smith M, Sheffield F.
Vaccine 1989: 7; 300-2.

Enhanced surveillance of non-toxigenic C.diphtheriae infections, CDR Weekly Report 1996; 6(4);29.

Manual for the management and control of diphtheria in the European Region
Begg N
Copenhagen: The Expanded Programme on Immunisation in the European Region of WHO, 1994.

Diphtheria: Manual for the Laboratory diagnosis of Diphtheria
Efstratiou A
Copenhagen : The Expanded Programme on Immunisation in the European Region of WHO, 1994.

Diphtheria Immunity in UK Blood Donors
Maple P A, Efstratiou A, George R C et al
Lancet 1995; 345 : 963-65

16 Haemophilus Influenzae Type b (Hib)

■ 16.1 Introduction

■ 16.1.1   Infections due to *Haemophilus influenzae* were an important cause of morbidity and mortality, especially in young children. Invasive disease is usually caused by encapsulated strains of the organism. Six capsular serotypes (a-f) are known to cause disease in man; however, over 99% of typeable strains causing invasive disease are type b. Non-typeable strains can occasionally cause invasive disease. Non-encapsulated strains are mainly associated with respiratory infections such as exacerbations of chronic bronchitis and otitis media.

■ 16.1.2   The most common presentation of invasive Hib disease is meningitis, frequently accompanied by bacteraemia. This presentation accounts for approximately 60% of all cases. 15% of cases present with epiglottitis, another potentially dangerous infection. Septicaemia, without any other concomitant infection, occurs in 10% of cases. The remainder is made up of cases of septic arthritis, osteomyelitis, cellulitis, pneumonia and pericarditis. The sequelae following Hib meningitis include deafness, convulsions and intellectual impairment. In studies conducted in Wales and Oxford, 8 to 11% had permanent neurological sequelae. The case fatality rate is 4 to 5%.

■ 16.1.3   Based on the Wales and Oxford studies, the estimated annual incidence of invasive Hib disease before the introduction of immunisation, was 34 per 100,000 children under the age of 5 years, ie. one in every 600 children developed some form of invasive Hib disease before their fifth birthday. The number of laboratory reports in England and Wales increased from 869 in 1983 to 1259 in 1989.

■ 16.1.4   The disease is rare in children under 3 months of age, but rises progressively during the first year, reaching a peak incidence between 10 and 11 months. Thereafter, the incidence declines steadily to 4 years of age after which infection becomes uncommon.

■ 16.1.5   Since the introduction of Hib immunisation, disease incidence has fallen dramatically. There were 39 laboratory reports of Hib infection in England and Wales in 1995 (9 in children less than one year of age), compared with 627 (229 in children under one year) in 1992. There was only one death in 1995. The decline in those under 1 year, at highest risk of invasive disease, was 96%. Notifications of *H. influenzae* meningitis (all ages, England and Wales) declined from 484 to 60 in the same period, a fall of 88%. The decrease in notifications for children less than one year is similar to that observed for laboratory reports. By March 1996, vaccine coverage by the second birthday was 95%.

16   Haemophilus Influenzae Type b (Hib)

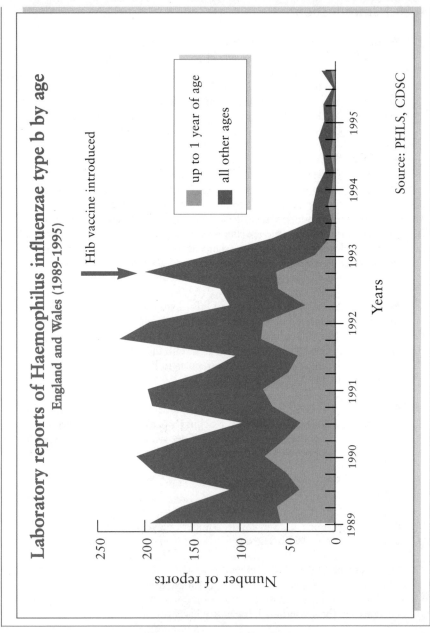

Laboratory reports of Haemophilus influenzae type b by age
England and Wales (1989-1995)

Hib vaccine introduced

up to 1 year of age

all other ages

Number of reports

Years

Source: PHLS, CDSC

16   Haemophilus Influenzae Type b (Hib)

■ 16.2 Vaccine

■ 16.2.1   Vaccines against Hib were first produced in the early 1970s. These vaccines contained purified capsular polysaccharide and were shown to be effective in protecting children against disease. However, the vaccines were not immunogenic in children under 18 months of age, the group in whom the risks of disease were highest. More recently, conjugate vaccines have been developed. Here the capsular polysaccharides have been linked to proteins, thereby improving the vaccine immunogenicity, especially in children less than one year of age. The capsular polysaccharides have been conjugated to diphtheria and tetanus toxoids, group B meningococcal outer membrane protein and a non-toxic derivative of diphtheria toxin (CRM197).

■ 16.2.2   The efficacy and safety of the conjugate Hib vaccines have been demonstrated in large field trials in Finland, the United States and in the UK. Vaccine efficacy exceeds 95% in infants immunised from 2 months of age. Studies comparing different vaccines, using the present United Kingdom primary schedule, have shown that 90 to 99% of children developed protective levels of antibody, following 3 doses (personal communication).

■ 16.2.3   Active surveillance of invasive Hib infections in fully immunised children started in September 1992 on a UK wide basis. By 1 April 1995, 35 true vaccine failures had been identified. Several of the cases had underlying conditions, such as immunoglobulin deficiency, that may have predisposed to vaccine failure. During the period of surveillance around seven million doses of Hib vaccine have been distributed. This is consistent with a vaccine efficacy in excess of 95%.

■ 16.2.4   The conjugate Hib vaccines are not live, containing non-replicating bacterial capsular antigens.

■ 16.2.5   The vaccine should be stored between 2-8°C but not frozen. If the vaccine is frozen, it should not be used.

■ 16.3   Route of administration and dosage

The dose of Hib vaccine is 0.5 ml. It should be given by deep subcutaneous or intramuscular injection, in a different limb from other concurrently administered vaccines. Recording the sites of injection of concurrently administered vaccines allows any local reactions to be attributed to the appropriate antigen or antigens.

16 Haemophilus Influenzae Type b (Hib)

■ 16.4 Recommendations

■ 16.4.1   Conjugate Hib vaccine, as a component of the primary course of childhood immunisation, is recommended for all infants from 2 months of age, in the absence of a genuine contraindication.

■ 16.4.2   The primary course consists of three doses of Hib vaccine with an interval of one month between each dose. If the primary course is interrupted, it should be resumed allowing one month intervals between the remaining doses.

■ 16.4.3   Recent studies undertaken by the PHLS have shown that there is no loss of immunogenicity or increase in reactogenicity when children are immunised with different sequences of Hib vaccines from different manufacturers. The studies compared tetanus conjugated Hib vaccine with CRM197 diphtheria mutant conjugate Hib vaccine. **Children who start a course of Hib vaccine on one product can therefore have the course completed with another product should the need arise. There is no need to recommence a course of Hib vaccine.**

■ 16.4.4   **There is now sufficient evidence of preservation of immunogenicity and no increase in reactogenicity to allow recommendation for Hib vaccines to be mixed with DTP vaccines for simultaneous administration.** Pasteur Merieux tetanus conjugate Hib vaccine (ActHib), a lyophilised powder, can be suspended with Pasteur Merieux DTP vaccine as the diluent for immediate administration. Evans DTP (0.5ml) can be mixed with SKB tetanus conjugate vaccine (Hiberix). The volume of the combined vaccine is 0.5ml and no further diluent is used. Evans DTP (0.5ml) can be mixed with Lederle Praxis CRM197 mutant diphtheria vaccine (HibTITER) giving a final volume of 1.0ml for simultaneous administration. Studies have shown that this volume of injected material is well tolerated.

■ 16.4.5   No reinforcing (booster) doses are recommended for children who have received three injections at the appropriate times.

■ 16.4.6   Children under the age of 13 months are at high risk of disease and should receive 3 doses of Hib vaccine, even if they have already commenced or completed their immunisations against Diphtheria, Tetanus, Pertussis and Poliomyelitis. Hib vaccine can be given at the same time as any other vaccines and any outstanding Hib doses should be given after the completion of the other antigens, separated by one month from the last Hib dose.

■ 16.4.7   Unimmunised children between 13 and 48 months should be given a single injection of Hib vaccine, either simultaneously with MMR vaccine, or singly if the MMR has already been given. Children in this age group are at lower risk of disease and the vaccine is effective after a single dose.

■ 16.4.8   Because the incidence of invasive disease falls sharply after 4 years, routine immunisation of older children and adults is not recommended.

■ 16.4.9   HIV positive individuals may receive Hib vaccine.

■ 16.4.10   Asplenic children and adults, irrespective of age or the interval from splenectomy, should receive a single dose of Hib vaccine. There are data to suggest that a single dose of Hib vaccine is immunogenic in splenectomised adults. Those under one year should be given three doses. At present, there are no data to indicate a need for further booster doses. When splenectomy is performed electively, the vaccine should be given ideally at least two weeks earlier.

■ 16.5   Adverse reactions

■ 16.5.1   Swelling and redness at the injection site have been reported at a rate of up to 10%, following the first dose. However, the size of these reactions was rarely sufficient to contraindicate further doses. These effects usually appear within 3 to 4 hours and resolve completely within 24 hours. The incidence of these reactions declines with subsequent doses, supporting the recommendation that courses of immunisation should be completed despite the occurrence of such reactions.

■ 16.5.2   When a severe local reaction (see 7.2.2) follows the administration of combined DTP/Hib vaccines, the course should be continued with the products given separately (DTP at one site, Hib at another site). Should a severe generalised reaction follow the administration of combined DTP/Hib vaccine, then Hib vaccine should be given at one site and DT vaccine at another.

■ 16.5.3   The addition of Hib vaccine to routine immunisation does not lead to an increase in the number of febrile convulsions that occur in the 72 hours after immunisation, compared to control periods.

16   Haemophilus Influenzae Type b (Hib)

■ 16.5.4   Surveillance in the UK of adverse events following Hib immunisation has not revealed any severe reactions that are not routinely reported after either DTP vaccine or MMR, which have most often been administered at the same time.

■ 16.6 Contraindications

■ 16.6.1   a. If the child is suffering from any acute illness, immunisation should be postponed until the child has recovered. Minor infections, without fever or systemic upset, are not reasons to postpone immunisation.

b. Immunisation should not proceed in children who have had a severe local reaction or a general reaction which can be confidently related to a preceding Hib immunisation, but see 16.5.2. When Hib vaccine has been given with DTP, generalised reactions are more likely to have been caused by the pertussis component of the DTP vaccine.

■ 16.6.2   Hib vaccine is not a live vaccine, but there is no evidence at present of its safety or lack of safety in pregnancy.

■ 16.7   Immunisation of cases and contacts of Hib disease

■ 16.7.1   Household contacts of a case of invasive Hib disease have an increased risk of contracting disease themselves. Any unimmunised household contact, under 4 years of age, should receive Hib vaccine (three doses if under 13 months, one dose if over 13 months and under 4 years). Independently of immunisation, rifampicin prophylaxis should be given to household contacts. The recommended dose is 20mg/kg/day (up to a maximum of 600mg daily) once daily for **four** days. Chemoprophylaxis is not indicated for those contacts aged under 4 years who have been fully immunised against Hib disease.

■ 16.7.2   The index case should also be immunised, irrespective of age.

■ 16.7.3   When a case occurs in a playgroup, nursery or creche, the opportunity should be taken to identify and immunise any unimmunised children under 4 years of age. Chemoprophylaxis should be offered to all room contacts - teachers and children - when **two or more** cases of Hib disease have occurred in a playgroup, nursery or creche, within 120 days.

There is little evidence, however, that children in such settings are at significantly higher risk of Hib disease than the general population of the same age.

■ 16.8   Supplies

Hib vaccines are manufactured by:

Pasteur Merieux MSD Ltd Tel. 01628 773200
Wyeth Lederle Vaccines Tel. 01628 414794
SmithKline Beecham Tel. 0181-913 4811 or 0181-913 4387.
Hib DTP combination vaccines are supplied by:
Pasteur Merieux MSD Ltd Tel. 01628 773200

They are supplied by Farillon (Tel. 01708 379000) as part of the National Childhood Immunisation Programme.

■ 16.9   Bibliography

A survey of invasive Haemophilus influenzae infections
B Nazareth, M P E Slack, A J Howard, P A Waight, N T Begg
Communicable Disease Report
Vol 2: Review No 2: 31 January 1992

A randomised, prospective field trial of a conjugate vaccine in the protection of infants and young children against invasive Haemophilus influenzae type b disease
Juhani Eskola et al
New England Journal of Medicine
Vol 323: No. 20: 1991:1381-1387

Immunisation of infants against Haemophilus influenzae type b in the UK
R Booy, E R Moxon
Archives of Disease in Childhood
1991: 66: 1251-1254

Efficacy in infancy of oligosaccharide conjugate Haemophilus influenzae type b (HbOC) vaccine in a United States population of 61 080 children
S B Black, H R Shinefield, B Fireman, R Hiatt, M Polen, E Vittinghoff
Pediatr Infect Dis J
1991: 10: 97-104

Safety and immunogenicity of oligosaccharide conjugate Haemophilus influenzae type b (HbOC) vaccine in infancy
S B Black, H Shinefield, D Lampert, B Fireman, R A Hiatt, M Polen, E Vittinghoff
Pediatr Infect Dis J
1991: Vol 10: No. 2

The efficacy in Navajo infants of a conjugate vaccine consisting of Haemophilus influenzae type b polysaccharide and neisseria meningitidis outer-membrane protein complex
M Santosham et al
The New England Journal of Medicine
Vol 324: No. 25: 1767

Chemoprophylaxis for Haemophilus influenzae type b. Cartwright KAV, Begg NT, Hull D. Br Med J 1991; 302 : 546-547

Use of vaccines and antibiotic prophylaxis in contacts and cases of Haemophilus influenzae type b (Hib) disease. Cartwright KAV, Begg NT, Rudd P. Communicable Disease Report 1994; 4: R16-17.

COVER (Cover Of Vaccination Evaluated Rapidly)/Korner: January-March 1996. Immunisation coverage statistics for children up to 2 years old in the UK. Communicable Disease Review 1996; 6 (30).

British Paediatric Association Surveillance Unit 9th Annual Report 1995. British Paediatric Association, London

Antibody responses and symptoms after DTP and either tetanus or diphtheria Haemophilus influenzae type b conjugate vaccines given for primary immunisation by separate or mixed injection.
Begg NT et al. Vaccine 1995; 13(16):1547-1550.

Interchangeability of conjugated Haemophilus influenzae type b vaccines during primary immunisation of infants.
Goldblatt D et al. BMJ 1996:312;817-8.

Changing patterns of invasive Haemophilus influenzae disease in England and Wales after the introduction of the Hib vaccination programme
Hargreaves R M et al
BMJ 1996; 312: 160-1

17 Hepatitis A

■ 17.1 Introduction

■ 17.1.1 Hepatitis A is transmitted by the faecal-oral route. Person to person spread is the most common method of transmission although contaminated food or drink may sometimes be involved. The incubation period is about 15-40 days and the disease is generally mild. Asymptomatic disease is common in children and severity tends to increase with age. Occasional cases of fulminant hepatitis may occur but there is no chronic carrier state and little likelihood of chronic liver damage.

■ 17.1.2 The incidence of hepatitis A shows a cyclical pattern in the UK, the most recent peak year being 1990 when 7,545 cases were reported to the Public Health Laboratory Service from England and Wales. As of 30 June 1996, there were 1,750 reports in 1995. Over 80% of cases are contracted in the UK and, whilst the majority of these are sporadic, outbreaks do occur.

■ 17.1.3 The prevalence of hepatitis A in countries outside Northern and Western Europe, North America, Australia and New Zealand is higher than in the UK. In 1995 approximately 220 (13%) of the cases notified to PHLS included a history of travel abroad in the six weeks before the onset of illness. The highest risk areas are the Indian subcontinent and the Far East, but the risk extends to Eastern Europe.

■ 17.2   Vaccine

■ 17.2.1   Hepatitis A vaccine is a formaldehyde-inactivated vaccine prepared from either the GBM or the HM 175 strain of hepatitis A virus (HAV) grown in human diploid cells. It is supplied as a suspension in pre-filled syringes.

■ 17.2.2   The vaccine should be stored at 2-8°C but not frozen, and should be protected from light. It should not be diluted or mixed with other vaccines in the same syringe.

■ 17.2.3   Immunogenicity studies show that levels of antibody produced after a primary course of vaccine administered intramuscularly

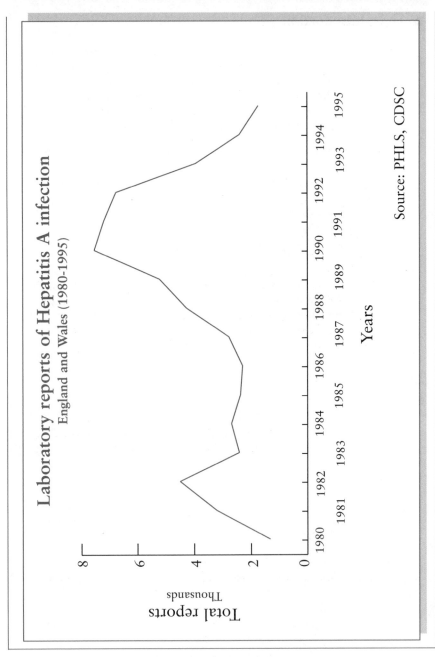

Laboratory reports of Hepatitis A infection
England and Wales (1980-1995)

Total reports
Thousands

Years

Source: PHLS, CDSC

are well in excess of those found after the administration of HNIG. The primary course produces anti-HAV antibodies which persist for at least one year and antibody persistence can be prolonged by administration of a booster dose of vaccine 6 to 12 months after the initial course.

■ 17.2.4   Human normal immunoglobulin may be administered at the same time as vaccine if protection is required less than 10 days after the first dose of hepatitis A vaccine.

■ 17.3   Recommendations

■ 17.3.1 Travellers

Protection against hepatitis A is recommended for travellers to areas of moderate or high HAV endemicity particularly if sanitation and food hygiene are likely to be poor. Active immunisation with hepatitis A vaccine is the preferred method of protection particularly for frequent travellers to such areas or for stays longer than three months. Immunisation is **not** considered necessary for those travelling to Northern or Western Europe (including Spain, Portugal and Italy), or to North America, Australia or New Zealand.

When practicable, testing for antibodies to hepatitis A virus prior to immunisation may be worthwhile in those aged fifty years or over, those born in areas of high or moderate hepatitis A endemicity and those who have a history of jaundice.

Similar considerations will apply to military and diplomatic personnel being posted or likely to be posted to hepatitis A virus endemic countries.

■ 17.3.2   Patients with chronic liver disease

Although patients with chronic liver disease are at no greater risk of acquiring hepatitis A infection, it can produce a much more serious illness in these patients who should therefore be considered for immunisation with hepatitis A vaccine. This will include intravenous drug misusers with chronic liver disease.

Hepatitis A

■ 17.3.3 Haemophiliacs

Transmission of hepatitis A has been associated with the use of Factor VIII and Factor IX concentrates where viral inactivation procedures do not destroy hepatitis A and it is especially important that haemophiliacs receiving such products should be immunised against hepatitis A. Because of the high incidence of previous infections with hepatitis B and hepatitis C and of pre-existing liver disease in haemophiliacs, infection with hepatitis A can be particularly severe and these haemophiliacs should also be immunised against hepatitis A. Those who are immunosuppressed may respond less well to vaccine, and post-immunisation testing for antibody should be considered.

Haemophiliacs should be immunised subcutaneously.

Haemophiliacs and patients with chronic liver disease should be checked for previous exposure before immunisation

■ 17.3.4 Occupational exposure

Immunisation is recommended for laboratory workers who are working directly with the virus.

There is no evidence that most health care workers are at increased risk of hepatitis A and routine immunisation is not indicated.

Outbreaks of hepatitis A have been associated with residential institutions for the mentally handicapped. Transmission does occur more readily in such institutions and immunisation of staff and residents may be appropriate in the light of local risk assessment. Similar considerations apply in other institutions where standards of personal hygiene are poor.

Infection in young children is likely to be sub-clinical and those working in day care centres and other settings with children who are not yet toilet-trained may be at increased risk of infection. Under normal circumstances, the risk of transmission to staff and children can be minimised by careful attention to personal hygiene but, for example, in the case of local community outbreaks the need for immunisation of staff and children should be discussed with the local Consultant in Communicable Disease Control or in Scotland the CPHM (CD & EH).

There is currently not enough evidence to suggest that immunisation of all sanitation workers against hepatitis A is justified and further epidemiological studies are needed to establish the risks in particular groups of workers. However raw untreated sewage is frequently contaminated with hepatitis A and a potential occupational risk exists in those workers who come into direct contact with untreated sewage. The Control of Substances Hazardous to Health (COSSH) Regulations 1994 require employers to undertake their own risk assessments and to bring into effect measures necessary to protect workers and others who may be exposed, so far as is reasonably practicable, against those risks. For those at risk of exposure to untreated sewage, immunisation against hepatitis A may be indicated as part of those measures.

Food packagers or food handlers in the United Kingdom have not been associated with HAV transmission sufficiently often to justify their immunisation as a routine measure.

■ 17.3.5 Homosexuals

Cases of hepatitis A in homosexual males have been reported in the United Kingdom. Immunisation should be offered to those whose sexual behaviour is likely to put them at risk.

■ 17.3.6 Outbreaks

There is evidence that the use of hepatitis A vaccine can interrupt ongoing community outbreaks of hepatitis A when given to a defined population. Further guidance on the management of outbreaks should be sought from the Consultant in Communicable Disease Control or from the PHLS Communicable Disease Surveillance Centre. In Scotland this should be from the CPHM (CD & EH) or from the Scottish Centre for Infection and Environmental Health. For post exposure prophylaxis for contacts of cases see section 17.9.

■ 17.4   Route of administration and dosage

■ 17.4.1 The immunisation regimen for adults consists of a single dose of vaccine. Antibodies produced in response to this persist for at least one year. A booster dose at 6-12 months after the initial dose results in more persistent antibodies and a substantial increase in antibody titre and will give immunity for up to 10 years.

■ 17.4.2 The immunisation regimen for children and adolescents up to 15 years consists of a single dose of vaccine (720 ELISA units of the HM 175 strain) administered intramuscularly and produces antibodies for at least a year. In order to obtain more persistent immunity for up to 10 years a booster dose (720 ELISA units) is recommended between six and twelve months after the primary course.

The former regimen for children and adolescents up to 15 years consisted of two doses of vaccine (360 ELISA units) administered intramuscularly two weeks to one month apart with a booster dose (360 ELISA units) recommended between six to twelve months after the primary course for prolonged immunity. Where initiated, the manufacturer recommends this regimen should be completed at this dosage.

The vaccine should be given intramuscularly in the deltoid region. It should not be given into the gluteal region because vaccine efficacy may be reduced; nor should it be administered intravenously, or intradermally and should not be routinely given subcutaneously, although the subcutaneous route should be used in haemophiliacs.

■ 17.4.3   **Dosage**

The dose in adults (16 years and over) is 1440 ELISA units (1ml) of the HM 175 strain or 160 Antigen units (0.5ml) of the GBM strain.

The dose in children/adolescents (1-15 years), in a separate presentation, is 720 ELISA units (0.5ml) of the HM175 strain. This will replace the earlier formulation where the dose was 360 ELISA units (0.5ml) (see 17.4.2).

■ 17.5 Adverse reactions

Adverse reactions are usually mild and confined to the first few days after immunisation. The most common reactions are mild transient soreness, erythema and induration at the injection site. General symptoms such as fever, malaise, fatigue, headache, nausea and loss of appetite are also reported less frequently.

It is important that all serious adverse reactions should be reported to the Committee on Safety of Medicines by the yellow card system.

■ 17.6 Contraindications

Immunisation should be postponed in individuals suffering from severe febrile illness.

The effect of HAV vaccine on fetal development has not been assessed. Since it is an inactivated vaccine, the risks to the fetus are likely to be negligible but, as with other vaccines in pregnancy, it should not be given unless there is a definite risk of infection.

■ 17.7 Supplies of Hepatitis A Vaccine

Pasteur Merieux MSD Ltd, Tel. 01628 773200
        Avaxim (adults) GBM strain

SmithKline Beecham, Tel. 0181-913 4290
        Havrix Monodose (adults)
        Havrix Monodose Junior (children and adolescents up to 15 years)
        Havrix Junior (children and adolescents up to 15 years)
        Havrix (all preparations) HM175 strain

■ 17.8 Immunoglobulin

■ 17.8.1 Human normal immunoglobulin (HNIG) offers short-term protection (up to about four months) against infection with hepatitis A to those in close contact with cases and to those travelling to areas where infection is more prevalent, particularly if sanitation and food hygiene are likely to be poor.

■ 17.8.2 Although infection is commonly subclinical in young children and severe infection uncommon, the decision to use HNIG may be influenced by the wish to protect parents and other adult contacts. Evidence suggests that, even if HNIG modifies disease rather than preventing infection, it is effective in preventing secondary cases.

■ 17.8.3 There is no evidence associating the administration of intramuscular immunoglobulin with transmission of HIV. Not only does the processing of the plasma from which it is prepared render it safe, but the plasma is derived from blood from donors screened for HIV, hepatitis B and hepatitis C.

■ **17.9   Recommendations**

Use of HNIG should be considered in the following circumstances:

a Contacts of cases of hepatitis A infection

Prophylaxis restricted to household and close contacts may be relatively ineffective in controlling further spread. If given to a wider social group of recent household visitors (kissing contacts and those who have eaten food prepared by the index case) spread may be more effectively prevented.

b Outbreaks

The appropriate approach to prophylaxis and the use of HNIG, with or without hepatitis A vaccine, should be discussed with the Consultant in Communicable Disease Control or CPHM (CD & EH) in Scotland.

In schools, particularly nursery and primary schools, HNIG may be used to protect teachers, adult helpers, including those responsible for cleaning the toilets, and the children and parents of children in the affected classes.

In closed communities where personal hygiene may be poor, widespread use of HNIG should be considered.

c Travellers

HNIG is an alternative to vaccine for those travelling occasionally and for short periods to countries outside Northern and Western Europe, North America, Australia and New Zealand. Hepatitis A vaccine is preferable for those visiting such countries frequently or staying for longer than three months (see 17.3.1).

Where practicable, testing for antibodies to hepatitis A virus prior to immunisation may be worthwhile in those aged fifty years or over, those born in areas of high or moderate endemicity and those who have a history of jaundice.

HNIG may interfere with the development of active immunity from live virus vaccines. It is therefore wise to administer live virus vaccines at least three weeks before the administration of immunoglobulin. If immunoglobulin has been administered first, then an interval of three months should be observed before administering a live virus vaccine.

This does not apply to yellow fever vaccine since HNIG does not contain antibody to this virus. For travellers, if there is insufficient time, the recommended intervals may have to be ignored, especially where polio vaccine is concerned. Alternatively, hepatitis A vaccine may be used in these circumstances.

■ 17.10 Dosage

At present, the dosage of HNIG is expressed either by weight (mg) or by volume (ml). 1ml of a 16% solution contains 160 mg. There are two dosage levels. The higher dose is recommended for those at greater risk (ie contacts) and for extended protection (ie those travelling abroad for 3-5 months).

Age	Low dose For travel lasting 2 months or less	High dose For travel lasting 3-5 months and for contacts
Under 10years	125 mg	250 mg
10years and over	250 mg	500 mg
or		
All ages	0.02-0.04 ml/kg	0.06-0.12 ml/kg

■ 17.11 Supplies

Bio-Products Laboratory Tel. 0181 905 1818
Scottish National Blood Transfusion Service Tel. 0131 664 2317
Northern Ireland Public Health Laboratory, Belfast City Hospital Tel. 01232 329241

Immuno (Gammabulin), Tel. 01732 458101

Kabi Pharmacia (Kabiglobulin), Tel. 01908 661101

For contacts and the control of outbreaks only:

PHLS Communicable Disease Surveillance Centre,
Public Health Laboratories, England and Wales Tel. 0181 200 6868

Scottish Centre for Infection and Environmental Health, Glasgow (Tel. 0141 9467120).

18   Hepatitis B

■ 18.1   Introduction

■ 18.1.1 Hepatitis B is transmitted parenterally and sexually. Transmission most commonly occurs following vaginal or anal intercourse, as a result of blood to blood contact, including injury with contaminated sharp instruments and sharing needles or other equipment by intravenous drug misusers, or by perinatal transmission from mother to child. Transmission has also rarely followed bites from infected persons. Transfusion-associated infection is now rare and adequate treatment of blood products has eliminated these as sources of infection in this country.

■ 18.1.2   The illness usually has an insidious onset, with anorexia, vague abdominal discomfort, nausea and vomiting, sometimes arthralgia and rash, which often progresses to jaundice. Fever may be absent or mild. The severity of the disease ranges from inapparent infections, which can only be detected by liver function tests and/or the presence of serological markers of acute HBV infection (eg HBsAg, antiHBc IgM), to fulminating cases of acute hepatic necrosis. Among cases admitted to hospital, the fatality rate is about 1%. The average incubation period is 40-160 days.

■ 18.1.3   About 2-10% of those infected as adults become chronic carriers of the hepatitis virus with hepatitis B surface antigen (HBsAg) persisting for longer than 6 months. Chronic carriage is more frequent in those infected as children and rises to 90% in those infected perinatally.

■ 18.1.4   Among carriers of the virus, those in whom hepatitis B **e-antigen** (HBeAg) is detected are most infectious. Those with **antibody** to HBeAg (anti-HBe) are generally of low infectivity.

■ 18.1.5   20 - 25% of hepatitis B carriers worldwide develop progressive liver disease with an active hepatitis leading in some patients to cirrhosis. The prognosis of the liver disease in such individuals is at present uncertain. Chronic hepatitis B carriers with liver disease are at increased risk of developing hepatocellular carcinoma.

■ 18.1.6   The number of overt cases of hepatitis in the UK is low and there has been a marked decrease in recent years. Reports of acute hepatitis B to the Public Health Laboratory Service fell from a peak of just under 2000 reports from England and Wales in 1984 to 629 reports in 1994. As of 30 June 1996, there were 612 reports in 1995. About two thirds of infections are asymptomatic and may therefore not be diagnosed.

Hepatitis B

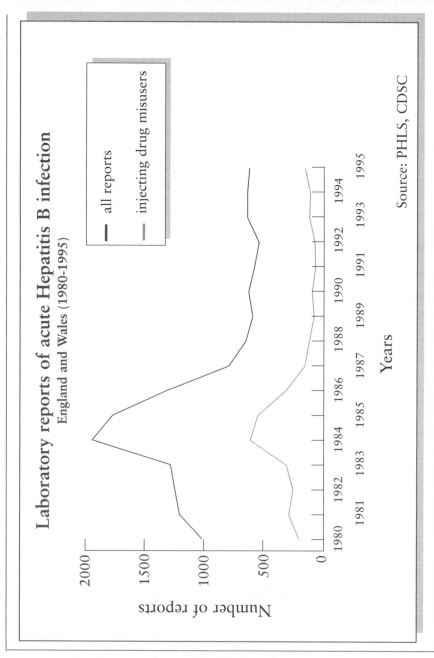

Laboratory reports of acute Hepatitis B infection
England and Wales (1980-1995)

Source: PHLS, CDSC

■ 18.1.7   The prevalence of surface antigenaemia is not known with certainty but recent figures suggest that it is in the order of 1 in 2500 in new blood donors. Ante-natal clinics in certain inner-city areas report hepatitis B carriage in up to 1 in 100 women.

■ 18.1.8   The prevalence of infection is increased among those with certain behavioural or occupational risk factors (see 18.4). The recent decrease in reports of acute hepatitis B has been seen in most of these risk groups. In some, such as health care workers, the decrease probably reflects successful immunisation policy and infection control measures. In other groups it may be linked to the modification of risk behaviours in response to the HIV/AIDS epidemic although the decrease has not been apparent in men who have sex with men.

Hepatitis B is the only sexually transmitted infection which may be prevented by immunisation.

■ 18.1.9   There are two types of immunisation product; a **vaccine** which produces an immune response, and a **specific immunoglobulin** (HBIG) which provides passive immunity and can give immediate but temporary protection after accidental inoculation or contamination with antigen positive blood. Passive immunisation with specific immunoglobulin does not affect the development of active immunity in response to vaccine and combined active/passive immunisation is recommended in certain circumstances (see 18.11)

ACTIVE IMMUNISATION

■ 18.2   Vaccine

■ 18.2.1   Hepatitis B vaccine contains hepatitis B surface antigen (HBsAg) adsorbed on aluminium hydroxide adjuvant. It is currently prepared from yeast cells using recombinant DNA technology. The plasma-derived vaccine is no longer marketed in the UK.

■ 18.2.2   The vaccine should be stored at 2-8°C but not frozen. **Freezing destroys the potency of the vaccine.**

■ 18.2.3   The vaccine is effective in preventing infection in individuals who produce specific antibodies to the hepatitis B surface antigen (anti-HBs). Overall, about 80-90% of individuals mount a response to the vaccine with anti-HBs levels > 10 miu/ml. Those over the age of 40 are less likely to respond. Patients who are immunodeficient or on immunosuppressive therapy may respond less well than healthy individuals and may require larger doses of vaccine or an additional dose.

An antibody level below 10 miu/ml is classified as a non-response to the vaccine whilst an antibody level of 100 miu/ml is considered to be protective. Those with antibody levels below 10 miu/ml two to four months after completing a primary course of immunisation will require HBIG for protection if exposed to infection (see 18.11). Poor responders (anti-HBs 10-100 miu/ml) should receive a booster dose and in non-responders (anti-HBs less than 10 miu/ml) a repeat course of vaccine should be considered.

Immunisation may take up to six months to confer adequate protection when the usual dose schedule is followed (see 18.5.1). Antibody titres should be checked in health care workers and babies born to hepatitis B carrier mothers two to four months after completion of the course. Post immunisation testing may also be indicated for other groups.

The duration of antibody persistence is not known precisely and there is no consensus on the need for booster doses. On present evidence it is felt that a single booster dose five years after completion of a primary course is sufficient to retain immunity in those who continue to be at risk of infection unless they have already received a booster dose following possible exposure to the virus (see 18.11.2).

Antibody levels greater than 100 miu/ml persist in some individuals for much longer than 5 years and there is some evidence that protective immunity is still present when antibody levels have fallen below 100 miu/ml.

■ 18.3   Recommendations

■ 18.3.1   Immunisation is recommended in individuals who are at increased risk of hepatitis B because of their lifestyle, occupation or other factors such as close contact with a case or carrier (see below). In some groups the risk is similar for all, but in other cases it will be necessary for an individual assessment of risk to be made. This is particularly the case with those who may be at risk because of their occupation. The Control of Substances Hazardous to Health (COSSH) Regulations 1994 require employers to undertake their own risk assessment and to bring into effect measures necessary to protect workers and others who may be exposed, as far as is reasonably practicable, against these risks.

NB. It is important that immunisation against hepatitis B does not encourage relaxation of good infection-control procedures.

■ 18.3.2 The vaccine should **not** be given to individuals known to be hepatitis B surface antigen positive, or to patients with acute hepatitis B, since in the former it would be unnecessary and, in the latter, ineffective.

Hepatitis B vaccine **may** be given to HIV positive individuals and should be considered in those not already known to be infected or immune. Response rates are in the order of 70%.

■ 18.4 Risk groups

Immunisation is recommended for the following groups:

■ 18.4.1   **Babies born to mothers who are chronic carriers of hepatitis B virus or to mothers who have had acute hepatitis B during pregnancy.**

Those providing antenatal care will need to take steps to identify infected mothers during pregnancy and make arrangements to ensure that babies born to these mothers receive a **complete** course of immunisation. This is best done by screening women early in pregnancy. Where this has not been done it should be possible to detect carrier mothers at the time of delivery and to provide vaccine to babies born to these mothers within 24 hours of birth.

Recent studies have shown that selective screening of ante-natal patients from groups with increased risks of having acquired hepatitis B fails to identify some carriers. This is due not only to a failure to correctly identify those with established risk factors but also to the existence of some carriers who have no obvious risks for hepatitis B. Antenatal clinics should therefore consider offering screening to all antenatal patients. Some clinics already do so.

Babies born to mothers who are HBeAg positive, who are HBsAg positive without e markers (or where e marker status has not been determined), or who have had acute hepatitis during pregnancy should receive HBIG as well as active immunisation (see 18.11). Hepatitis B vaccine, but not HBIG, is recommended for babies born to mothers who are hepatitis B surface antigen positive but known to be anti-HBe positive.

Hepatitis B

	Baby should receive	
	Hepatitis B vaccine	HBIG
Mother is HBsAg positive and HBeAg positive	+	+
Mother is HBsAg positive without e markers (or where they have not been determined)	+	+
Mother had acute hepatitis B during pregnancy	+	+
Mother is HBsAg positive and anti-HBe positive	+	-

■ **18.4.2   Parenteral drug misusers**

■ **18.4.3   Individuals who change sexual partners frequently,** particularly homosexual and bisexual men, and men and women who are prostitutes. Hepatitis B is the only sexually transmitted infection which can be prevented by immunisation.

■ **18.4.4   Close family contacts of a case or carrier**

Sexual partners are most at risk but close household contacts may also be at increased risk.

Contacts should have their hepatitis B markers checked to see if they have already become infected. Contacts who are HBsAg, anti-HBs or anti-HBc positive do not require immunisation but, in the case of sexual partners, it may be unwise to delay administration of the first dose of the vaccine whilst awaiting test results. Advice should be given regarding the use of condoms until immunity is established.

Sexual contacts of patients with acute hepatitis B should also receive HBIG (see 18.11).

■ **18.4.5   Families adopting children from countries with a high prevalence of hepatitis B** (particularly some in Eastern Europe, SE Asia and S America) may be at risk as these children could be chronic carriers. When the status of the child to be adopted is not known, families adopting children from any high prevalence country should be counselled as to the risks and offered immunisation against hepatitis B. There are grounds to consider testing such children because there could be benefits from referring an infected child for further management.

■ **18.4.6**   **Haemophiliacs,** those receiving regular blood transfusions or blood products, or those carers responsible for the administration of such products.

■ **18.4.7**   **Patients with chronic renal failure.** The response to hepatitis B vaccine is poor in those who are immunocompromised. Only 60% of patients on haemodialysis develop anti-HBs and therefore, in addition to those already on haemodialysis, the immunisation of all patients with chronic renal failure is recommended, as soon as it is anticipated they may require dialysis or transplantation. A better response among patients with chronic renal failure may be obtained if higher doses of vaccine (e.g. 40 mcg) are used.

■ **18.4.8**   **Health care workers including students and trainees** who have direct contact with patients' blood or blood-stained body fluids or with patients' tissues.

This group will include doctors, surgeons, dentists, nurses, midwives, laboratory workers and mortuary technicians but immunisation should also be considered for any other staff who are at risk of injury from blood stained sharp instruments, contamination of surface lesions by patients' blood or blood-stained body fluids, or of being deliberately injured or bitten by patients. Advice should be obtained from the appropriate Occupational Health Department.

■ **18.4.9**   **Staff and residents of residential accommodation for those with severe learning disabilities (mental handicap).**

A higher prevalence of hepatitis B carriage has been found among certain groups of those with learning disabilities (mental handicap) in residential accommodation than in the general population. Close daily living contact, and the possibility of behavioural problems, may lead to staff and other clients being at increased risk of infection.

Similar considerations may apply to children and staff in day care settings and special schools for those with severe learning disability. Decisions on immunisation should be made on the basis of local risk assessments.

■ 18.4.10 **Other occupational risk groups.**

In some occupational groups, such as morticians and embalmers, there is an established risk of hepatitis B and immunisation is recommended. The incidence of infection is not apparently greater than in the population as a whole for members of the police, ambulance, fire and rescue services. Nevertheless, there may be individuals within these occupations who are at higher risk and who should be considered for immunisation. Such a selection has to be decided locally by the occupational health services or as a result of appropriate medical advice following the necessary risk assessment. Immunisation is available on request to all Prison Service staff in regular contact with prisoners.

■ 18.4.11 **Inmates of custodial institutions.**

Guidance on immunisation of prisoners against hepatitis B issued by the Director of Health Care to Heads of Health Care in HM Prison Service recommends that immunisation against hepatitis B should be offered to all prisoners.

■ 18.4.12 **Those travelling to areas of high prevalence** who intend to seek employment as health care workers or those who plan to remain there for lengthy periods and who may therefore be at increased risk of acquiring infection as the result of medical and dental procedures carried out in those countries.

Short term tourists or business travellers are not generally at increased risk of infection unless they place themselves at risk by their sexual behaviour when abroad.

■ 18.5 Route of administration and dosage

■ 18.5.1   The basic immunisation regimen consists of three doses of vaccine, with the first dose at the elected date, the second dose one month later and the third dose at six months after the first dose.

An accelerated schedule has also been used where more rapid immunisation is required, for example for travellers or following exposure to the virus, when the third dose may be given at two months after the initial dose with a booster dose at 12 months. This dosage schedule for the rapid acquisition of immunity can be used to prevent perinatal transmission if given to neonates born to hepatitis B carrier mothers.

The vaccine should normally be given intramuscularly. The injection should be given in the deltoid region, though the anterolateral thigh is the preferred site in infants. **The buttock must not be used because vaccine efficacy may be reduced.**

In patients with haemophilia, the subcutaneous or intradermal route may be used. The likelihood of an effective antibody response is, however, reduced following use of the intradermal route and doctors are advised that until such time as the manufacturers apply for and are granted variations to their product licences for the intradermal route of administration, the use of this route is on their own personal responsibility. (For intradermal dose see 18.5.2). The response may be poor in those who are immunosuppressed and further doses of vaccine may be required.

■ 18.5.2   **Dosage**

Currently licensed products contain different concentrations of antigen per ml. The particular manufacturers dosage schedules should be adhered to.

Engerix B (SmithKline Beecham)

Age 0-12 years 10 mcg (0.5ml)	**Adults** 20 mcg (1.0 ml)

The intradermal dose (**but see 18.5.1**) of Engerix B is 2 micrograms (0.1ml)

H-B-VaxII (Pasteur Merieux MSD)

Age 0-10 years 5 mcg (0.5ml)	**Adults** 10 mcg (1.0ml)

■ 18.6 Adverse reactions

Hepatitis B vaccine is generally well tolerated and the most common adverse reactions are soreness and redness at the injection site. Injection intradermally may produce a persisting nodule at the site of the injection, sometimes with local pigmentation changes. Other reactions which have been reported include fever, rash, malaise and an influenza-like syndrome, arthritis, arthralgia, myalgia and

Serious suspected neurological reactions such as Guillain Barré syndrome and demyelinating disease have very rarely been reported although a causal relationship with hepatitis B vaccine has not been established.

It is important that all serious adverse reactions should be reported to the Committee on Safety of Medicines by the yellow card system.

■ 18.7 Contraindications

Immunisation should be postponed in individuals suffering from severe febrile illness.

■ 18.8   Pregnancy

Hepatitis B infection in pregnant women may result in severe disease for the mother and chronic infection of the newborn. Immunisation should not be withheld from a pregnant woman if she is in the high risk category.

Information available on the outcome in those immunised during pregnancy does not reveal any cause for concern.

■ 18.9   Supplies of Hepatitis B vaccine

Engerix B: SmithKline Beecham. Tel. 0181 913 4290
H-B-Vax II: Pasteur Merieux MSD Ltd. Tel. 01628 773200

■ 18.10   Post-exposure prophylaxis

■ 18.10.1 Specific hepatitis B immunoglobulin (HBIG) is available for passive protection and is normally used in combination with hepatitis B vaccine to confer passive/active immunity after exposure. Guidance is given in 'Exposure to hepatitis B virus; guidance on post exposure prophylaxis'. PHLS Hepatitis Subcommittee. *CDR Review* 1992:2;R97-R101. A summary of this guidance is given in the following table.

■ 18.10.2 Whenever immediate protection is required, immunisation with the vaccine should be combined with simultaneous administration of hepatitis B immunoglobulin (HBIG) at a different site. It has been shown that passive immunisation with HBIG does not suppress an active immune response. A single dose of HBIG (usually 500iu for adults; 200iu for the newborn) is sufficient for healthy individuals. If infection has already occurred at the time of immunisation, virus multiplication may not be inhibited completely, but severe illness and, most importantly, the development of the carrier state may be prevented.

■ 18.10.3   Immunoglobulin should be administered as soon as possible after exposure. In babies born to hepatitis B carrier mothers it should be given not later than 48 hours after birth (but see 18.11.1) and in other types of exposure it should preferably be given within 48 hours and certainly no later than a week after exposure.

■ 18.10.4   There is no evidence associating the administration of HBIG with acquisition of HIV infection. Not only does the processing of the plasma from which it is prepared render it safe, but the screening of blood donations is now routine practice.

■ 18.11   Groups requiring post-exposure prophylaxis

■ 18.11.1   **Babies** born to mothers who are HBeAg positive carriers, who are HBsAg positive without e markers (or where e marker status has not been determined), or who have had acute hepatitis during pregnancy.

Active/passive immunisation is recommended (see 18.4.4). All babies of HBsAg positive mothers should receive hepatitis B vaccine but only those whose mothers are e-antigen positive, HBsAg positive without e-markers (or where e-marker status has not been determined) or had acute hepatitis during pregnancy will require HBIG. The first dose of vaccine should be given at birth or as soon as possible thereafter. HBIG should be given at a contralateral site at the same time; arrangements for the supply of HBIG should be made well in advance. If administration of HBIG is delayed for more than 48 hours, advice should be sought from a local Consultant in Communicable Disease Control, CPHM (CD & EH), a Consultant in Medical Microbiology/Consultant Virologist or from the PHLS Communicable Disease Surveillance Centre or SCIEH.

■ 18.11.2   Persons who are accidentally inoculated, or who contaminate the eye or mouth or fresh cuts or abrasions of the skin, with blood from a known HBsAg positive person. Individuals who sustain such accidents should wash the affected area well with soap and

Hepatitis B

HBV Prophylaxis for reported exposure incidents

HBV status of person exposed	Significant exposure				Non-significant exposure	
	HBsAg positive source	Unknown source	HBsAg negative source	Continued risk	No further risk	
≤ 1 dose HB vaccine pre-exposure	Accelerated course of HB vaccine* HBIG x 1	Accelerated course of HB vaccine*	Initiate course of HB vaccine	Initiate course of HB vaccine	No HBV prophylaxis. Reassure	
≥ 2 doses HB vaccine pre-exposure (anti-HBs not known)	One dose of HB vaccine followed by second dose one month later	One dose of HB vaccine	Finish course of HB vaccine	Finish course of HB vaccine	No HBV prophylaxis. Reassure	
Known responder to HB vaccine (anti-HBs > 10 miU/ml)	Consider booster dose of HB vaccine	Consider booster dose of HB vaccine	Consider booster dose of HB vaccine	Consider booster dose of HB vaccine	No HBV prophylaxis. Reassure	
Known non-responder to HB vaccine (anti-HBs <10 miU/ml 2-4 months post-immunisation	HBIG x 1 Consider booster dose of HB vaccine	HBIG x 1 Consider booster dose of HB vaccine	No HBIG Consider booster dose of HB vaccine	No HBIG Consider booster dose of HB vaccine	No prophylaxis. Reassure	

* An accelerated course of vaccine consists of doses spaced at 0, 1 and 2 months.
A booster dose may be given at 12 months to those at continuing risk of exposure to HBV.
Source: PHLS Hepatitis Subcommittee. CDR Review 1992;2;R97-R101. (Further details and explanation of definitions are contained in this article.)

warm water and seek medical advice. Advice about prophylaxis after such accidents should be obtained by telephone from the nearest Public Health Laboratory or from the CPHM on call for the local Health Board in Scotland. Advice following accidental exposure may also be obtained from the Hospital Control of Infection Officer or the Occupational Health Services.

Health care workers who have already been successfully immunised should be given a booster dose of vaccine unless they are known to have adequate protective levels of antibody.

■ 18.11.3 Sexual partners (and in some circumstances a family contact judged to be at high risk) of individuals suffering from acute hepatitis B, and who are seen within one week of onset of jaundice in the contact.

■ 18.12 Dosage

Hepatitis B immunoglobulin is available in 2ml ampoules containing 200 iu and 5ml ampoules containing 500 iu.

> *Newborn*   200iu as soon as possible after birth

If administration of HBIG is delayed for more than 48 hours see 18.11.1.

> *Children*
> | | |
> |---|---|
> | Age 0-4 years | 200iu |
> | Age 5-9 years | 300iu |

> *Adults and children aged 10 years or more*   *500iu*

For adults and children not exposed at birth, HBIG should be given preferably within 48 hours and not later than a week after exposure.

■ 18.13 Supplies of Hepatitis B Immunoglobulin

Public Health Laboratory Service: either from the Communicable Disease Surveillance Centre (Tel. 0181-200 6868) or via local Public Health Laboratories.

In Scotland, Hepatitis B Immunoglobulin is held by the Blood Transfusion Service:

Aberdeen   (01224) 681818
Dundee   (01382) 645166
Edinburgh   (0131) 5365360
Glasgow   (01698) 373315/8
Inverness   (01463) 704212/3

In Northern Ireland, Hepatitis B Immunoglobulin is held by the Public Health Laboratory, Belfast City Hospital, Belfast. Tel (01232) 329241.

Note: Supplies of this product are limited and demands should be restricted to patients in whom there is a clear indication for its use.

HBIG for use in hepatitis B recipients of liver transplants should be obtained from The Bioproducts Laboratory, Dagger Lane, Elstree, Herts

■ 18.14 Bibliography

Exposure to hepatitis B virus; guidance on post exposure prophylaxis. PHLS Hepatitis Subcommittee. *CDR Review* 1992:2;R97-R101.

Protecting health care workers and patients from hepatitis B. HSG(93)40 Department of Health. (Available from Communicable Disease Branch, Department of Health, Room 736, Wellington House, 133-155 Waterloo Road, London SE1 8UG)

Guidance for clinical health care workers: Protection against blood borne virus infections; Recommendations of the Expert Advisory Group on AIDS and the Advisory Group on Hepatitis. (*In preparation*) Replaces Guidance for clinical health care workers: Protection against infection with HIV and Hepatitis Viruses; Recommendations of the Expert Advisory Group on AIDS. HMSO 1990

■ 19.1   Introduction

■ 19.1.1 Information on specific immunoglobulins is provided in the chapters on particular vaccines.

■ 19.1.2 All immunoglobulins are prepared from the blood of donors who are negative for hepatitis B surface antigen (HBsAg) and for antibody to human immunodeficiency viruses types 1 and 2 (HIV), and to hepatitis C virus (HCV). The materials are treated to inactivate viruses.

■ 19.2   Human Normal Immunoglobulin (HNIG)

■ 19.2.1 This is prepared from the pooled plasma of blood donors and contains antibody to measles, varicella, hepatitis A and other viruses which are currently prevalent in the population. Immunoglobulin prepared by Bio Products Laboratory, and supplied as below, is available in 1.7ml ampoules containing 250mg, and 5ml vials containing 750mg. It is given by intramuscular injection. It must be stored at 0-4°C and the expiry date on the packet must be observed. It has a shelf life of three years when correctly stored. Unused portions of a vial must be discarded.

■ 19.2.2 Recommendations for the use of HNIG for prophylaxis of measles and hepatitis A are given in 22.9.1 and 17.9 respectively. It is not recommended for prevention of mumps (22.9.2) or rubella (22.9.3).

■ 19.2.3 HNIG may interfere with the immune response to live virus vaccines which should therefore be given at least three weeks before or three months after an injection of HNIG. This does not apply to yellow fever vaccine since HNIG obtained from donors in the UK is unlikely to contain antibody to this virus. For travellers going abroad this interval may not be possible. In the case of live polio vaccine, this is likely to be a booster dose for which the possible inhibiting effect of HNIG is less important.

Immunoglobulin

■ 19.3   Supplies

Central Public Health Laboratory Tel. 0181-200 6868.
Public Health Laboratories, England and Wales.
Blood Transfusion Service, Scotland (see 18.13).
Bio Products Laboratory Tel. 0181-905 1818.
Northern Ireland: Public Health Laboratory, Belfast City Hospital,
Tel. 01232 329241.
Immuno. Tel. 01732 458101 (Gammabulin).
Pharmacia and Upjohn Ltd. Tel. 01908 661101(Kabiglobulin).

■ 19.4   Specific Immunoglobulins

These are available for tetanus, hepatitis B, rabies and varicella-zoster. They are
prepared from the pooled plasma of blood donors who have a recent history of
infection or immunisation, or who on screening are found to have suitably high
titres of antibody. Recommendations for their use are given in the relevant
chapters.

■ 19.5   Supplies

Anti-tetanus immunoglobulin
　　Regional Blood Transfusion Centres.
　　Immuno (Tetabulin) Tel. 01732 458101.
　　Scotland: Blood Transfusion Service (see 18.13 for telephone numbers).
　　Northern Ireland: Blood Transfusion Service Tel. 01232 321414 (issued
　　via hospital pharmacies).
　　Bio Products Laboratory Tel 0181 905 1818.

Anti-hepatitis B immunoglobulin
　　CDSC Tel. 0181-200 6868.
　　Public Health Laboratories, England and Wales.
　　Scotland: Blood Transfusion Service (see 18.13 for telephone numbers).
　　Northern Ireland: Public Health Laboratory, Belfast City Hospital, Tel.
　　01232 329241.
　　Belfast Tel. 01232 894628.
　　Bio Products Laboratory Tel 0181 905 1818.

Anti-rabies immunoglobulin
Central Public Health Laboratory (Virus Reference Laboratory) Tel. 0181-200 4400.
Northern Ireland: Public Health Laboratory, Belfast City Hospital, Tel. 01232 329241.
Scotland: Blood Transfusion Service (see 18.13 for telephone numbers).
Bio Products Laboratory 0181 905 1818.

Anti-Varicella-zoster immunoglobulin
Communicable Disease Surveillance Centre.
Tel. 0181-200 6868.
Public Health Laboratories, England and Wales.
Bio Products Laboratory Tel. 0181 905 1818.
Northern Ireland: Public Health Laboratory, Belfast City Hospital Tel. 01232 329241.
Scotland: Blood Transfusion Service (see 18.13 for telephone numbers).

20   Influenza

■ 20.1   Introduction

■ 20.1.1   Influenza is an acute viral infection of the respiratory tract affecting all age groups and characterised by the abrupt onset of fever, chills, headache, myalgia and sometimes prostration. A dry cough is almost invariable and there may be a sore throat. It is usually a self-limiting disease with recovery in two to seven days, but can be a serious illness and may be complicated by bronchitis, secondary bacterial pneumonia and (in children) otitis media. The greatest morbidity and mortality from influenza is among those with underlying disease, particularly chronic respiratory and cardiac disease, and especially if they are also elderly. Primary influenzal pneumonia is a rare complication but carries a high case fatality rate.

■ 20.1.2   Influenza is highly infectious, and, with an incubation period of 1-3 days, can spread rapidly especially in institutions. Epidemics occur unpredictably, and are generally associated with a large number of excess deaths mainly among the elderly. Even in winters when the incidence is low, 3,000-4,000 deaths may be attributed to influenza.

■ 20.1.3   Serological studies show that asymptomatic infections also occur.

■ 20.1.4   Two types of influenza virus are responsible for most clinical illness: influenza A and influenza B. Outbreaks of infection with influenza A occur most years and these are the usual cause of epidemics. Influenza B infection can also cause outbreaks, usually between outbreaks of influenza A; they tend to be less extensive and to be associated with less severe illness.

■ 20.1.5   Influenza A viruses are antigenically labile due to changes in the principal surface antigens, haemagglutinin (H) and neuraminidase (N). Minor changes ('antigenic drift') occur progressively from season to season. Major changes ('antigenic shift') due to acquisition of a 'new' haemagglutinin result periodically in the emergence of new sub-types which, because populations may have little immunity to them, can cause epidemics or pandemics.

■ 20.1.6   Influenza B viruses are subject to antigenic drift but with less frequent changes.

Influenza

■ 20.1.7   The World Health Organisation monitors influenza viruses throughout the world and makes recommendations each year about the strains to be included in vaccines for the forthcoming winter.

■ 20.2 Influenza vaccine

■ 20.2.1   Influenza vaccine is prepared each year using virus strains or genetic reassortants similar to those considered most likely to be circulating in the forthcoming winter. The highly purified viruses are grown in embryonated hens' eggs, chemically inactivated and then further treated and purified. Current vaccines are trivalent containing two type A and one type B sub-types and in recent years have given a good match with subsequently circulating viruses. A monovalent vaccine containing the antigens of only one strain of virus might be more appropriately produced if a new virus with epidemic or pandemic potential emerged.

■ 20.2.2   Two types of vaccine are available: 'split virus' vaccines contain virus components prepared by treating whole viruses with organic solvents or detergents and then centrifuging; 'surface antigen' vaccines contain highly purified haemagglutinin and neuraminidase antigens prepared from disrupted virus particles. The vaccines are equivalent in efficacy and adverse reactions.

■ 20.2.3   Currently available influenza vaccines give 70-80% protection against infection with influenza virus strains related to those in the vaccine. In the elderly, protection against infection may be less, but immunisation has been shown to reduce the incidence of bronchopneumonia, hospital admissions and mortality. Protection lasts for about one year. To provide continuing protection, annual immunisation is necessary with vaccine containing the most recent strains.

■ 20.2.4   Manufacture of influenza vaccine is complex and conducted to a tight schedule. Manufacturers may not be able to respond to unexpected demands for vaccine at short notice.

■ 20.2.5   The vaccines should be stored at 2-8°C and protected from light. They must not be frozen. They should be allowed to reach room temperature and shaken well before they are given.

Influenza

■ 20.3   Recommendations

■ 20.3.1   Selective immunisation is recommended to protect those who are most at risk of serious illness or death should they develop influenza. Annual influenza immunisation is therefore strongly recommended for adults and children with any of the following:

a. chronic respiratory disease, including asthma

b. chronic heart disease

c. chronic renal failure

d. diabetes mellitus

e. immunosuppression due to disease or treatment, including asplenia or splenic dysfunction.

The risk from influenza is greater for the elderly with these conditions and increases if two or more risk conditions co-exist.

■ 20.3.2   Immunisation is also recommended for those living in nursing homes, residential homes and other long stay facilities where rapid spread is likely to follow introduction of infection.

■ 20.3.3   Immunisation of fit children and adults, including health care and other key workers, is not recommended as a routine.

■ 20.3.4   The final decision as to who should be offered immunisation is a matter for the patient's medical practitioner but should take into account the risk of influenza infection exacerbating the underlying disease as well as the risk of serious illness from influenza.

■ 20.3.5   Any changes to these recommendations, and details of the composition and doses of each year's vaccines, are issued by the Departments of Health in annual letters from the Chief Medical Officers.

Influenza

■ 20.4   Increasing the uptake of influenza vaccine

■ 20.4.1   Although uptake of influenza vaccine has increased in recent years, reports suggest that it is still under-used in the recommended risk groups. The single most important factor in patients accepting influenza immunisation is that their doctor recommended it. General practitioners can improve uptake by compiling a register of those patients for whom it is recommended, from chronic disease, computer, patient or prescription records, or as patients are seen during the year. Sufficient vaccine can then be ordered in advance and patients invited to planned immunisation sessions or appointments.

■ 20.5   Route of administration and dosage

■ 20.5.1   *Adults and children aged 13 years and over:*
a single injection of 0.5ml im or deep sc
Children aged 4-12 years:
0.5ml im or deep sc, repeated 4-6 weeks later if receiving influenza vaccine for the first time
Children aged 6 months-3 years:
0.25ml im or deep sc, repeated 4-6 weeks later if receiving influenza vaccine for the first time.

■ 20.5.2   The deltoid muscle is the recommended site for adults and older children. For infants and young children the preferred site is the anterolateral aspect of the thigh.

■ 20.5.3   Antibody levels may take up to 10-14 days to rise. Influenza activity is not usually significant before the middle of November, and therefore the ideal time for immunisation is October/early November.

■ 20.5.4   Patients should be warned that many other organisms cause respiratory infections similar to influenza during the influenza season which influenza vaccine will not prevent; patients may otherwise become disillusioned with the vaccine especially in a non-epidemic year.

■ 20.5.5   Influenza vaccine may be given at the same time as pneumococcal vaccine, at a different site, **but note that for most patients pneumococcal vaccine is given once only (see 25.3 and 25.5).**

■ 20.6   Adverse reactions

■ 20.6.1 Influenza vaccine is usually well tolerated apart from occasional soreness at the immunisation site. In rare instances it can, however, cause:

a. Fever, malaise, myalgia and/or arthralgia beginning 6 to 12 hours after immunisation and lasting up to 48 hours.

b. Immediate reactions such as urticaria, angio-oedema, bronchospasm and anaphylaxis, most likely due to hypersensitivity to residual egg protein.

■ 20.6.2 Guillain-Barré syndrome has been reported very rarely after immunisation with influenza vaccine, although a causal relationship has not been established.

■ 20.6.3 Influenza vaccine contains inactivated virus and cannot cause influenza.

20.7   Contraindications

■ 20.7.1 The vaccines are prepared in hens' eggs and should not be given to individuals with known anaphylactic hypersensitivity to egg products.

■ 20.7.2 There is no evidence that influenza vaccine prepared from inactivated virus causes damage to the fetus. However, it should not be given during pregnancy unless there is a specific indication.

20.8   Amantadine in the prevention of influenza

■ 20.8.1 Amantadine hydrochloride is an effective antiviral agent against influenza A and may be used prophylactically to control an outbreak proven to be due to, or occurring during an epidemic of, influenza A in the following circumstances:

a. For unimmunised patients in the 'at risk' groups for two weeks while the vaccine takes effect.

Influenza

b. For patients in the 'at risk' groups for whom immunisation is unavailable or contraindicated, for the duration of the outbreak.

c. For health care workers and other key personnel to prevent disruption of services during a major epidemic.

■ 20.8.2 The recommended dose is 100mg daily. Higher doses are associated with a greater incidence of adverse reactions.

■ 20.8.3 Adverse reactions include insomnia, restlessness and anxiety, nausea and anorexia. Epileptic fits have occasionally occurred, mainly in the elderly taking doses higher than 100 mg/day.

■ 20.8.4 Amantadine should not be used for prophylaxis of influenza outside these recommendations, or for prophylaxis and treatment in the same household, as there is evidence that drug resistant virus may emerge.

■ 20.9 Supplies

■ 20.9.1 Demand for influenza vaccine sometimes increases unpredictably in response to speculation about influenza illness in the community. It is therefore recommended that practices compile registers of their risk patients (see 20.3.1 and 20.3.2), and order sufficient vaccine for their needs, well in advance of the immunisation season.

■ 20.9.2 Information on current vaccines is given in the latest CMO letter from the Departments of Health. At the time of publication, vaccines are available from:

Evans Medical Ltd, Tel. 0345 451500 (local rate) or 01372 364000
Pasteur Merieux MSD Ltd, Tel. 01628 773200
SmithKline Beecham plc, Tel. 0800 616482
Solvay Healthcare Ltd, Tel. 01703 476171

Influenza

■ 20.10 Bibliography

Influenza: diagnosis, management and prophylaxis
Wiselka M
BMJ 1994; 308: 1341-5

Excess mortality from epidemic influenza: 1957-1966
Housworth J, Langmuir AD
Am J Epidemiol 1974; 100: 40-8

Pneumonia and influenza deaths during epidemics
Barker WH, Mullooly JP
Arch Int Med 1982; 142: 85-9

Deaths in Great Britain associated with the influenza epidemic of 1989/90
Ashley J, Smith T, Dunnell K
Population Trends 1991; 62: 16-20

Reduction in mortality associated with influenza vaccine during 1989-90
epidemic
Ahmed A'EH, Nicholson KG, Nguyen-Van-Tam JS
Lancet 1995; 346: 591-95

Study of the effectiveness of influenza vaccination in the elderly in the
epidemic of 1989/90 using a general practice database
Fleming DM, Watson JM, Nicholas S, Smith GE, Swan AV
Epidemiol and Infection 1995; 115: 581-9

What are the complications of influenza and can they be prevented?
Experience from the 1989 epidemic of H3N2 influenza A in general practice.
Connolly AM, Salmon RL, Lervy B, Williams DH
BMJ 1993; 306:1452-4

The efficacy of influenza vaccine in elderly persons: a meta-analysis and
review of the literature
Gross PA, Hermogenes AW, Sacks HS et al
Ann Int Med 1995; 123: 518-27

Influenza immunisation status and viral respiratory tract infections in patients
with chronic airflow limitation
Fox R, French N, Davies L et al
Respir Med 1995; 89: 559-61

Influenza

Influenza vaccination on renal transplant patients is safe and serologically effective
Grekas D et al
Int J Clin Pharm Therapy and Toxicol 1993; 31: 553-6

Influenza infection and diabetes mellitus: a case for annual vaccination
Diepersloot RJA, Bouter KP, Hoekstra JBL
Diabetes Care 1990; 13: 876-82

Adverse reactions to influenza vaccine in elderly people: randomised double blind placebo controlled trial
Govaert ThME, Dinant GJ, Aretz K et al
BMJ 1993; 307: 988-90

Influenza immunisation: policies and practices of general practitioners in England, 1991/92
Nguyen-Van-Tam J
Health Trends 1993; 25: 101-5

Immunisation against influenza among people aged over 65 living at home in Leicestershire during the winter 1991-2
Nicholson K
BMJ 1993; 306: 974-6

Simultaneous administration of influenza and pneumococcal vaccines
De Stefano F, Goodman R A, Noble G R et al
JAMA, 1982; 247: 2551-2554

Current Status of amantadine and rimantadine as anti-influenza A agents
World Health Organisation Memorandum
Bull WHO 1985; 63: 51-6.

Emergence and possible transmission of amantadine-resistant viruses during nursing home outbreaks of influenza A(H3N2)
Mast EE, Harmon MW, Gravenstein S et al
Am J Epidemiol 1991; 134: 988-97

■ 21.1   Introduction

Japanese encephalitis is a mosquito-borne viral encephalitis caused by a flavivirus antigenically related to St Louis encephalitis virus. It occurs throughout South East Asia and the Far East where it is the leading cause of viral encephalitis. Illness ranges from asymptomatic infection (about 1 in 200 infections is estimated to become clinically apparent) to severe encephalitis with a high mortality and a high rate (approximately 30%) of permanent neurological sequelae in survivors. It is endemic in rural areas, especially where rice growing and pig farming coexist, and epidemics occur in both rural and urban areas. Highest transmission rates occur during and just after wet seasons, when mosquitoes are most active, but seasonal patterns vary both within individual countries and from year to year.

■ 21.2   Vaccine

A formalin-inactivated whole cell vaccine derived from mouse brains is available in the UK but is unlicensed and must therefore be given on a named patient basis. The vial contains a single dose of vaccine which should be reconstituted with 1.3ml of Sterile Water for Injection. (For storage recommendations, see 21.6).

■ 21.3   Recommendations

■ 21.3.1   Immunisation is recommended for travellers to South East Asia and the Far East who will be staying for a month or longer in endemic areas, especially if travel will include rural areas. The risk to an individual traveller is difficult to assess, but areas where rice growing and pig farming coexist and journeys towards the end of the Monsoon season (roughly June-September) are likely to increase the risk. Occasionally immunisation should be considered for shorter trips where there is a high risk of exposure, eg extensive outdoor activities in endemic areas. More detailed country by country information is contained in the UK Health Departments' book 'Health Information for Overseas Travel'.

■ 21.3.2   Precautions against mosquito bites should be taken by all travellers to SE Asia.

Japanese
Encephalitis

■ 21.4 Route of administration and dosage

■ 21.4.1   The recommended vaccine schedule is three doses of 1ml by deep subcutaneous injection on days 0, 7-14 and 28. Full immunity takes up to a month to develop. A two dose schedule at 0 and 7-14 days is said to give short term immunity in 80% of vaccinees.

■ 21.4.2   One additional subcutaneous dose of 1ml is recommended a month after the initial course for those over 60 years of age.

■ 21.4.3   For children under three years of age, the dose for each injection is 0.5ml by deep subcutaneous injection.

■ 21.4.4   The duration of protection is not known. Neutralising antibody persists for at least two years after a 3-dose primary course. A booster may be given after this time.

■ 21.5   Adverse reactions

■ 21.5.1   Local reaction at the injection site may occur.

■ 21.5.2   Allergic reactions, mainly urticaria, but also angioneurotic oedema and dyspnoea, occur occasionally within minutes or up to two weeks after receiving the vaccine. Caution is therefore required with the use of this vaccine; it is recommended that recipients are kept under observation at the immunisation centre for about 30 minutes after being given the vaccine and that the course is completed at least ten days prior to departure.

■ 21.5.3   It is important that any suspected adverse reaction is reported to the supplier and to the Committee on Safety of Medicines on a yellow card. Reports to the supplier will be passed to the Department of Health.

■ 21.6   Contraindications

■ 21.6.1   Fever or acute infection.

■ 21.6.2   History of anaphylactic hypersensitivity.

■ 21.6.3 Immunisation is not advised in pregnancy or in those with cardiac, renal or hepatic disorders, leukaemia, lymphoma or other generalised malignancy because of lack of data on its efficacy and adverse reactions in these conditions.

■ 21.7 Storage

■ 21.7.1 The vaccine should be stored below 10°C prior to reconstitution. Exposure of the vaccine to direct sunlight should be avoided.

■ 21.7.2 The reconstituted vaccine should be used immediately and not stored.

■ 21.8 Supplies

Biken lyophilised vaccine, produced in Japan, is available in single doses from Cambridge Selfcare Diagnostics Ltd, Tel: 0191 261 5950.

■ 21.9 Bibliography

Health Information for Overseas Travel
UK Health Departments and the PHLS Communicable Disease Surveillance Centre. London: HMSO, 1995

Japanese encephalitis - inactivated Japanese encephalitis virus vaccine
WHO Weekly Epidem Rec 1994; 69: 113-20

Inactivated Japanese encephalitis vaccine: Recommendations of the ACIP
Centers for Disease Control. MMWR 1993; 42 (RR-1):3-4

Systemic allergic reactions to Japanese encephalitis vaccines
Nazareth B, Levin J, Johnson H, Begg N
Vaccine 1994; 12 : 666

22   Measles, Mumps and Rubella

■ **22.1 Introduction** (for rubella see also Chapter 28)

■ 22.1.1 **Measles** is an acute viral illness transmitted via droplet infection. Clinical features include, coryza, conjunctivitis, bronchitis, Koplik spots, rash and fever. The incubation period is about ten days, with a further two to four days before the rash appears. It is highly infectious from the beginning of the prodromal period to four days after the appearance of the rash. Measles is a notifiable disease.

■ 22.1.2 Fulfilment of criteria of a case definition is not a requirement for notification of measles but recent experience shows that few cases, notified according to clinical diagnosis, are measles. Correctly diagnosed cases tend to be those occurring in older children and in outbreaks. The presence of the following features may improve the accuracy of clinical diagnosis: rash for at least three days, fever for at least one day, and at least one of the following - cough, coryza or conjunctivitis.

■ 22.1.3 The diagnosis of measles (and mumps and rubella) can now be confirmed through non-invasive means. Detection of specific IgM in saliva samples, ideally taken from three days after the onset of rash or parotid swelling, has been shown to be highly sensitive and specific for confirmation of these infections, when compared with serological tests used as standards. Whenever possible, saliva samples should be obtained from all notified cases. Advice on this procedure can be obtained from the local Consultant in Communicable Disease Control, or Public Health Laboratory or Consultant in Public Health Medicine (CPHM) Communicable Disease and Environmental Health (CD & EH) in Scotland.

■ 22.1.4 Complications of measles have been reported in one in 15 notified cases, and include otitis media, bronchitis, pneumonia, convulsions and encephalitis. Encephalitis has an incidence of one in 5000 cases, has a mortality of about 15%, and 20% to 40% of survivors have residual neurological sequelae. Electro-encephalographic changes have been reported after apparently uncomplicated measles as well as in cases with frank encephalitis. Complications are more common and severe in poorly nourished and chronically ill children; **it is therefore particularly important that such children should be immunised against measles.**

■ 22.1.5 Case fatality rates for measles are age-related. They are high in children under one year of age, are lowest in children aged 1 to 9 years and then rise again with advancing age. Before 1988, more than half the acute measles deaths occurred in previously healthy children who had not been immunised.

■ 22.1.6 In children receiving immunosuppressive treatment, particularly for leukaemia, measles was a major cause of morbidity and mortality. Between 1970 and 1983, 19 children in remission from acute lymphatic leukaemia died from measles, and of 51 children who died in their first remission in 1974-84, measles was the cause of death in nearly a third.

■ 22.1.7 Subacute sclerosing panencephalitis (SSPE) is a rare but fatal late complication of measles infection. Most often it follows early measles infection which may not necessarily have been recognised. Measles immunisation protects against SSPE.

■ 22.1.8 Notification of measles began in England and Wales in 1940, and until the introduction of vaccine in 1968 annual notifications varied between 160,000 and 800,000, the peaks occurring in two year cycles. By the late 1980s, annual notifications had fallen only to between 50,000 and 100,000. This limited effect came about because coverage was never sufficiently high to have an effect on virus transmission. Between 1970 and 1988, there continued to be an average of 13 acute measles deaths each year. In countries where high coverage was achieved shortly after the introduction of measles immunisation, the epidemic cycle was more effectively suppressed and very low levels of measles were observed.

■ 22.1.9 Following the introduction of MMR vaccine in October 1988 and the achievement of coverage levels in excess of 90%, notifications of measles fell progressively to the lowest levels since records began, in 1940. In 1993, there were only 9612 measles notifications. Since 1988, there have been only 11 deaths due to measles recorded in England and Wales. Most of these have been due to neurological conditions and only 4 have been due to acute measles illness.

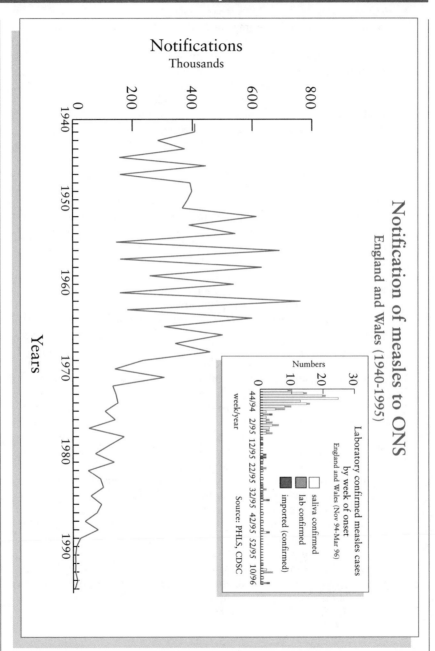

Notification of measles to ONS
England and Wales (1940-1995)

Notifications
Thousands

Years

Laboratory confirmed measles cases
by week of onset
England and Wales (Nov 94-Mar 96)

Numbers

week/year

44/94 2/95 12/95 22/95 32/95 42/95 52/95 10/96

saliva confirmed
lab confirmed
imported (confirmed)

Source: PHLS, CDSC

■ 22.1.10 The high coverage of MMR vaccine and the ensuing reduction of transmission meant that after 1988, children who had not been immunised no longer had the opportunity to be exposed to measles infection and remained susceptible until early teenage. A rising proportion of school age children were therefore susceptible to measles, as confirmed by age stratified sero-epidemiology. Analysis of epidemiological data, by mathematical modelling, predicted the high probability of a major resurgence of measles affecting for the greater part the school age population. Similar measles epidemics had been seen in many other countries following periods of low incidence, achieved through high immunisation coverage.

■ 22.1.11 In 1993, small outbreaks of measles began to occur in England and Wales and predominantly affected secondary school children. In Scotland, a measles epidemic, affecting the west of the country, led to 138 teenagers being admitted to one infectious disease unit alone.

■ 22.1.12 A national immunisation campaign was implemented in November 1994 throughout the United Kingdom. Over 8 million children aged between 5 and 16 years were immunised with measles/ rubella vaccine. As a consequence, susceptibility to measles in the target population fell by about 85% and only very few confirmed cases of measles have occurred in school children. The few confirmed cases that now occur, mostly in adults or children too young to be protected by immunisation, can often be linked to importation of the virus from abroad. Reports of serious adverse reactions to the vaccine were very rare (0.007%).

■ 22.1.13 **Mumps** is an acute viral illness characterised by parotid swelling which may be unilateral or bilateral; some cases are asymptomatic. The incubation period is 14-21 days and mumps is transmissible from several days before the parotid swelling to several days after it appears. Complications include pancreatitis, oophoritis and orchitis; even when the latter is bilateral there is no firm evidence that it causes sterility. Neurological complications including meningitis and encephalitis may precede or follow parotitis, and can also occur in its absence. Before the introduction of MMR vaccine, mumps was the cause of about 1200 hospital admissions each year in England and Wales. In the under 15 age group it was a common cause of viral meningitis; it can also cause permanent unilateral deafness at any age.

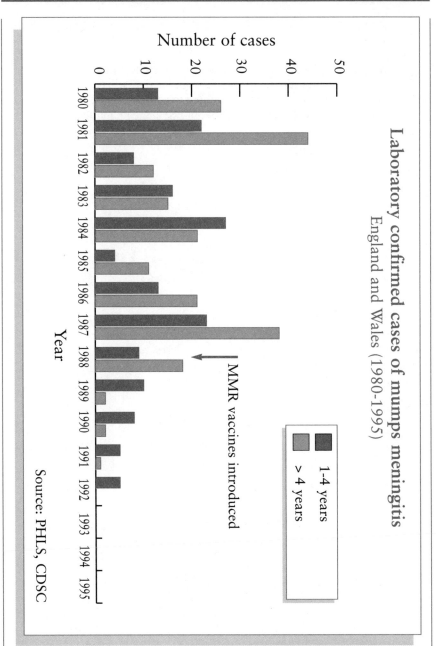

Laboratory confirmed cases of mumps meningitis
England and Wales (1980-1995)

Number of cases

Year

MMR vaccines introduced

1-4 years
> 4 years

Source: PHLS, CDSC

■ 22.1.14 Mumps was made a notifiable disease in the UK in October 1988.

■ 22.1.15 Notifications have fallen progressively; in 1995 there were only 2021 notifications. The incidence of the disease has declined dramatically in all ages, including those too old to have been immunised. Laboratory testing shows that most notified cases are not mumps.

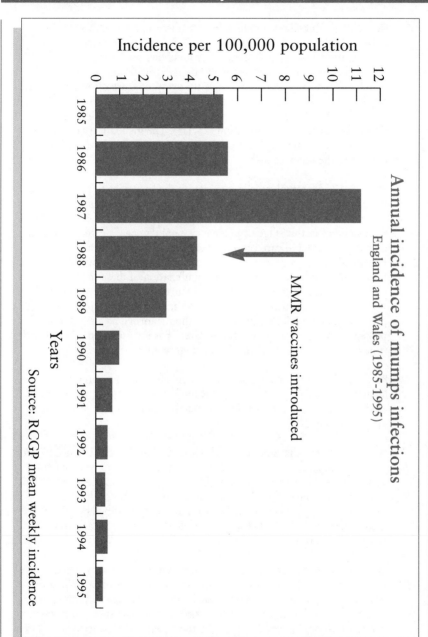

Annual incidence of mumps infections
England and Wales (1985-1995)

Incidence per 100,000 population

MMR vaccines introduced

Years

Source: RCGP mean weekly incidence

■ 22.1.16 **Rubella** is a mild infectious disease, previously common among children aged four to nine years. It causes a transient erythematous rash, lymphadenopathy involving post-auricular and sub-occipital glands and occasionally in adults, arthritis and arthralgia. Clinical diagnosis is unreliable since the symptoms are often fleeting and can be caused by other viruses; in particular, the rash is not diagnostic of rubella. **A history of "rubella" should never be accepted without serological or saliva confirmation** (28.1.7). The incubation period is 14-21 days and the period of infectivity from one week before until four days after the onset of rash.

■ 22.1.17 Maternal rubella infection in the first eight to ten weeks of pregnancy results in fetal damage in up to 90% of infants and multiple defects are common. The risk of damage declines to about 10-20% by 16 weeks and after this stage of pregnancy, fetal damage is rare. Fetal defects include mental handicap, cataract, deafness, cardiac abnormalities, retardation of intra-uterine growth and inflammatory lesions of brain, liver, lungs and bone-marrow. Any combination of these may occur; the only defects which commonly occur alone are perceptive deafness and pigmentary retinopathy following infection after the first eight weeks of pregnancy. Some infected infants may appear normal at birth but perceptive deafness may be detected later. **For investigation of suspected rubella or exposure to rubella in pregnant women see 28.1.5.**

■ 22.1.18 Before the introduction of rubella immunisation, there were as many as 70 cases of Congenital Rubella Syndrome (CRS) during epidemic years; the ratio of therapeutic abortions to cases of CRS was approximately 10:1.

■ 22.1.19 Rubella immunisation was introduced in the UK in 1970 for pre-pubertal girls and non-immune women with the aim of protecting women of child-bearing age from the risks of rubella in pregnancy. This policy was not intended to prevent the circulation of rubella, but to increase the proportion of women with antibody to rubella; this increased from 85-90% before 1970 to 97-98% by 1987 and has remained at this level.

■ 22.1.20 Although the selective immunisation policy was effective in reducing the number of cases of CRS and terminations of pregnancy, it became apparent that the elimination of rubella in pregnancy could never be achieved by this means. The few remaining rubella susceptible women continued to be exposed to rubella by their own and their friends' children.

■ 22.1.21 The inclusion of rubella vaccine in 1988, with measles and mumps vaccines, as MMR, was intended to interrupt circulation of rubella amongst young children, thereby protecting susceptible adult women. Rubella was made a notifiable disease in 1988.

■ 22.1.22 A considerable decline in rubella in young children followed but in 1993, there was a large increase in both notifications and laboratory confirmed cases of rubella. Many of these cases occurred in males in colleges and universities. However, there was also an increase in the number of reports of rubella infections in pregnant women. These rose from 2 in 1992 to 23 in 1993; there were 8 in 1995. Outbreaks of rubella have continued predominantly in young males and there will continue to be a small number of infections in pregnant women, through contact with young men in this country or acquired abroad.

Measles, Mumps and Rubella

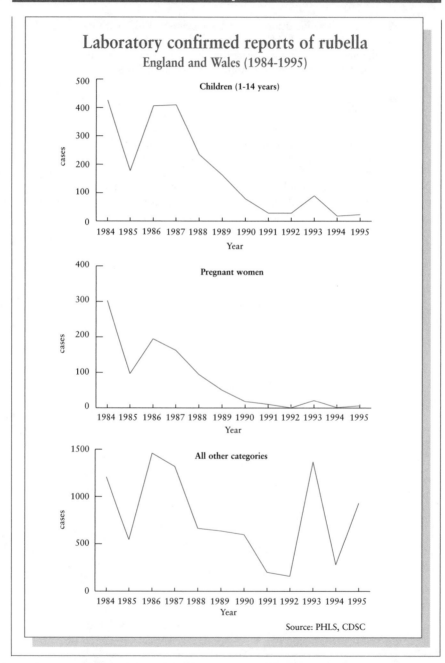

Laboratory confirmed reports of rubella
England and Wales (1984-1995)

■ 22.1.23 Sero-epidemiological surveillance has showed high levels of susceptibility to rubella in males aged 10-40 years compared to women of this age. This difference had resulted from the effect of the selective rubella immunisation programme which was targeted only at females. The inclusion of rubella vaccine with measles vaccine in the national immunisation campaign of 1994 has reduced susceptibility to rubella in males aged up to 16 years by about 85%. This will prevent these males from transmitting rubella to susceptible pregnant women in the future. Outbreaks of rubella, as presently being seen, can be expected to stop.

■ 22.1.24 For reporting of CRS, see 28.9.

■ 22.2 MMR Vaccine

■ 22.2.1 This is a freeze-dried preparation containing live attenuated measles, mumps and rubella viruses. It must be stored in the dry state at 2-8°C (**not** frozen) and protected from light. It should be reconstituted with the diluent supplied by the manufacturer and used within one hour. Immunisation provides protection for around 90% of recipients for measles and mumps and over 95% for rubella. Vaccine-induced antibody to rubella has been shown to persist for at least 18 years in the absence of endemic disease. Since the vaccine viruses are not transmitted, there is **no risk of infection** from vaccinees.

■ 22.2.2 One vaccine is currently available:

MMR II (Merck); Enders' Edmonston strain measles, RA 27/3 rubella, Jeryl Lynn mumps.

■ 22.2.3 Single antigen measles, mumps and rubella vaccines are available. (See 28.7 for rubella vaccine supplies).

■ 22.3 Route of administration and dosage

0.5ml is given by intramuscular or deep subcutaneous injection.

■ 22.4   Recommendations

■ 22.4.1 Evidence shows that a single dose of MMR vaccine confers protection in around 90% of individuals for measles and mumps and 95% for rubella. Therefore, if 92% of children are given MMR vaccine, with 90% efficacy for the measles component, only 83% are protected from each year's birth cohort. The accumulation over time of these susceptible children is sufficient to allow the re-emergence of epidemics of measles. This potential for epidemics can be prevented with a two dose programme.

■ 22.4.2 Beginning 1 October 1996, all children, except those with a valid contraindication, should receive 2 doses of MMR vaccine. These are recommended to be given shortly after the first birthday and before school entry.

■ 22.4.3 MMR vaccine should be given irrespective of a history of measles, mumps or rubella infection.

■ 22.4.4 MMR vaccine can be given to children **of any age** whose parents request it, and no opportunity should be missed to ensure that this is done. If the primary immunisations of DTP, polio and Hib have not been completed by the time that MMR vaccine is due, they can be given at the same time using separate syringes and different sites. For maximum effect, vaccine must be given soon after the first birthday.

■ 22.4.5 If parents do not wish MMR vaccine to be given at the same time as other injected vaccines, then OPV should be given with MMR and the child recalled for the other vaccines as soon as possible; in these circumstances no three week interval between immunisations is necessary.

■ 22.4.6 When children who have not received their first dose of MMR attend for their pre-school boosters (DT and polio vaccines), they should be offered the first MMR and arrangements made for a second dose to be given three months after the first dose.

■ 22.4.7 There is a group of children who were too young to be included in the measles rubella immunisation campaign of 1994 and who have already been given their pre-school boosters. These children should be recalled and given MMR vaccine. Similarly, any children known not to have received measles and rubella vaccine, should be offered MMR vaccine.

■ 22.4.8 When children attend for their school leaving immunisations, there is an opportunity to check that all recommended immunisations have been completed. Boys and girls who have not had measles and rubella vaccine, should be offered MMR vaccine. There is no contraindication to the simultaneous administration of MMR, Td and OPV.

■ 22.4.9 MMR vaccine can be given to non-immune adults and should be considered for those in long-term institutional care who may not have developed immunity. Entry into college, university or other centres for further education provides an opportunity to check the immunisation history. Students who have not received MR or MMR vaccine should be offered MMR immunisation.

■ 22.4.10 Children with a personal or close family history of convulsions **should** be given MMR vaccine, provided the parents understand that there may be a febrile response. As for all children, advice for reducing fever should be given. Doctors should seek specialist paediatric advice rather than refuse immunisation. Dilute immunoglobulin as formerly used with measles vaccine for such children is no longer used since it may inhibit the immune response to the rubella and mumps components.

■ 22.4.11 Unimmunised children in the following groups are at particular risk from measles infection and should be immunised with MMR vaccine:

a. Children with chronic conditions such as cystic fibrosis, congenital heart or kidney disease, failure to thrive, Down's syndrome.

b. Children from the age of one year upwards in residential or day care, including playgroups and nursery schools.

■ 22.4.12 As vaccine-induced **measles** antibody develops more rapidly than that following natural infection, MMR vaccine can be used to protect susceptible contacts during a **measles** outbreak. To be effective the vaccine must be administered within three days of exposure. If there is doubt about a child's immunity, vaccine should be given since there are no ill effects from vaccinating individuals who are already immune. Immunoglobulin is available for individuals for whom vaccine is contraindicated (22.9.1). NB. **Antibody responses to the rubella and mumps components of MMR vaccine are too slow for effective prophylaxis after exposure to these infections.**

■ 22.4.13 Re-immunisation is necessary when vaccine has been given before 12 months of age.

■ 22.4.14 Measles virus inhibits the response to tuberculin, so that a false negative tuberculin test **may** be found for up to a month following MMR vaccine.

■ 22.4.15 HIV positive individuals may be given MMR vaccine in the absence of contraindications.

■ 22.5 Adverse reactions

■ 22.5.1 **Following the first dose of MMR vaccine,** malaise, fever and/or a rash may occur, most commonly about a week after immunisation and last about two to three days. In a study of over 6000 children aged one to two years, the symptoms reported were similar in nature, frequency, time of onset and duration to those commonly reported after measles vaccine. During the sixth to eleventh days after vaccine, febrile convulsions occurred in 1/1000 children, the rate previously reported in the same period after measles vaccine. Parotid swelling occurred in about 1% of children of all ages up to four years, usually in the third week and occasionally later.

■ 22.5.2 Up until September 1992, MMR vaccines containing the Urabe strain of mumps virus were in routine use. These vaccines were found to be rarely associated with mumps meningitis, most often occurring around three weeks after immunisation. **No cases have been confirmed in association with the presently used Jeryl Lynn mumps vaccine.** When mumps virus is isolated from the cerebro-spinal fluid, laboratory tests can distinguish between wild and vaccine strains. Advice should be sought from the National Institute for Biological Standards and Control (Tel. 01707 654753).

■ 22.5.3 Thrombocytopenia, which usually resolves spontaneously, occurs in about 1 in 24,000 children given a first dose of MMR at 12 - 15 months.

■ 22.5.4 Arthropathy (arthralgia or arthritis) has been reported to occur rarely after MMR immunisation. If it occurs other than 14-21 days after immunisation, it is unlikely to have been caused by the vaccine.

■ 22.5.5 Because MMR vaccine contains live attenuated viruses, it is biologically plausible for it to cause cases of encephalitis. However, a recent review of the published evidence on encephalitis, and measles or MMR immunisation, concluded that the evidence is inadequate to accept or reject a causal relationship between measles or mumps vaccine and encephalitis or encephalopathy. This suggests that if there is a risk of encephalitis or encephalopathy, induced by the vaccine, it is exceptionally small.

■ 22.5.6 23 cases of neurological disease following measles immunisation were investigated in the United States between 1965 and 1967. 18 cases were characterised as 'encephalitis'. The interval from immunisation to the onset of symptoms ranged from 3 to 24 days. The estimated rate of encephalitis within a four week period of measles immunisation was 1.5 cases per 1 million distributed doses of vaccine. The background rate of encephalitis (unrelated to immunisation) was 2.8 cases per 1 million children for any 4 week period. The authors of the study concluded that 'no single clinical or epidemiological characteristic appears consistently in the reports of cases of possible neurological sequelae of measles immunisation'.

■ 22.5.7 **After a second dose of MMR vaccine,** adverse reactions are considerably less common than after the first dose. One study showed no increase in fever or rash after re-immunisation of college students compared to unimmunised controls. Only 3 cases of thrombocytopenia were reported in association with the immunisation of over 8 million children in the November 1994 measles/rubella campaign. This suggests that the risk in children receiving a second dose is considerably less than in children receiving a first dose. An analysis of adverse reactions reported through the US Vaccine Adverse Events Reporting System in 1991-93 showed fewer reactions among children aged 6 to 19 years, considered to be second dose recipients, than among those aged 1-4 years, considered first dose recipients.

■ 22.5.8 Three cases of Guillain-Barré syndrome (GBS) were reported following the November 1994 MR immunisation campaign. Between one and eight cases would have been expected in this population over this period of time in the absence of an immunisation campaign. Analysis of reporting rates of GBS from acute flaccid paralysis surveillance undertaken in the Region of the Americas has shown no increase in rates of GBS following measles immunisation campaigns when over 70 million children were immunised. It was concluded from this evidence that measles immunisation does not cause GBS.

■ 22.5.9 Parents should be told about possible symptoms after immunisation and given advice for reducing fever, including the use of paracetamol in the period five to ten days after immunisation. They should also be reassured that post-immunisation symptoms are **not** infectious.

■ 22.5.10 Serious reactions should be reported to the Committee on Safety of Medicines using the yellow card system.

■ 22.6   Contraindications

(i) If a child is suffering from an acute illness, immunisation should be postponed until recovery has occurred. Minor infections without fever or systemic upset are not reasons to postpone immunisation. Antibody responses and incidence of adverse reactions were the same in children with or without acute mild illness, when given MMR vaccine. The acute illnesses were upper respiratory tract infection, diarrhoea or otitis media.

(ii) Children with untreated malignant disease or altered immunity; those receiving immunosuppressive or X-ray therapy or high-dose steroids (see 7.3.1 to 7.3.7).

(iii) Children who have received another live vaccine - including BCG - within three weeks (but see 7.5.2 for polio).

(iv) Children with allergies to neomycin or kanamycin.

(v) If MMR vaccine is given to adult women, pregnancy should be avoided for one month, as for rubella vaccine (see 28.4 and 28.6 (i)).

(vi) MMR vaccine should not be given within three months of an injection of immunoglobulin.

■ 22.7   Allergy to egg

There is increasing evidence that MMR vaccine can be given safely to children even when they have previously had an anaphylactic reaction (generalised urticaria, swelling of the mouth and throat, difficulty in breathing, hypotension or shock) following food containing egg. A combined total of 1265 patients from 16 studies has been reported. None of 284 patients with histories of egg hypersensitivity confirmed by oral challenge, had any adverse reactions. MMR was administered safely to 1209 patients with positive skin tests to egg. There were only 2 reports of symptoms suggestive of anaphylaxis (0.16%). The combined data indicate that over 99% of children who are allergic to eggs can safely receive MMR vaccine. Dislike of egg, or refusal to eat it, is **not** a contraindication. If there is concern, paediatric advice should be sought with a view to immunisation under controlled conditions such as admission to hospital as a day case.

■ 22.8   Supplies

MMR vaccines are supplied by Farillon (Tel. 01708 379000) as part of the National Childhood Immunisation Programme.

MMR II (Merck); Enders' Edmonston strain measles, RA 27/3 rubella, Jeryl Lynn mumps. Pasteur Merieux MSD Ltd (Tel. 01628 773200)

■ 22.9   Immunoglobulin (and see Chapter 19).

■ 22.9.1   Measles

Children and adults with compromised immunity (7.3.1 to 7.3.7) who come into contact with measles should be given human normal immunoglobulin (HNIG) as soon as possible after exposure. Testing for measles antibody may delay the administration of HNIG and neither immunisation nor low level antibody guarantees immunity to measles in the immunocompromised.

Children under 12 months in whom there is a particular reason to avoid measles, (such as recent severe illness), can also be given immunoglobulin; MMR vaccine should then be given after an interval of at least three months, at around the usual age.

Dose:
To prevent an attack:

Age	Dose
Under 1 year	250 mg
1-2 years	500 mg
3 and over	750 mg

To allow an attenuated attack:

Under 1 year	100 mg
1 year or over	250 mg

An interval of at least three months must be allowed before subsequent MMR immunisation.

Dilute immunoglobulin as previously used with measles vaccine for children with a history of convulsions is no longer used since it may inhibit the immune response to rubella and mumps.

■ 22.9.2 **Mumps**

HNIG is no longer used for post-exposure protection since there is no evidence that it is effective. Mumps-specific immunoglobulin is no longer available.

■ 22.9.3 **Rubella**

Post-exposure prophylaxis does **not** prevent infection in non-immune contacts and is therefore **not** recommended for the protection of pregnant women exposed to rubella. It may however reduce the likelihood of clinical symptoms which may possibly reduce the risk to the fetus. It should only be used when termination of pregnancy for proved rubella infection is unacceptable to the pregnant woman, when it should be given as soon as possible after exposure; serological follow-up of recipients is essential.

Dose   750 mg

■ 22.10 Supplies of HNIG:

Communicable Disease Surveillance Centre. Tel. 0181 200 6868
Public Health Laboratories, England and Wales.
Blood Transfusion Service, Scotland (see 18.13 for telephone numbers).
Bio Products Laboratory Tel. 0181 905 1818.
Northern Ireland: Public Health Laboratory, Belfast City Hospital,
Tel. 01232 329241.
Immuno, Tel. 01732 458101. (Gammabulin).
Pharmacia and Upjohn Ltd, Tel. 01908 661101(Kabiglobulin).

■ 22.11 Bibliography

Severity of notified measles.
Miller C L.
BMJ 1978; i: 1253.

Deaths from measles.
Miller C L.
BMJ 1985; 290: 443-444.

Mortality and morbidity caused by measles in children with malignant disease
attending four major treatment centres: a retrospective view.
Gray M, Hann I M, Glass S, Eden O B, Morris Jones P, Stevens R F.
BMJ 1987; 295: 19-22.

Measles serology in children with a history of measles in early life.
Adjaye N, Azad A, Foster M, Marshall W C, Dunn H.
BMJ 1983; 286: 1478.

Live measles vaccine: a 21 year follow up.
Miller C L.
BMJ 1987; 295: 22-24.

Safe administration of mumps/measles/rubella vaccine in egg-allergic children.
Greenberg M A, Birx D L.
J. Pediatrics 1988; 113: 504-6.

Safe immunisation of allergic children against measles, mumps and rubella.
Juntenen-Backman K, Peltola H, Backman A, Salo O P.
Am. J. Dis. Children 1987; 141: 1103-5.

Virus meningitis and encephalitis in 1979.
Noah N D, Urquart A M.
J. Infection 1980; 2: 379-83.

Big bang for immunisation. Editorial.
Sir John Badenoch.
BMJ 1988; 297: 750-1.

Surveillance of antibody to measles, mumps and rubella by age.
Morgan-Capner P, Wright J, Miller C L, Miller E.
BMJ 1988; 297: 770-2.

Surveillance of symptoms following MMR vaccine in children.
Miller C L et al.
Practitioner 1989; 233: 69-73.

Mumps meningitis and MMR vaccination.
Lancet 1989, ii: 1015-1016.

Mumps viruses and mumps, measles, and rubella vaccine.
Forsey T, Minor P D.
BMJ 1989; 299: 1340.

Egg hypersensitivity and measles/mumps/rubella vaccine administration.
Beck S A, Williams L W, Shirrell M, Burks A W
Paediatrics 1991; 88: 5: 913-917.

Vaccine safety versus vaccine efficacy in mass immunisation programmes
Nokes D J, Anderson R M
Lancet 1991: 338: 1309-1312

Safe administration of the measles vaccine to children allergic to eggs.
James J M, Burks A W, Robertson P K, Sampson H A.
N Eng J Med; 1995;332:19,1262-1266.

Measles in 1995 - transmission interrupted in schoolchildren.
Communicable Disease Report 1995;5(21):

Adverse events following measles-mumps-rubella and measles vaccinations in
college students.
Chen R T et al. Vaccine 1991;9:297-9.

Rubella surveillance to June 1994: third joint report from the PHLS and the National Congenital Rubella Surveillance Programme.
Miller E et al.
CDR Review 1994;4(R12):R146-52.

The epidemiology of subacute sclerosing panencephalitis in England and Wales, 1970 to 1989.
Miller C, Farrington C P and Harbert K.
International J of Epidemiology 1992;21:998-1006.

Risk of aseptic meningitis after measles, mumps and rubella vaccine in UK children.
Miller E et al.
Lancet 1993;341:979-82.

An outbreak of measles in Trafford.
Richardson J A, Quigley C.
CDR Review 1994;4(R6):R73-5.

Complications of mumps vaccines.
Balraj V, Miller E.
Reviews in Medical Virology 1995;5:219-27.

Adverse Events Associated with Childhood Vaccines -Evidence Bearing on Causality.
Stratton K R, Howe C J and Johnston R B.
Institute of Medicine, National Academy Press, Washington D.C. 1994 : p130.

A new method for active surveillance of adverse events from diphtheria/tetanus/pertussis and measles/mumps/rubella vaccines.
Farrington P, Pugh S, Colville A, Flower A, Nash J, Morgan-Capner P, Rush M, Miller E
Lancet 1995; 345;567-569

Salivary diagnosis of measles: A study of notified cases in the United Kingdom, 1991-93
Brown D, Ramsay M, Richards A, Miller E
BMJ 1994, 308 1015-1017

Measles in secondary school children; implications for vaccination policy
Calvert N, Cutts F, Miller E, Brown D, Munro J
CDR 1994; 4; No. 6, R70-R73

Adverse Reactions to Measles/Rubella Vaccine
Current Problems in Pharmacovigilance 1995; 21: pp 9-10.

For rubella references see Chapter 28.

23 Meningococcal

■ 23.1 Introduction

■ 23.1.1 Meningococcal meningitis and septicaemia are systemic infections caused by *Neisseria meningitidis*. Meningococci are Gram negative diplococci which are divided into antigenically distinct groups, the commonest of which in the UK are B, C, A, Y and W135. They are further subdivided by type and sulphonamide sensitivity.

■ 23.1.2 Group B strains account for approximately two thirds of all isolates submitted to the Public Health Laboratory Service Meningococcal Reference Laboratory. Group C strains contribute about one third, but some years can be higher. Group A strains are rare in this country (less than 2%) but are the epidemic strains in other parts of the world.

■ 23.1.3 Irregular upsurges of meningococcal infection occur in the United Kingdom with the last previous wave in the mid 1970s. The present upsurge began in 1984: there were peaks in 1989/90 and 1995/6. The disease is commonest in the winter. An association has been demonstrated between the seasonal onset of influenza activity and meningococcal disease. The incidence of meningococcal disease is highest in infants followed by one to five year old children, but the recent increase of Group C disease has been associated with an increased incidence in school age children and young adults.

Meningococcal

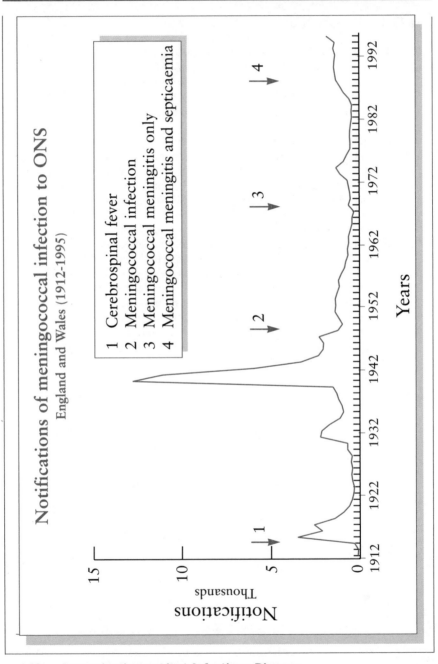

Notifications of meningococcal infection to ONS
England and Wales (1912-1995)

1 Cerebrospinal fever
2 Meningococcal infection
3 Meningococcal meningitis only
4 Meningococcal meningitis and septicaemia

Years

Notifications
Thousands

Meningococcal

■ 23.1.4 The carriage rate for all meningococci in the normal population is about 10% although rates vary with age; about 25% of young adults may be carriers at any one time.

■ 23.1.5 Meningococci are transmitted by droplet spread or direct contact from carriers or from individuals in the early stages of the illness; the probable route of invasion is via the nasopharynx. The incubation period is two to three days, and the onset of disease varies from fulminant to insidious with mild prodromal symptoms. Early symptoms and signs are usually malaise, pyrexia and vomiting. Headache, photophobia, drowsiness or confusion, joint pains and a typical haemorrhagic rash of meningococcal septicaemia may develop. **Early on, the rash may be non-specific.** The rash, which may be petechial or purpuric, does not blanche and this can be confirmed readily by gentle pressure with a glass, when the rash can be seen to persist. Patients may present in coma. In young infants particularly, the onset may be insidious and the classical signs absent. The diagnosis should be suspected in the presence of vomiting, pyrexia, irritability and, if still patent, raised anterior fontanelle tension.

■ 23.1.6 Overall mortality from meningococcal infection is around 7-8% and has changed little for 20 years. Meningitis is the commonest presentation, but in about 15-20% of cases, features of septicaemia predominate. Mortality is 3-5% in meningitis and 15-20% in septicaemia. Current expert advice endorses the importance of early recognition, prompt antibiotic treatment and speedy referral to hospital for all suspected cases. Benzylpenicillin is the antibiotic of choice and should be administered by the general practitioner before transfer to hospital. The recommended dose is 1,200 mg for adults and children aged 10 years or more, 600 mg for children aged 1 to 9 years, and 300 mg for those aged less than 1 year. Benzylpenicillin should be withheld if there is a known history of anaphylaxis following previous penicillin administration. Although benzylpenicillin may reduce the chance of isolating the causative organism, this is outweighed by the benefit to the patient, and new techniques are becoming available that facilitate the diagnosis of meningococcal disease even after antibiotics have been given.

Meningococcal

■ 23.2   Vaccine

■ 23.2.1 Currently available meningococcal vaccine is a purified, heat stable, lyophilised extract from the polysaccharide outer capsule of Neisseria meningitidis, effective against serogroup A and C organisms. Vaccine contains 50mcg each of the respective purified bacterial capsular polysaccharides. **There is no available vaccine effective against Group B organisms.**

■ 23.2.2 A serological response is detected in more than 90% of recipients and occurs five to seven days after a single injection. The response is strictly Group specific and confers no protection against Group B organisms. Young infants respond less well than adults with little response to the Group C polysaccharide below 18 months and similar lack of response to Group A polysaccharide below three months. Vaccine induced immunity lasts approximately three to five years; in younger children a more rapid decline in antibody has been noted. Conjugated vaccines on the same lines as Hib vaccines are presently being investigated for suitability for infant use to protect against Group C meningococcal infections.

■ 23.2.3 Vaccine must be stored at 2-8°C and the diluent must not be frozen. Vaccine should be reconstituted immediately before use with the diluent supplied by the manufacturer.

■ 23.3   Route of administration and dosage

A single dose of 0.5ml is given by deep subcutaneous or intramuscular injection to adults and children from two months of age.

■ 23.4   Recommendations

■ 23.4.1 Routine immunisation with meningococcal vaccine is not recommended as the overall risk of meningococcal disease is very low, Group B organisms are the major cause of disease in the United Kingdom and a considerable number of cases of meningococcal disease from Group C organisms occur in children too young to be protected with presently available vaccines.

■ 23.4.2 Asplenic children and adults, irrespective of age or the interval from splenectomy, should receive a single dose of meningococcal vaccine before travelling to areas where there is an increased risk of Group A infection. Otherwise the vaccine should be restricted to groups for whom it is otherwise specifically recommended (see 23.4.3 to 23.4.5).

■ 23.4.3 **Contacts of cases:** Close contacts of cases of meningococcal meningitis have a considerably increased risk of developing the disease in the subsequent months, despite appropriate chemoprophylaxis. The recommended schedule for prophylaxis is rifampicin 600mg every 12 hours for **two** days in adults, 10mg/kg dose for children over one year of age and 5mg/kg for children less than one year. Ciprofloxacin as a single dose of 500mg is an alternative for adults but is not yet licensed in the UK for this purpose. Ceftriaxone 250mg intramuscularly can be given to pregnant contacts, but is not licensed in the UK for this purpose. Immediate family or close contacts of cases of Group A or Group C meningitis should be given meningococcal vaccine in addition to chemoprophylaxis. The latter should be given first and the decision to offer vaccine should be made when the results of typing are available. Vaccine should not be given to contacts of Group B cases.

■ 23.4.4 **Local Outbreaks:** In addition to sporadic cases, outbreaks of meningococcal infections with Group C organisms tend to occur in closed or semi-closed communities such as schools and military establishments. Immunisation has been shown to be effective in controlling epidemics, reducing infection rates but not carriage rates. Advice on the use of meningococcal vaccines is available from:

PHLS Communicable Disease Surveillance Centre
(0181-200 6868).

Public Health Laboratory Service
Meningococcal Reference Laboratory
(0161 445 2416).

Scottish Centre for Infection and Environmental Health
(0141 946 7120).

Scottish Meningococcal and Pneumococcal Reference Laboratory
(0141 201 3836).

Meningococcal vaccine has no part to play in the management of outbreaks of Group B meningococcal meningitis.

■ 23.4.5 **Travel:** In some areas of the world the risk of acquiring meningococcal infection is much higher than in this country particularly for those visitors who live or travel 'rough', such as backpackers, and those living or working with local people. Immunisation is recommended for longer visits (generally a month or more), especially if backpacking or living or working with local people, to:

(i) Sub-Saharan Africa:
Epidemics, mainly Group A infections, occur throughout tropical Africa particularly in the Savanna in the dry season which varies from country to country and can be unpredictable. More detailed country by country information is contained in the UK Health Departments' book 'Health Information for Overseas Travel'.

(ii) the area around Delhi, and Nepal, Bhutan and Pakistan.

(iii) Since 1988, following an outbreak of Group A meningococcal meningitis in 1987, Saudi Arabia has required immunisation of people coming to the Haj annual pilgrimage.

■ 23.4.6 Meningococcal vaccine may be given to HIV positive individuals in the absence of contraindications.

■ 23.5 Adverse Reactions

■ 23.5.1 Generalised reactions are rare although pyrexia occurs more frequently in young children than in adults.

■ 23.5.2 Injection site reactions occur in approximately 10% of recipients and last for approximately 24-48 hours.

■ 23.5.3 Serious reactions should be reported to the Committee on Safety of Medicines using the yellow card system

■ 23.6   Contraindications

■ 23.6.1 Immunisation should be postponed in individuals suffering from an acute febrile illness.

■ 23.6.2   Although there is no information to suggest that meningococcal vaccine is unsafe during pregnancy, it should only be given when this is unavoidable, ie. when there is true risk of disease. During an epidemic of meningococcal meningitis in Brazil, no adverse events were reported in pregnant women receiving vaccine.

■ 23.6.3   A severe reaction to a preceding dose of meningococcal vaccine is a contraindication to further doses.

■ 23.7   Supplies

The following meningococcal vaccines are licensed and available:

Mengivac (A+C), Pasteur Merieux MSD Ltd 01628 773200

AC Vax, SmithKline Beecham   0800 616482

■ 23.8   Bibliography

Antibody response to serogroup A and C polysaccharide vaccines in infants born to mothers vaccinated during pregnancy.
McCormick J B, Gusman H H et al.
J Clin. Invest, 1980; 65 : 1141-1144.

Meningococcus Group A vaccine in children three months to five years of age. Adverse reactions and immunogenicity related to endotoxin content and molecular weight of the polysaccharide.
Peltola H, Kayhty H, Kuronen T, Haque N, Sanna S, Makela P H.
J. Pediatr. 1978; 92 : 818-822.

Kinetics of antibody production to Group A and Group C meningococcal polysaccharide vaccines administered during the first six years of life; prospects for routine immunisation of infants and children.
Gold R, Lepow M L, Goldschneider I, Draper T F, Gotschlich E C.
J Infect Dis 1979; 140 : 690-7.

Secondary cases of meningococcal infection among close family and household contacts in England and Wales, 1984-7.
Cooke R P D, Riordan T, Jones D M, Painter M J.
BMJ 1989; 298: 555-558.

Control of meningococcal disease: guidance for Consultants in Communicable Disease Control, PHLS Meningococcal Infections Working Group and Public Health Medicine Environmental Group. CDR Review 1995:5(R13):R189-195

Control of meningococcal disease : guidance for microbiologists Kaczmarski E B, Cartwright KAV, CDR Review 1995;5(R13):R196-98

24   Pertussis

■ 24.1   Introduction

■ 24.1.1   Pertussis is a highly infectious bacterial disease caused by *Bordetella pertussis* and spread by droplet infection; the incubation period is seven to ten days. A case is infectious from seven days after exposure to three weeks after the onset of typical paroxysms. The initial catarrhal stage has an insidious onset and is the most infectious period. An irritating cough gradually becomes paroxysmal, usually within one to two weeks, and often lasts for two to three months. In young infants, the typical 'whoop' may never develop and coughing spasms may be followed by periods of apnoea. Pertussis may be complicated by bronchopneumonia, repeated post-tussive vomiting leading to weight loss, and by cerebral hypoxia with a resulting risk of brain damage. Severe complications and deaths occur most commonly in infants under six months of age.

■ 24.1.2   Before the introduction of pertussis immunisation in the 1950s, the average annual number of notifications in England and Wales (E and W) exceeded 100,000. In 1972, when vaccine acceptance was over 80%, there were only 2069 notifications of pertussis.

■ 24.1.3   Because of public anxiety about the safety and efficacy of the vaccine, acceptance rates fell to about 30% in 1975 and major epidemics with over 100,000 notified cases followed (in E and W) in 1977/79 and 1981/83. However increased vaccine uptake, resulting from the return of professional and public confidence, cut short the next epidemic which died away in 1986, well below the levels of the previous two. In 1992, when uptake had risen to 92%, there were only 2309 notifications, the lowest annual total since 1972. In keeping with the cyclical pattern of pertussis epidemics, notifications rose in 1993, but only reached 4091. By 1995, coverage by the second birthday was 94%; there were 1873 notifications. This is the lowest annual figure ever recorded.

Pertussis

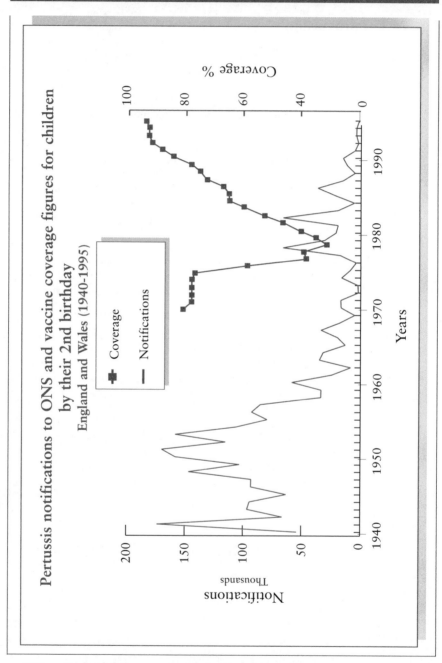

Pertussis notifications to ONS and vaccine coverage figures for children
by their 2nd birthday
England and Wales (1940-1995)

■ 24.1.4   Until the mid 1970s, mortality from pertussis was about one per 1000 notified cases with a higher rate for infants under one year. In 1978 however when there were over 65,000 notifications (in E and W), only 12 deaths were notified. The actual number of deaths due to pertussis is undoubtedly higher since not all cases in infants are recognised. In 1990, there were six deaths from pertussis, all in infants under four months of age. The timing of routine pertussis immunisation was accelerated in 1990; from 1991 to 1995 only five deaths attributed to pertussis were reported (in England and Wales), all in infants too young to be immunised.

■ 24.1.5   Since the anxieties in the mid 1970s concerning pertussis vaccine, studies have confirmed that a full course of vaccine confers protection in over 80% of recipients; in those not fully protected the disease is usually less severe. The two large epidemics which followed the reduction in vaccine acceptance are additional evidence of the effectiveness of pertussis vaccine in the prevention of disease. In Regions with particularly low vaccine coverage, pertussis notifications in 1986 were significantly higher than those in Regions with high coverage.

■ 24.2 Vaccine

■ 24.2.1   Pertussis vaccine is a suspension of killed *Bordetella pertussis* organisms with an estimated potency of not less than four International Units in each 0.5ml of vaccine. The vaccine is usually given as a triple vaccine combined with diphtheria and tetanus vaccines (DTP), with an adjuvant such as aluminium hydroxide. The plain vaccine is no longer supplied as it is less immunogenic and causes more systemic reactions, especially fever.

■ 24.2.2   Adsorbed diphtheria/tetanus/pertussis vaccine (DTP): one 0.5ml dose consists of a mixture in isotonic buffer solution of diphtheria toxoid and tetanus toxoid adsorbed on to aluminium hydroxide gel, together with not more than 20,000 million Bordetella pertussis organisms. The potency of the diphtheria component is not less than 30 iu; that of the tetanus component not less than 60 iu and that of the pertussis component not less than an estimated 4 iu. Thiomersal is added as a preservative to a final concentration of 0.01%.

Pertussis

■ 24.2.3   At present, there is no supplier of monovalent **whole cell** pertussis vaccine. As an alternative, an **acellular** monovalent preparation (Acellular Pertussis Vaccine (APV)) is available for use on a 'named patient' basis. This vaccine contains approximately 3 μg of highly purified pertussis toxin (PT), 36 μg of filamentous haemagglutinin (FHA) and small quantities of Pertactin (or 69 kilodalton outer membrane protein) and type 2 fimbriae. The vaccine is adsorbed onto alum hydroxide and phosphate gel and contains thiomersal preservative.

■ 24.2.4   The vaccines should be stored between 2-8°C, but not frozen. If the vaccine is frozen, it should not be used. Vaccine that has been frozen can be identified by the following test: using an ampoule of DTP vaccine that has not been frozen as a control, shake both ampoules, inspect the contents, leave the ampoules to stand for 15 - 30 minutes and inspect again. Frozen vaccine remains cloudy with clumps of flocculated material.

■ 24.2.5   Protect the vaccine from light. Disposal should be by incineration at a temperature not less than 1100°C at a registered waste disposal contractor.

■ 24.3   Route of administration and dosage

The dose of DTP and APV is 0.5ml, given by deep subcutaneous or intramuscular injection.

■ 24.4   Recommendations

■ 24.4.1   Adsorbed pertussis vaccine as a component of the primary course of immunisation against diphtheria, tetanus and pertussis (DTP) is recommended for all infants from two months of age, unless there is a genuine contraindication (see Chapter 7).

■ 24.4.2   The primary course consists of **three doses with an interval of one month between each dose** (see Chapter 11). If the primary course is interrupted it should be resumed but not repeated, allowing appropriate intervals between the remaining doses.

■ 24.4.3   Monovalent acellular pertussis vaccine can be given when the pertussis component has been omitted from earlier immunisations. Children who have received a full course of immunisation against diphtheria and tetanus should be given three doses of monovalent pertussis vaccine at monthly intervals. APV has been made available solely for this purpose and should not be used in place of the existing DTP for routine primary immunisation.

■ 24.4.4   Where the primary course of diphtheria/tetanus immunisation has been started and the parent wishes pertussis vaccine to be added, DTP vaccine may be used for the subsequent doses, followed by acellular pertussis vaccine at monthly intervals to complete the three doses. Similarly, children presenting for their pre-school diphtheria/tetanus booster who have not previously been immunised against pertussis should be given triple vaccine as the first dose, with two subsequent doses of acellular pertussis vaccine at monthly intervals.

■ 24.4.5   Research from the UK and other countries shows that local reactions and pyrexias occur less often after acellular pertussis vaccine than after whole cell vaccine, especially when the immunisation is given **after** 6 months of age. When the primary immunisation against pertussis was not completed because of a local reaction or pyrexia, it can be completed with acellular pertussis vaccine.

■ 24.4.6   The low uptake of pertussis vaccine from 1975-1985 left a considerable number of unimmunised older children who received DT vaccine only. Such children can be immunised with monovalent acellular pertussis vaccine, both for their own protection and for that of young siblings under the age of immunisation; **there is no upper age limit.**

■ 24.4.7   No reinforcing dose of pertussis vaccine is currently recommended after a course of three injections.

■ 24.4.8   **Children with problem histories:**
When there is a personal or family history of **febrile** convulsions, there is an increased risk of these occurring after pertussis immunisation. In such children, **immunisation is recommended** but advice on the prevention of fever should be given at the time of immunisation.

In a recent British study, children with a family or personal history of **epilepsy** were immunised with pertussis vaccine without any significant adverse events. These childrens' developmental progress has been normal. In children with **a close family history** (first degree relatives) **of idiopathic epilepsy**, there may be a risk of developing a similar condition, irrespective of vaccine. **Immunisation is recommended for these children and for those with a personal history of epilepsy** (see below). Advice on the prevention of pyrexia should be given.

Where there is a still evolving neurological problem, immunisation should be deferred until the condition is stable. **Children whose epilepsy is well controlled may receive pertussis vaccine.** When there has been a documented history of cerebral damage in the neonatal period, immunisation should be carried out unless there is evidence of an evolving neurological abnormality. If immunisation is to be deferred, then this should be stated on the neonatal discharge summary. **Where there is doubt, appropriate advice should be sought from a Consultant Paediatrician, District (Health Board) Immunisation Co-ordinator or Consultant in Communicable Disease Control rather than withholding vaccine.**

■ 24.4.9   HIV positive individuals may receive pertussis vaccine in the absence of contraindications.

■ 24.4.10   If pertussis vaccine is contraindicated, then DT should be offered. There may be an opportunity at a later date to complete pertussis immunisation using APV.

■ 24.5   Adverse reactions

■ 24.5.1   a. Swelling and redness at the injection site are common. A small painless nodule may form at the injection site; this usually disappears and is of no consequence. The incidence of local reactions and pyrexias has been shown to be lower following the accelerated schedule than the previous extended schedule.

b. Crying, screaming and fever may occur after pertussis vaccine in triple vaccine; they may also occur after vaccine which does not contain the pertussis component. Attacks of high pitched screaming, episodes of pallor, cyanosis, limpness, convulsions, as well as local reactions have been reported after both adsorbed DTP and DT vaccines. Both local and systemic reactions were more common after the plain preparations which did not contain adjuvant.

c. More severe neurological conditions, including encephalopathy and prolonged convulsions, resulting in permanent brain damage and death, have been reported after pertussis vaccine. But similar illnesses can develop from a variety of causes in the first year of life in both immunised and unimmunised children and there is no specific test which can identify cases which may be caused by pertussis vaccine. Therefore, no wholly reliable estimate of the risk of such complications due to the vaccine can be made.

d. For these reasons, there has been considerable public and professional anxiety about the safety of pertussis vaccine. In Great Britain, between 1976 and 1979, a total of 1182 children with serious acute neurological illnesses were reported to the National Childhood Encephalopathy Study (NCES). Only 39 of these children had recently had pertussis vaccine and in many of these, the association of the neurological illnesses with immunisation could have occurred by chance.

e. Analysis of the results of the NCES showed that, after taking this into account, the vaccine may very rarely be associated with the development of severe acute neurological illness in children who were previously apparently normal; most of these children suffered no apparent harm. The occurrence of a severe encephalopathy after pertussis immunisation was sometimes associated with long-term residual neurological damage, but the evidence is insufficient to indicate whether or not DTP increases the overall risk of chronic neurological dysfunction. **The number of cases in the NCES, even after three years of intensive case finding, was too small to show conclusively whether or not the vaccine could cause permanent brain damage if such damage occurs at all.**

f. These conclusions have been confirmed by a recent large case control study from the United States that found no significant increased risk of serious acute neurological illness in the seven days after DTP vaccine in children under 2 years of age.

g. In the USA, a group of children who had had convulsions or hypotonic-hyporesponsive episodes within 48 hours of DTP were reviewed six to seven years later; there was no evidence of serious neurological damage or intellectual impairment as a result of these episodes. In another American study, while an association was demonstrated between the first febrile convulsion and the scheduled age of pertussis immunisation, no relationship was demonstrated between immunisation and the age of onset of epilepsy.

h. A major review of studies on adverse events after pertussis vaccine was published by the United States Institute of Medicine in 1991. This concluded that the evidence did not indicate a causal relationship between pertussis vaccine and infantile spasms, hypsarrhythmia, Reye's syndrome and Sudden Infant Death syndrome.

i. Neurological complications after pertussis disease are considerably more common than after vaccine.

j. Cot deaths (Sudden Infant Death Syndrome) occur most commonly during the first year of life and may therefore coincide with the giving of DTP vaccine. However studies have established that this association is temporal rather than causal. The incidence of SIDS appears to be lower in children who have had pertussis vaccine than in those who have not.

■ 24.5.2   Recently available data from linkage of hospital admission records with immunisation details shows that **there is no increase in the likelihood of a febrile convulsion requiring admission to hospital in the week following pertussis containing vaccine, compared with the background risk, if children are immunised before 6 months of age.** Immunisation with pertussis containing vaccine **after** 6 months of age is associated with an increased risk of febrile convulsion, particularly with the third dose.   If a febrile convulsion occurs after a dose of triple vaccine, specialist advice should be sought before continuing with any immunisation.   Children having such convulsions are at increased risk of further febrile convulsions following subsequent immunisations. However, these risks can be minimised by appropriate measures to prevent fever (eg paracetamol and tepid sponging) and **immunisation is recommended.**

■ 24.5.3   It has been suggested that pertussis vaccine is linked with the development of asthma. A recent double-blind study of pertussis vaccines found no significant differences between DTP immunised children and controls for reported wheezing, itchy rash or sneezing. The results suggest that there is no reason to withhold pertussis immunisation because of fear of subsequent asthma or allergy.

■ 24.5.4   When pertussis vaccine is genuinely contraindicated, immunisation against diphtheria and tetanus should still be considered.

■ 24.5.5   Severe or unusual reactions to pertussis vaccine must be reported to the Committee on Safety of Medicines using the yellow card system.

■ 24.6   Contraindications to pertussis immunisation

■ 24.6.1   a. If the child is suffering from any acute illness, immunisation should be postponed until the child has recovered. Minor infections without fever or systemic upset are not reasons to postpone immunisation.

b. Immunisation should not be carried out in children who have a history of a general reaction to a preceding dose. In these children, immunisation should be completed with DT vaccine. Where there has been a local reaction or a pyrexia, acellular pertussis vaccine may be used (see 24.4.5). The following reactions should be regarded as severe:

Local: an extensive area of redness and swelling which becomes indurated and involves most of the antero-lateral surface of the thigh or a major part of the circumference of the upper arm.

General: fever equal to or more than 39.5°F within 48 hours of vaccine; anaphylaxis; bronchospasm; laryngeal oedema; generalised collapse. Prolonged unresponsiveness; prolonged inconsolable or high-pitched screaming for more than 4 hours; convulsions or encephalopathy occurring within 72 hours.

■ 24.6.2 A personal or family history of allergy is **not** a contraindication to immunisation against pertussis, nor are stable neurological conditions such as cerebral palsy or spina bifida. For other 'false contraindications' see 7.6 and 7.7.

Where there is doubt, appropriate advice should be sought from a consultant paediatrician, District (Health Board) Immunisation Co-ordinator or Consultant in Communicable Disease Control, rather than withholding vaccine.

■ 24.7   Management of outbreaks

Since a course of three injections is required to protect against pertussis, vaccine cannot be used to control an outbreak.

■ 24.8   Supplies

DTP vaccines are manufactured by Evans Medical Ltd. (Tel. 0345 451500 or 01372 364000) and
Pasteur Merieux MSD Ltd (Tel. 01628 773200)
Acellular pertussis vaccine is manufactured by Wyeth Lederle Vaccines. (Tel. 01628 414794)
These vaccines are supplied by Farillon (Tel. 01708 379000) as part of the National Childhood Immunisation Programme.

For supplies of single antigen acellular pertussis vaccine in Northern Ireland, contact:
Regional Pharmacist,
Procurement Co-ordinator
Eastern Health and Social Services Board
12-21 Linenhall Street
Belfast
BT2 8BS
Tel. 01232 321313

In Scotland, supplies through Scottish Health Care Services Division of the Common Services Agency (0131-552 6255).

■ 24.9   Bibliography

Infants and children with convulsions and hypotonic/hyporesponsive episodes following DTP immunisation; follow-up evaluation.
Barraff L J, Shields W D et al.
Pediatrics 1988; 81; 789-794.

Relationship of pertussis immunisation to the onset of neurological disorders: a retrospective epidemiological study.
Shields W D, Nielson C et al.
J. Pediatrics 1988: 81; 801-805.

Vaccination and cot deaths in perspective.
Roberts S C.
Arch. Dis. Child. 1987: 12; 754-9.

DHSS Whooping Cough: Reports from the Committee on Safety of Medicines and the Joint Committee on Vaccination and Immunisation. HMSO 1981.

Severity of notified whooping cough.
Miller C L and Fletcher W B.
BMJ 1976, (1), 117-119.

Pertussis immunisation and serious acute neurological illness in children.
Miller D L, Ross E M, Alderslade R, Bellman M H, Rawson N S B.
BMJ 1981: 282; 1595-1599.

Symptoms after primary immunisation with DTP and with DT vaccine.
Pollock T M, Miller E, Mortimer J Y, Smith G.
Lancet 1984: ii; 146-159.

Efficacy of pertussis vaccination in England.
PHLS Epidemiological Research Laboratory and 21 Area Health Authorities.
BMJ 1982: 285; 357-359.

Communicable Disease Report Oct-Dec 1986.
Community Medicine 1987: 9; 176-181

Immunogenicity of combined diphtheria, tetanus and pertussis vaccine given
at 2, 3 and 4 months versus 3, 5 and 9 months of age.
Lancet 1991, i, 507-510
Booy R, Aitken SJM, Taylor S, Tudor-Williams G et al.

Risk of serious acute neurological illness after immunisation with
diphtheria/tetanus/pertussis vaccine:
JAMA 1994, 271: 37
Gale JL, Thapa PB, Wassilak SGF et al.

Adverse Effects of Pertussis and Rubella Vaccines
National Academy Press, Washington DC, 1991.
Institute of Medicine.

Pertussis immunisation in children with a family or personal history of
convulsions: a review of children referred for specialist advice.
Health Trends 1994, 26: 23-4.
Ramsay M, Begg N, Holland B and Dalphinis J.

Sudden Infant Death Syndrome and Diphtheria-Tetanus-Pertussis-Poliomyelitis
vaccination status.
Jonville-Bera AP, Autret E, Laugier J.
Fundam. Clin. Pharmacol. 1995; 9: 263-70.

Pertussis

A new method for active surveillance of adverse events from
diphtheria/tetanus/pertussis and measles/mumps/rubella vaccines.
Farrington P et al.
Lancet 1995; **345**: 567-69.

Pertussis vaccination and asthma: is there a link?
Odent MR, Culpin EE, Kimmel T.
JAMA, 1994; **272**: 592-293.

Lack of Assosiation between Pertussis Vaccination and Symptoms of Asthma
and Allergy
Nillson L et al.
JAMA, 1996; **275**: 760.

25   Pneumococcal

■ 25.1   Introduction

■ 25.1.1   Invasive pneumococcal disease (pneumonia, bacteraemia and meningitis) is a major cause of morbidity and mortality, especially among the very young, the elderly, those with an absent or non-functioning spleen and those with other causes of impaired immunity. The pneumococcus is the commonest cause of community acquired pneumonia. Pneumococcal pneumonia is estimated to affect 1/1000 adults each year and has a mortality of 10-20%. The pneumococcus is also one of the most frequently reported causes of bacteraemia and meningitis. During 1995, 3,897 laboratory isolates from blood or CSF were reported to the Public Health Laboratory Service. Recurrent infections may occur associated with abnormalities such as fractures of the skull.

■ 25.1.2   *Streptococcus pneumoniae* (the pneumococcus) is an encapsulated Gram positive coccus. 84 capsular types have been characterised, of which 8-10 cause two thirds of the serious infections in adults and about 85% of infections in children. Immunity to infection is complicated, but depends greatly on type specific anti-capsular antibodies. However the level of antibody required for protection is not currently known.

■ 25.1.3   Antimicrobial resistance among *S. pneumoniae* is increasing in the UK and worldwide and susceptibility to penicillin, cephalosporin and macrolide antimicrobials can no longer be assumed. In 1994, 2.5% of bacteraemia and meningitis isolates reported to the PHLS in England and Wales showed full or intermediate resistance to penicillin and 11.2% were resistant to erythromycin.

■ 25.2   Pneumococcal Vaccine

■ 25.2.1   Pneumococcal vaccine is a polyvalent vaccine containing 25 microgrammes of purified capsular polysaccharide from each of 23 capsular types of pneumococcus which together account for about 90% of the pneumococcal isolates causing serious infection in Britain. It is supplied in a single dose vial.

■ 25.2.2   Most healthy adults develop a good antibody response to a single dose of the vaccine by the third week following immunisation. Antibody response is not so reliable in young children, those with immunological impairment (including an absent or dysfunctional spleen) and those being treated with immunosuppressive therapy. Antibody response in children under two years of age is likely to be poor.

■ 25.2.3   Many studies of efficacy have found it difficult to reach firm conclusions, but overall efficacy in preventing pneumococcal pneumonia is probably 60-70%. The vaccine is less effective in children under two years of age and in those with immunosuppression. It has been relatively ineffective in patients with multiple myeloma, Hodgkins and non-Hodgkins lymphoma, especially during treatment, and in chronic alcoholism. It does not prevent otitis media or exacerbations of chronic bronchitis, and since so much pneumococcal meningitis is in young children and those with skull defects, its scope for preventing this disease is limited.

■ 25.2.4   Antibody levels usually begin to wane after about five years, but may decline more rapidly in asplenic patients and children with nephrotic syndrome.

■ 25.2.5   Vaccine should be stored unopened at 2-8°C and inspected before being given to check that it is clear, colourless and without suspended particles.

■ 25.3   Recommendations

■ 25.3.1   Pneumococcal vaccine is recommended for all those aged two years or older in whom pneumococcal infection is likely to be more common and/or dangerous, ie those with:

i.   Asplenia or severe dysfunction of the spleen, including homozygous sickle cell disease and coeliac syndrome

ii. Chronic renal disease or nephrotic syndrome

iii. Immunodeficiency or immunosuppression due to disease or treatment, including HIV infection at all stages

iv. Chronic heart disease

v.   Chronic lung disease

vi. Chronic liver disease including cirrhosis

vii. Diabetes mellitus

■ 25.3.2   Where possible, the vaccine should be given, together with advice about the increased risk of pneumococcal infection, four to six weeks (but at least two weeks) before splenectomy and before courses of chemotherapy. If this is not practicable, as in traumatic splenectomy, the vaccine should be given as soon as possible after recovery from the operation, and before discharge from hospital. If not given before chemotherapy and/or radiotherapy, immunisation should be delayed until at least six months after completion of therapy.

■ 25.3.3   **Additional measures for asplenic and hyposplenic patients:** Haemophilus influenzae b, influenza, and in some circumstances meningococcal vaccines are additionally recommended and antibiotic prophylaxis (usually phenoxymethyl penicillin) is advisable at least until the age of 16 years. New guidelines have recently been published and a patient card and information sheet are available from the Department of Health (details at the end of this chapter).

■ 25.3.4   It is recommended that GPs actively identify and contact unimmunised asplenic patients to offer them advice and to immunise them.

■ 25.3.5   It is also recommended that GPs identify patients on their lists in the other groups for whom vaccine is recommended (25.3.1) and that doctors take opportunities to immunise those who have not previously been immunised:

i.   at routine GP or hospital consultations

ii. on discharge after hospital admission

iii. when immunising against influenza.

■ 25.3.6   Pneumococcal vaccine may be given at the same time as influenza vaccine, at a different site, but note that whereas influenza vaccine must be given annually, for most patients pneumococcal vaccine is given once only and re-immunisation may cause adverse reactions (see 25.5 and 25.6.2).

Pneumococcal

■ 25.4   Route of administration and dosage

A single dose of 0.5ml is given subcutaneously or intramuscularly preferably into the deltoid muscle or lateral aspect of the mid thigh. Intradermal injection may cause severe local reaction. The vaccine must not be given intravenously. The vaccine is used as supplied. No dilution or reconstitution is necessary.

■ 25.5   Re-immunisation

Re-immunisation is not normally advised (see 25.6.2) except, after 5-10 years, in individuals in whom antibody levels are likely to have declined more rapidly such as those with no spleen, with splenic dysfunction or with nephrotic syndrome. A few centres are able to measure antibody levels in cases where there is doubt about the need for re-immunisation. This should first be discussed with a local haematologist.

■ 25.6 Adverse Reactions

■ 25.6.1 Mild soreness and induration at the site of injection and, less commonly, a low grade fever may occur.

■ 25.6.2 Re-immunisation with the earlier 12 and 14-valent vaccines produced more severe reactions in some recipients, especially if less than three years had elapsed since the first injection. Reactions correlated with high levels of circulating antibodies. The same considerations are likely to apply to re-immunisation with the 23-valent vaccine.

■ 25.7   Contraindications

■ 25.7.1 Pneumococcal vaccine should not be given during an acute infection. The vaccine is not recommended in pregnancy or in women who are breast feeding.

■ 25.7.2 Re-immunisation within three years of a previous dose of pneumococcal vaccine is contraindicated.

■ 25.8   Supplies

■ 25.8.1   Pneumococcal vaccine is supplied by Pasteur Merieux MSD Ltd. (Tel: 01628 773200).

■ 25.8.2   A patient card and information sheet for asplenic and hyposplenic patients is available from: Department of Health, PO Box 410, Wetherby, LS23 7LL Fax: 01937 845 381, or in Scotland from: Public Health Policy Unit, Scottish Office Department of Health, Room 18, St Andrew's House, Edinburgh EH1 3DE.

■ 25.9   Bibliography

Streptococcus pneumoniae: virulence factors, pathogenesis and vaccines.
Alonsodevelasco E, Verheul AFM, Verhoef J, Snippe H.
Microbiol Rev 1995; 59: 591-603.

Community-acquired pneumonia in adults in British hospitals in 1982-83: A survey of aetiology, mortality, prognostic factors and outcome.
Br Thoracic Society Research Committee, Q J Med 1987; 62: 195-220.

Hospital study of adult community-acquired pneumonia.
MacFarlane J T, Ward M J, Finch R D, Macrae A D,
Lancet 1982; ii: 255-8.

Community acquired pneumonia
Bartlett JG, Mundy LM
N Engl J Med 1995; 333: 1618-24

Pneumococcal bacteraemia and meningitis in England and Wales 1982-92
Aszkensay OM, George RC, Begg NT
Comm Dis Rep 1995; 5: R45-50

Antibiotic resistant pneumococci in the United Kingdom.
George R C, Ball L C, Cooper P G,
CDR 1992; 2: R37-43

Prevalence of antibiotic resistance and serotypes in pneumococci in England and Wales : results of observational surveys in 1990 and 1995
Johnson A P, Speller D C E, George R C et al
BMJ, 1996; 312: 1454-6

Pneumococcal

PHLS surveillance of antibiotic resistance, England and Wales: emerging resistance in Streptococcus pneumoniae
Speller DCE, Johnson AP, Cookson BD et al
Emerging Infect Diseases 1996; 2: 57-58

Efficacy of pneumococcal vaccination in adults: a meta-analysis of randomised controlled trials
Fine MJ, Smith MA, Carson CA et al
Arch Int Med 1994; 154: 2666-77

Pneumococcal polysaccharide vaccine efficacy: An evaluation of current recommendations
Butler JC, Breiman RF, Campbell JF et al
JAMA 1993; 270: 1826-31

Immunogenicity of pneumococcal revaccination in patients with chronic disease
Davidson M, Bulkow LR, Grabman J et al
Arch Int Med 1994; 154: 2209-14

Immunogenicity and safety of a 23-valent pneumococcal polysaccharide vaccine in healthy children and in children at increased risk of pneumococcal infection
Lee H-J, Kang J-H, Henrichsen J et al
Vaccine 1995; 13: 1533-8

Guidelines for the prevention and treatment of infection in patients with an absent or dysfunctional spleen.
Working Party of the British Committee for Standards in Haematology
Clinical Haematology Task Force
BMJ 1996; 312: 430-4

26   Poliomyelitis

■ 26.1   Introduction

■ 26.1.1   Poliomyelitis is an acute illness following invasion of the gastro-intestinal tract by one of the three types of polio virus (1, 2 and 3). The virus has a high affinity for nervous tissue and replicates in motor neurones. The infection may be clinically inapparent, or range in severity from a non-paralytic fever to aseptic meningitis or paralysis. Symptoms include headache, gastro-intestinal disturbance, malaise and stiffness of the neck and back, with or without paralysis. The infection rate in households with young children can reach 100%. The proportion of inapparent to paralytic infections may be as high as 1000 to one in children and 75 to one in adults, depending on the polio virus type and the social conditions. Poliomyelitis remains endemic in some developing countries where it occurs in epidemics. In countries where the disease incidence is low, but transmission is still occurring, polio cases are seen sporadically or as outbreaks amongst unimmunised individuals. Transmission is through contact with the faeces or pharyngeal secretions of an infected person. In industrialised countries, transmission is most likely to be through the oro-pharyngeal route.

■ 26.1.2   The incubation period ranges from three to 21 days. Cases are most infectious from seven to ten days before and after the onset of symptoms; virus may be shed in the faeces for up to six weeks or longer.

■ 26.1.3   Inactivated poliomyelitis vaccine (Salk) was introduced in 1956 for routine immunisation, and was replaced by attenuated live oral vaccine (Sabin) in 1962. **Individuals born before 1958 may not have been immunised and no opportunity should be missed to immunise them in adult life.** Since the introduction of vaccine, notifications of paralytic poliomyelitis (in England and Wales) have dropped from nearly 4,000 in 1955 to a total of 35 cases between 1974-1978. This included 25 cases during 1976 and 1977, in which infection with wild virus occurred in unimmunised persons, demonstrating the continuing need to maintain high levels of immunisation uptake. From 1985-95, 28 cases were reported. 19 were vaccine associated (14 recipients, 5 contacts), 6 were imported; the source of infection could not be found in 3 cases, but in none of whom could wild virus be detected.

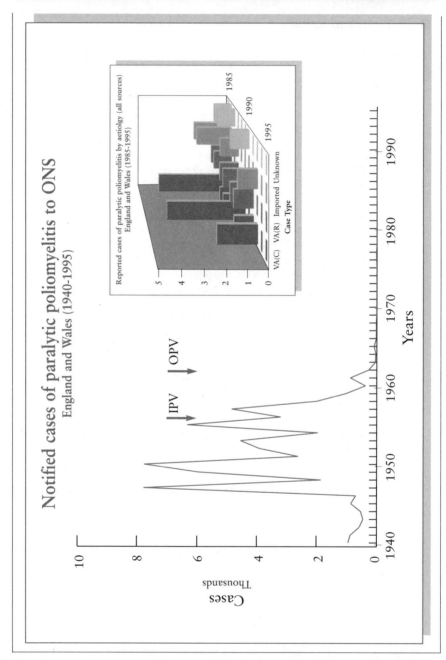

Notified cases of paralytic poliomyelitis to ONS
England and Wales (1940-1995)

Reported cases of paralytic poliomyelitis by aetiolgy (all sources)
England and Wales (1985-1995)

■ 26.1.4 By March 1996, coverage for poliomyelitis immunisation was 96% by the second birthday.

■ 26.1.5 The World Health Organisation has included the UK among the countries which are likely to have eliminated indigenous poliomyelitis due to wild virus. **In any case of childhood acute flaccid paralysis (AFP), including Guillain Barré syndrome, it is essential to obtain two faecal samples 24 to 48 hours apart, as soon as possible after the onset of paralysis for viral examination. Ideally, faecal samples should also be obtained from household and other close contacts.** In the Region of the Americas, where there has been no single case of wild virus poliomyelitis since August 1991, it was recommended that faecal samples should be obtained from at least 5 close contacts of each childhood AFP case.

■ 26.1.6 In September 1994, after 3 years with no single case of wild virus poliomyelitis, an international commission certified that polio virus transmission had been interrupted in the region of the Americas and polio could be considered to have been eliminated from that region.

■ 26.2 Poliomyelitis vaccine (Live and Inactivated)

■ 26.2.1 **Live Oral polio vaccine (OPV)** is routinely used for immunisation in the UK, always given by mouth. It contains live attenuated strains of poliomyelitis virus types 1, 2 and 3 grown in cultures of monkey kidney cells or in human diploid cells. The attenuated viruses become established in the intestine and promote antibody formation both in the blood and in the gut epithelium, providing local resistance to subsequent infection with wild poliomyelitis viruses. This reduces the frequency of symptomless excretion of wild poliomyelitis virus in the community. OPV inhibits simultaneous infection by wild polio viruses and is thus of value in the control of epidemics. Vaccine strain poliomyelitis virus may persist in the faeces for up to six weeks after OPV. This provides an additional community benefit as contacts of recently immunised children may be protected through acquisition of vaccine virus.

■ 26.2.2 Whilst a single dose of polio vaccine may give protection, a course of three doses produces long-lasting immunity to all three polio virus types.

■ 26.2.3 OPV manufactured by SmithKline Beecham should be stored at 2-8°C and OPV manufactured by Evans should be stored at 0-4°C. The expiry date should be checked before use. Vaccine stored unopened at the temperature recommended by manufacturers is stable, but once the containers are open it may lose its potency. Protect from light. Any vaccine remaining in opened containers at the end of an immunisation session must be discarded.

■ 26.2.4 Enhanced potency inactivated polio vaccine (eIPV) contains polio viruses of all three types inactivated by formaldehyde. It should be stored at 2-8°C but not frozen. 0.5ml is given by subcutaneous injection (26.6.1). A course of three injections at monthly intervals produces long-lasting immunity to all three polio virus types. IPV can be given from 2 months of age.

■ 26.2.5 When IPV has been given previously, subsequent immunisation can be carried out using OPV if appropriate. Similarly, when OPV has been used initially, immunisation can be completed with IPV if needed.

■ 26.3 Recommendations

■ 26.3.1 Primary immunisation of infants and children

Oral polio vaccine is recommended for infants from two months of age. **The primary course consists of three separate doses with intervals of one month between each dose (see 11.1), given at the same time as diphtheria/tetanus/pertussis and Hib vaccine.** The dose of vaccine should be repeated if it is regurgitated.

■ 26.3.2 Breast-feeding does not interfere with the antibody response to OPV and immunisation should not be delayed on this account.

■ 26.3.3 Faecal excretion of vaccine virus can last up to six weeks and may lead to infection of unimmunised contacts; such infection may provide protection of previously susceptible individuals, but see 7.3, 7.4, 7.7.5, and 26.3.4.

■ 26.3.4 The contacts of a recently immunised baby should be advised of the need for strict personal hygiene, particularly for washing their hands after changing the baby's napkins.

Unimmunised adults can be immunised at the same time as their children (see 26.5). There is no need to boost previously immunised individuals.

■ 26.3.5 Babies in Special Care Units should be given IPV whilst remaining in the Unit, or alternatively, be given OPV at the time of discharge. Where IPV has been given, immunisation can be completed subsequently with OPV.

■ 26.3.6 Recently immunised children may be taken swimming, even if they have been given OPV. Similarly, there is no risk of an unimmunised child contracting vaccine associated poliomyelitis from a recently immunised child if they are taken swimming. In such public places, care must be taken to dispose of soiled napkins without contaminating facilities that others might use.

■ 26.4   Reinforcing immunisation in children

A reinforcing dose of oral poliomyelitis vaccine (OPV) should be given before school entry at the same time as the reinforcing dose of diphtheria and tetanus vaccine; a further dose of OPV should be given at 15-19 years of age before leaving school.

■ 26.5   Immunisation of adults

■ 26.5.1 A course of three doses of OPV at intervals of four weeks is recommended for the primary immunisation of adults. **No adult should remain unimmunised against poliomyelitis (see 26.1.3).**

■ 26.5.2 Reinforcing doses for adults are not necessary **unless** they are at special risk, such as:

a. Travellers to areas or countries where poliomyelitis is epidemic or endemic. (See 'Health Information for Overseas Travel' 1995 Edition).

b. Health care workers in possible contact with poliomyelitis cases.

■ 26.5.3   Health care workers requiring polio vaccine, either for primary immunisation or for boosting prior to travel to a polio infected country, may be given OPV. They must be reminded of the need for strict personal hygiene, especially if their work brings them into contact with immunosuppressed individuals. There is no known case of nosocomial vaccine related contact poliomyelitis involving a health care worker and an immunosuppressed patient.

■ 26.5.4   For those exposed to a continuing risk of infection, a single reinforcing dose is desirable every ten years.

■ 26.6   Polio vaccines and immunocompromised individuals

■ 26.6.1   Inactivated polio vaccine (IPV) is available for the immunisation of individuals for whom a live vaccine is contraindicated (see 7.3 and 7.4). It should also be used for siblings and other household contacts of immunosuppressed individuals. A primary course of three doses of 0.5ml with intervals of one month should be given by subcutaneous injection and can be given from 2 months of age. A course started with OPV can be completed or reinforced with IPV and vice versa. Reinforcing doses should be given as for OPV.

■ 26.6.2   HIV positive asymptomatic individuals **may** receive live polio vaccine but excretion of the vaccine virus in the faeces may continue for longer than in normal individuals. Household contacts should be warned of this and reminded of the need for strict personal hygiene, including hand-washing after nappy changes for an HIV positive infant.

■ 26.6.3   For HIV positive symptomatic individuals, IPV may be used instead of OPV at the discretion of the clinician.

■ 26.7   Adverse reactions

■ 26.7.1   Cases of vaccine-associated poliomyelitis have been reported in recipients of OPV and in contacts of recipients. In England and Wales there is an annual average of one recipient and one contact case in relation to over two million doses of oral vaccine. Contact cases would be eliminated if all children and adults were immunised. The possibility of a very small risk of poliomyelitis induced by OPV cannot be ignored but is insufficient to warrant a change in immunisation policy. The need for strict personal hygiene for contacts of recent vaccinees must be stressed.

■ 26.7.2   Any such cases following immunisation with poliomyelitis vaccine should be reported to the Committee on Safety of Medicines using the yellow card system.

■ 26.8   Contraindications - OPV

(i) Acute or febrile illness; immunisation should be postponed.

(ii) Vomiting or diarrhoea; immunisation should be postponed.

(iii) Treatment involving high-dose corticosteroids or immunosuppression including general radiation (see 7.3).

(iv) Malignant conditions of the reticulo-endothelial system such as lymphoma, leukaemia, and Hodgkin's disease, and where the normal immunological mechanism may be impaired as for example, in hypogammaglobulinaemia. (See 7.3).

(v) Although adverse effects on the fetus have not been reported, oral polio vaccine should not be given to women during the first four months of pregnancy unless there are compelling reasons, such as travel to an endemic poliomyelitis area.

■ 26.8.1   OPV **may** be given at the same time as inactivated vaccines and with other live vaccines except oral typhoid vaccine (see 33.6.2). When BCG is given to infants, there is no need to delay the primary immunisations which include polio vaccine, because the latter viruses replicate in the intestine to induce local immunity and serum antibodies, and three doses are given.

■ 26.8.2   OPV may contain trace amounts of penicillin, neomycin, polymyxin and streptomycin but these do not contraindicate its use except in cases of extreme hypersensitivity.

■ 26.8.3   OPV should **not** be used for the siblings and other household contacts of immunosuppressed children; such contacts should be given IPV.

■ 26.8.4 OPV should be given either three weeks before or three months after an injection of normal immunoglobulin. This may not always be possible in the case of travellers going abroad, but as in such cases the OPV is likely to be a booster dose, the possible inhibiting effect of immunoglobulin is less important.

■ 26.9 Contraindications to IPV

(i) Acute or febrile illness; immunisation should be postponed.

(ii) IPV may contain trace amounts of polymyxin B and neomycin but these do not contraindicate its use except in cases of extreme hypersensitivity. It does not contain penicillin.

■ 26.10 Management of outbreaks

After a single case of paralytic poliomyelitis from wild virus, a dose of OPV should be given immediately to all persons in the neighbourhood of the case (with the exception of individuals with genuine contraindications such as immunodeficiency, to whom IPV should be given) regardless of a previous history of immunisation against poliomyelitis. In previously unimmunised individuals the three dose course must be completed. If there is laboratory confirmation that a vaccine-derived polio virus is responsible for the case, immunisation of further possible contacts is unnecessary since no outbreaks associated with vaccine virus have ever been documented. If the source of the outbreak is uncertain, it should be assumed to be a 'wild' virus and appropriate control measures instituted.

■ 26.11 Supplies

a. Oral poliomyelitis vaccine, manufactured by SmithKline Beecham in 10 x 1 dose packs and in dropper tubes of ten doses, is available from Farillon (Tel 01708 379000) for use in childhood immunisation programmes and in adults. 10 x 1 dose packs of Evans' Oral poliomyelitis vaccine may also be available in 1997.

b. Inactivated polio vaccine (IPV) is supplied in single dose ampoules and can be obtained only when required for use in named patients.

England: Farillon (Tel 01708 379000).

Wales: the Welsh Health Common Service Authority, Cardiff. Tel. 01222 500500.
Scotland: Common Services Agency, Trinity Park House, South Trinity Park Road, Edinburgh EH5 35H (Tel 0131 552 6255 ext 2283).

Northern Ireland: Regional Pharmacist Procurement Coordinator, Eastern Health and Social Services Board, 12-21 Linenhall St., Belfast (Tel 01232 321313).

■ 26.12 Bibliography

Paralytic poliomyelitis in England and Wales 1976-77.
Collingham K E, Pollock T M, Roebuck M O.
Lancet 1978: (i); 976-977.

Effect of breast feeding on sero-response of infants to oral polio vaccine.
John T J, et al.
Pediatrics 1976: 57; 47-53.

Immunity of children to diphtheria, tetanus and poliomyelitis.
Bainton D, Freeman M, Magrath D I et al.
BMJ 1979: (i); 854-857.

Prevalence of antibodies to polio virus in 1978 among subjects aged 0-88 years.
Roebuck M, Chamberlain R.
BMJ 1982: 284; 697-700.

Prevalence of antibody to polio virus in England and Wales 1984-86.
White P, Green J.
BMJ 1986: 293; 1153-1155.

Paralytic poliomyelitis in England and Wales 1985 - 91.
Joce R, Wood D, Brown D Begg N
Br Med J 1992: 305; 79-82.

Progress towards poliomyelitis eradication
Expanded Programme on Immunisation
Weekly Epidemiological Record. 1996;7:53

COVER (Cover Of Vaccination Evaluated Rapidly)/Körner:
January to March 1996. Immunisation coverage statistics for children
up to 2 years old in the UK.
Communicable Disease Report 1996; 6: 30.

27 Rabies

■ 27.1 Introduction

■ 27.1.1 Rabies is an acute viral infection resulting in encephalomyelitis. The incubation period is generally between two and eight weeks, but may range from nine days to two years or more. The onset of illness is insidious. Early symptoms may include paraesthesiae around the site of the wound, fever, headache and malaise. The disease may then present with spasms, or with hydrophobia, hallucinations and maniacal behaviour progressing to paralysis and coma, or as an ascending flaccid paralysis and sensory disturbance. Rabies is almost always fatal, death resulting from respiratory paralysis. There is no treatment.

■ 27.1.2 Infection is usually via the bite of a rabid animal. Rarely, transmission of the virus has occurred through mucous membranes. It does not occur through intact skin. Virus is present in some tissues and fluids of patients with rabies, but person-to-person spread of the disease has not been documented with the exception of six cases acquired through corneal grafts. No case of indigenous human rabies has been reported in the United Kingdom since 1902 although cases occur from time to time in persons infected abroad.

■ 27.1.3 Rabies in animals occurs in all continents except Australasia and Antarctica. Canine rabies is endemic throughout most of Asia, Africa and Latin America. In Europe foxes are the predominant host but many other animals become infected including dogs and cats, cattle, horses, badgers, martens and deer; mass oral immunisation campaigns have reduced the numbers of reported cases of animal rabies in recent years. In the United States, rabies in animals has become more prevalent since the 1950s; skunks, raccoons and bats account for 85% of animal cases. The UK has been free of indigenous animal rabies since 1922 apart from the identification of a single rabid bat on the Sussex coast in 1996.

■ 27.2 Vaccine

■ 27.2.1 Rabies human diploid cell vaccine (HDCV) is a freeze dried suspension of Wistar rabies virus strain PM/WI 38 1503-3M cultured in human diploid cells and inactivated by beta-propiolactone. The potency of the reconstituted vaccine is not less than 2.5 International Units per 1ml dose. It contains traces of neomycin.

■ 27.2.2   The freeze dried vaccine should be stored at 2-8°C and not frozen. It should be used immediately after reconstitution with the diluent supplied and any unused vaccine discarded after one hour. It may be given by deep subcutaneous, intramuscular or intradermal injection (see 27.4.3 and 27.4.5) usually into the deltoid region.

■ 27.2.3 **Rabies-specific immunoglobulin**

Human rabies immunoglobulin (HRIG) is obtained from the plasma of immunised human donors. It is used after exposure to rabies to give rapid protection until rabies vaccine, which should be given at the same time, becomes effective.

■ 27.3   Recommendations

■ 27.3.1 **Pre-exposure (prophylactic) immunisation**

Pre-exposure immunisation with human diploid cell rabies vaccine should be offered, and is available free from the NHS, to:

a. Laboratory workers handling the virus.

b. Those who, in the course of their work, regularly handle imported animals e.g.

- at animal quarantine centres
- at zoos
- at research and acclimatisation centres where primates and other imported animals are housed
- at ports e.g. certain Customs and Excise officers
- carrying agents authorised to carry imported animals
- veterinary and technical staff at the Ministry of Agriculture, Fisheries and Food (MAFF), the Scottish Office, Agriculture, Environment and Fisheries Department, (SOAEFD) and the Department of Agriculture for Northern Ireland (DANI).
- inspectors appointed by local authorities under the Diseases of Animals Act. (This does not include all local authority dog wardens for whom the risk of exposure is low and for whom post exposure prophylaxis in the event of an incident is likely to be more appropriate.)

c. Licensed bat handlers

d. Workers in enzootic areas abroad who by the nature of their work are at special risk of contact with rabid animals (e.g. veterinary staff or zoologists).

e. Health workers who are likely to come into close contact with a patient with rabies.

■ 27.3.2   Pre-exposure immunisation is also recommended for those living or travelling in enzootic areas who may be exposed to unusual risk of being infected or are undertaking especially long journeys in remote parts where medical treatment may not be immediately available. (More detailed country by country advice is contained in the UK Health Departments' book 'Health Information for Overseas Travel'). For these individuals, the vaccine is not supplied free from the NHS.

■ 27.4   Route of administration and dosage

■ 27.4.1   For primary pre-exposure protection, three doses of 1.0ml of HDCV should be given, on days 0, 7 and 28, by deep subcutaneous or intramuscular injection in the deltoid region. (The antibody response may be reduced if the gluteal region is used.)

■ 27.4.2   For travellers who are not animal handlers, two doses of 1.0ml by deep subcutaneous or intramuscular injection four weeks apart can be expected to give immunity in 98% of recipients and may be acceptable if post exposure treatment is likely to be readily available. For those at continued exposure a further dose should be given 6-12 months later.

■ 27.4.3   **Use of the intradermal route:** When more than one person is to be immunised, the vaccine may be administered in smaller doses (0.1ml) by the intradermal route in either of the above schedules. The intradermal route may also be used for rapid immunisation of, for example, staff caring for a patient with rabies, giving 0.1ml of vaccine intradermally into each limb (0.4ml in all) on the first day of exposure to the patient. **Intradermal immunisation is reliable only if the whole of the 0.1ml dose is properly given into the dermis and should only be given by those experienced in the intradermal technique. It should not be used in those taking chloroquine for malaria prophylaxis as this suppresses the antibody response. The use of the intradermal route is on the doctor's own responsibility as this is not covered by the manufacturer's Product Licence.**

Rabies

■ **27.4.4 Reinforcing doses:** Where post-exposure treatment is readily available, as in the UK, reinforcing doses are not normally required for individuals who have received three doses of vaccine unless exposure occurs (when post exposure treatment should be given) or unless exposure is regular and continuous (e.g. laboratory workers handling the virus, licensed bat handlers).

■ 27.4.5 For those at regular and continuous risk in the UK, and where post-exposure treatment is not readily available and there is continued risk, single reinforcing doses of vaccine should be given at two to three year intervals, the interval to be reviewed after 2-3 reinforcing doses (but see 27.4.6 and 27.5.1).

■ 27.4.6 The three dose primary pre-exposure course produces protective antibody in virtually 100% of recipients and makes routine post-immunisation serological testing unnecessary. Serological testing is advised for those who work with live virus. They should have their antibodies tested every six months, and be given reinforcing doses of vaccine as necessary to maintain protective levels. Serological testing is otherwise only advised for those who have had a severe reaction to a previous dose of vaccine to confirm the need for a reinforcing dose.

■ 27.4.7 All travellers to enzootic areas should also be informed by their medical advisers of the practical steps to be taken if an animal bite is sustained (see 27.4.8).

■ 27.4.8 Post exposure treatment

In the event of possible exposure, firstly, as soon as possible after the incident, the wound should be thoroughly cleansed by scrubbing with soap and water under a running tap for five minutes. Secondly, the name and address of the owner of the animal should be obtained and the animal observed for ten days to see if it begins to behave abnormally. If necessary, the assistance of local officials should be sought. Thirdly, advice should be taken from a local doctor. If the animal is wild or a stray and observation is impossible, the doctor will know if rabies occurs in the locality and if immunisation is advised.

■ 27.4.9 For travellers returning to this country who report an exposure (break in skin or contamination of mucosal surface) to an animal abroad, treatment, including cleaning the wound as above, should be started as soon as possible while enquiries are made about the prevalence of rabies in the country concerned and, where possible, the ownership and condition of the biting animal. Information should be sought from the PHLS Virus Reference Division, London (0181-200 4400); in Scotland, the Scottish Centre for Infection and Environmental Health (0141-946 7120); in Northern Ireland, the Public Health Laboratory, Belfast City Hospital (01232 329241).

■ 27.4.10 Subsequent treatment will depend on the risk of rabies in the country concerned and the immune status of the individual, and **each incident has to be judged on its merits. Points to consider include if the animal is indigenous (native) or not, its behaviour, the site and severity of bite and whether the bite was provoked.**

■ 27.4.11 Summary of post-exposure prophylaxis:

Rabies risk in country of incident	Unimmunised/incompletely immunised individual*	Fully immunised individual
No Risk (27.4.13)	None	None
Low Risk (27.4.15)	5 doses HDCV	2 doses HDCV
High Risk (27.4.17)	5 doses HDCV plus human rabies specific immunoglobulin	2 doses HDCV

*persons who have been immunised by the intradermal route, or who have received fewer than 3 doses of vaccine, or whose last dose of vaccine was given more than 2 years previously.

■ 27.4.12 **NO RISK:** generally no rabies post exposure prophylaxis needed, however each incident needs to be judged separately (see 27.4.10).

Rabies

■ 27.4.13 The following countries are considered 'no risk':

Europe: *Cyprus, Faroe Is, Finland, Gibraltar, Greece, Iceland, Ireland, Malta, Norway (mainland), Mainland Spain exc N.African coast, Sweden, United Kingdom, Portugal, Italy (except the Northern & Eastern borders).*

Americas: *Bermuda, St Pierre & Miquelon, Anguilla, Antigua & Barbuda, Bahamas, Barbados, Cayman Is, Dominica, Guadaloupe, Jamaica, Martinique, Montserrat, Netherlands Antilles, St Christopher & Nevis, St Lucia, St Martins, St Vincent & the Grenadines, Turks & Caicos Is, Virgin Is.*

Asia: *Japan, Singapore, Taiwan.*

Oceania: *American Samoa, Australia, Belau, Cook Is, Federated States of Micronesia, Fiji, French Polynesia, Guam, Kiribati, New Caledonia, New Zealand, Niue, Northern Mariana Is, Papua New Guinea, Samoa, Solomon Is, Tonga, Vanuatu, Western Samoa.*

■ 27.4.14 **LOW RISK:** vaccine only required:

a   Previously unimmunised individuals should be given five doses of 1.0ml HDCV, one each on days 0, 3, 7, 14 and 30.

b   Previously fully immunised individuals should be given two doses of 1.0ml HDCV, one on day 0 and one between days 3-7.

Vaccine must be given by deep subcutaneous or intramuscular injection into the deltoid region (not gluteal) or, in a child, the anterolateral aspect of the thigh.

■ 27.4.15 The following countries are considered low risk:

France, Belgium, Germany, Luxembourg, Netherlands, Switzerland, Denmark, USA and Canada.

If the animal can be reliably observed and remains well for 10 days, immunisation may not be required.

■ 27.4.16 **HIGH RISK**

a. Previously unimmunised individuals should be given immunoglobulin as well as vaccine as follows:

i. Immunoglobulin: human rabies specific immunoglobulin 20iu/kg body weight, up to half the dose infiltrated in and around the wound after cleansing and the rest given by intramuscular injection;

ii. Vaccine: five doses of 1.0ml HDCV by deep subcutaneous or intramuscular injection into the deltoid muscle (not the buttocks) or, in children, anterolateral thigh, one each on days 0, 3, 7, 14 and 30.

b Previously fully immunised individuals: two doses of 1.0ml HDCV given as above, the first on day 0 and the second between days 3-7. Immunoglobulin treatment is not needed.

■ 27.4.17 Countries considered high risk are:

Parts of Mexico, El Salvador, Guatemala, Peru, Colombia, Ecuador, India, Nepal, Pakistan, Philippines, Sri Lanka, Thailand, Vietnam. Also most other countries in Asia, Africa and South America.

■ 27.4.18 Up to date advice should be obtained from the Virus Reference Division, Central Public Health Laboratory, Colindale, London (0181-200 4400) or in Scotland from the Scottish Centre for Infection and Environmental Health (0141 946 7120) as the country-by-country risk groups may change.

■ 27.4.19 Human rabies is a notifiable disease. In the event of a case of human rabies, the Consultant in Communicable Disease Control (in Scotland, the Chief Administrative Medical Officer) should be informed.

■ 27.5   Adverse reactions

■ 27.5.1   HDCV may cause local reactions such as redness, swelling or pain at the site of injection within 24-48 hours of administration. Systemic reactions such as headache, fever, muscle aches, vomiting, and urticarial rashes have been reported. Anaphylactic shock has been reported from the USA and Guillain-Barré syndrome from Norway. Reactions may become more severe with repeated doses.

■ 27.5.2   HRIG may cause local pain and low grade fever but no serious adverse reactions have been reported.

■ 27.5.3   Suspected adverse reactions should be reported to the Committee on Safety of Medicines using the yellow card system.

■ 27.6   Contraindications

■ 27.6.1   There are no absolute contraindications to HDCV, although if there is evidence of hypersensitivity, subsequent doses should not be given except for post-exposure treatment.

■ 27.6.2   Pre-exposure vaccine should only be given to pregnant women if the risk of exposure to rabies is high.

■ 27.7   Supplies

■ 27.7.1   Human diploid cell vaccine (HDCV) is available from Pasteur Merieux MSD Ltd (Tel. 01628 773200).

HDCV for pre-exposure immunisation of those at occupational risk is available from the PHLS Virus Reference Division, Tel. 0181-200 4400. For others, it can be obtained through local pharmacies by private prescription.

For post-exposure use, vaccine is supplied by centres listed in the PHLS Directory. Information may be obtained from the PHLS Virus Reference Division, the Scottish Centre for Infection and Environmental Health or Northern Ireland Public Health Laboratory, Belfast City Hospital, Lisburn Road, Belfast BT9 7AB.

■ 27.7.2 Human rabies immunoglobulin (HRIG) is manufactured by Bio Products Laboratory (BPL) and supplied through some Public Health Laboratories (see above), also BPL and the Scottish National Blood Transfusion Service. Supply centres in Scotland for HDCV and HRIG are listed in the Scottish Office Home and Health Department, Memorandum on Rabies. In Northern Ireland, HDCV and HRIG are available from The Public Health Laboratory, Belfast City Hospital (Tel. 01232 329241).

■ 27.8 Bibliography

WHO Expert Committee on Rabies, 8th report
WHO Technical Report Series, 824, WHO Geneva 1992

Antibody response to human diploid cell rabies vaccine
Cabasso VJ, Dobkin MB, Roby RE, Hammar AH
Appl Microbiol 1974; 27: 553-61

Evaluation of a human diploid cell strain rabies vaccine: final report of a three year study of pre-exposure immunisation
Turner GS, Nicholson KG, Tyrrell DAJ, Aoki FY
J Hyg Camb 1982; 89: 101-10

Longevity of rabies antibody titre in recipients of human diploid cell rabies vaccine
Briggs DJ, Schwenke JR
Vaccine 1992; 10: 125-9

Zoonoses control. WHO consultation on intradermal application of human rabies vaccines
WHO Weekly Epidem Record 1995; 70: 336-7

Multisite intradermal rabies vaccination
Nicholson KG, Prestage H, Cole PJ et al
Lancet 1981; ii: 915-8

Post-exposure rabies vaccination during pregnancy: Effect on 202 women and their infants
Chutivongse S, Wilde H, Benjavongkulchai M et al
Clin Infect Dis 1995; 20: 818-20

Efficacy of rabies vaccines against Duvenhage virus isolated from the European house bats (Eptesicus serotinus), classic rabies and rabies-related viruses
Fekadu M, Shaddock J H, Sanderlin D W, Smith J S
Vaccine 1988; 6: 533

Rabies

28 Rubella

■ 28.1 Introduction

■ 28.1.1 Rubella is a mild infectious disease, most common in unimmunised populations among children aged four to nine years. In the UK, young men are most commonly affected (see 22.1.22). It causes a transient erythematous rash, lymphadenopathy involving post-auricular and sub-occipital glands and occasionally in adults, arthritis and arthralgia. Clinical diagnosis is unreliable since the symptoms are often fleeting and can be caused by other viruses; in particular the rash is not diagnostic of rubella. **A history of rubella should therefore not be accepted without serological evidence of previous infection.** The incubation period is 14-21 days, and the period of infectivity is from one week before until four days after the onset of rash.

■ 28.1.2 Maternal rubella infection in the first eight to ten weeks of pregnancy results in fetal damage in up to 90% of infants and multiple defects are common: the Congenital Rubella Syndrome (CRS). The risk of damage declines to about 10-20% by 16 weeks; after this stage of pregnancy fetal damage is rare. Fetal defects include mental handicap, cataract, deafness, cardiac abnormalities, retardation of intra-uterine growth, and inflammatory lesions of brain, liver, lungs and bone-marrow. Any combination of these defects may occur; the only defects which commonly occur alone are perceptive deafness and pigmentary retinopathy following infection after the first eight weeks of pregnancy. Some infected infants may appear normal at birth but perceptive deafness may be detected later. In 1995, there were only 8 laboratory confirmed rubella infections in pregnant women, reported to CDSC, compared with 164 in 1987. Rubella associated terminations of pregnancy fell from over 750 in 1972 to 22 in 1993. Since the introduction of MMR vaccine, CRS cases, reported to the National Congenital Rubella Surveillance Programme, have fallen to around 5 cases annually.

Rubella

Rubella terminations due to disease/contact or immunisation, reported to ONS.
England and Wales (1971-1994)

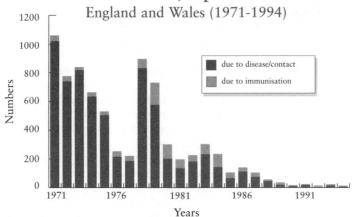

- due to disease/contact
- due to immunisation

Confirmed cases of Congenital Rubella Syndrome and Congenital rubella infection.
England and Wales (1971-1994)

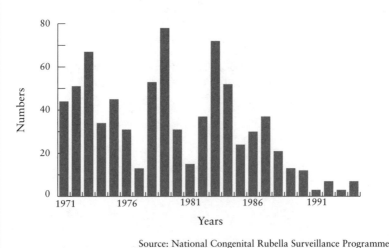

Source: National Congenital Rubella Surveillance Programme

Rubella

■ 28.1.3   Rubella was made a notifiable disease in the UK in 1988. For notification of cases of CRS (see 28.10).

■ **28.1.4   Confirmation of rubella infection in pregnant women**

Because the rash is not diagnostic and also because infection can occur with no clinical symptoms, acute rubella can only be confirmed by laboratory tests.

■ **28.1.5   Investigation of pregnant women exposed to rubella**

All pregnant women with suspected rubella or exposed to rubella must be investigated serologically, irrespective of a history of immunisation, clinical rubella or a previous positive rubella antibody result.

As soon as possible after the exposure to rubella, a blood sample should be taken and sent to the laboratory with **date of LMP and date of exposure. Close collaboration between virologists and clinicians is essential for the accurate interpretation of serological results.** Further specimens may be needed based on the initial results.

■ 28.1.6   As some patients may have more than one exposure to a person with a rubella like illness, or because exposure may occur over a prolonged period, it is important to know the dates of the first and last exposures.

■ 28.1.7   Confirmation of acute rubella infection is recommended in all suspected cases. Saliva samples are appropriate for children but serological samples are essential for pregnant women. Either technique can be used for non-pregnant women and all men; the most convenient test should be used.

■ 28.2   Rubella vaccine

■ 28.2.1   The rubella virus was isolated in cell cultures in 1962. Vaccines are prepared from strains of attenuated virus and have been licensed in the UK since 1970. All rubella vaccine used in the UK contains the Wistar RA 27/3 strain grown in human diploid cells (see 2.7).

■ 28.2.2 Rubella vaccine is a freeze dried preparation. It must be protected from light, stored in the dried state at 2-8°C (not frozen) and reconstituted with the diluent fluid supplied by the manufacturer; it must be used within one hour of reconstitution.

■ 28.2.3 One dose of vaccine produces an antibody response in over 95% of vaccinees; there is no evidence that protection following immunisation wanes with time. In girls who were among the first to be immunised in the UK in 1968, vaccine-induced antibody has shown little decline. In countries where rubella is no longer endemic, vaccine-induced antibody has been shown to persist for at least 18 years. Protection against clinical rubella appears to be long-term even in the presence of declining antibody.

■ 28.2.4 Rubella re-infection can occur in individuals with both natural and vaccine-induced antibody. Occasional cases of CRS after reinfection in pregnancy have been reported; although the risk to the fetus cannot be quantified precisely, it is considered to be low.

■ 28.2.5 Susceptible pregnant women will continue to be at risk of rubella infection in pregnancy until the transmission of rubella virus is interrupted. This will occur when the present school population reaches adulthood (see 22.1.23).

■ 28.2.6 The vaccine virus is not transmitted from vaccinees to susceptible contacts. Thus there is no risk to pregnant women from contact with recently immunised individuals.

■ 28.3 Route of administration and dosage

For both children and adults the dose is 0.5ml given by subcutaneous or intramuscular injection.

■ 28.4 Recommendations (and see Chapter 22)

■ 28.4.1 All boys and girls should be immunised with rubella containing vaccine (MMR) at 12 - 15 months and again at approximately 4 years. A history of rubella should be disregarded because of the unreliability of diagnosis. Young people of either sex, attending for their school-leaving Td and polio immunisations should be offered MMR vaccine if they have not previously had rubella (or measles) vaccine.

■ 28.4.2   Immigrants who have entered the UK after the age of school immunisation are particularly likely to require immunisation. Approximately two in five of the children currently born with congenital rubella syndrome are of Asian origin.

■ 28.4.3   General practitioners are uniquely placed to ensure that all women of child-bearing age have been screened for rubella antibody and immunised where necessary with single antigen rubella vaccine. Opportunities for screening also arise during ante-natal care, and at family planning, infertility and occupational health clinics. In such cases general practitioners must be informed of the results. Every effort must be made to identify and immunise sero-negative women. **All women should be informed of the result of their antibody test and be given evidence that rubella immunisation has been given.**

■ 28.4.4   Serological testing of non-pregnant women should be performed whenever possible before immunisation but need not be undertaken where this might interfere with the acceptance or delivery of vaccine. Pregnancy should be avoided for one month.

■ 28.4.5   Women should be screened for rubella antibodies at least in the first pregnancy,irrespective of a previous positive rubella antibody result. Very occasionally, laboratory errors or errors during reporting may result in patients who are sero-negative being reported as sero-positive. When there are documented results available of two tests using a specific method, both confirming the presence of rubella antibody, then further screening in pregnancy is unnecessary, unless contact with suspected rubella or a rubella-like rash occurs.

■ 28.4.6   Women found to be seronegative on ante-natal screening should be immunised after delivery and before discharge from the maternity unit. If anti-D immunoglobulin is required, the two may be given at the same time in different sites with separate syringes. While it has now been established that anti-D immunoglobulin does not interfere with the antibody response to vaccine, blood transfusion does inhibit the response in up to 50% of vaccinees. In such cases a test for antibody should be performed eight weeks later, with re-immunisation if necessary. If rubella vaccine is not given post-partum before discharge, the general practitioner **must** be informed of the need for this. Alternatively it can be given at the post-natal visit. **All women found on antenatal screening to be susceptible to rubella should be immunised after delivery, before the next pregnancy.**

■ 28.4.7　To avoid the risk of transmitting rubella to pregnant patients, **all health service staff, both male and female,** should be screened and those seronegative immunised with rubella vaccine.

■ 28.4.8　Rubella vaccine **may** be given to HIV positive individuals in the absence of contraindications.

■ 28.5　Immunisation in pregnancy:

■ 28.5.1　Because of the known association between wild rubella virus and CRS, there were concerns that the attenuated vaccine virus could carry this risk. Active surveillance in USA, UK and Germany has found no case of Congenital Rubella Syndrome following inadvertent immunisation shortly before or during pregnancy. There is no evidence that the vaccine is teratogenic.

■ 28.5.2　Termination of pregnancy following immunisation should therefore **not** be recommended. The potential parents should be given this information before considering termination.

■ 28.5.3　As with any live viral vaccine however, immunisation of pregnant women should be avoided where feasible (see 7.2.3).

■ 28.5.4　Pregnant women who are found to be susceptible to rubella should be immunised after delivery.

■ 28.5.5　Enquiring about the date of the last menstrual period is not necessary as it would not prevent immunisation being given just before conception occurs, nor would it prevent immunisation in the early stage before pregnancy is recognised, but see 28.7.

■ 28.6　Adverse reactions

■ 28.6.1　Mild reactions such as fever, sore throat, lymphadenopathy, rash, arthralgia and arthritis may occur following immunisation. Symptoms usually begin one to three weeks after immunisation and are transient; joint symptoms are more common in women than in young girls. One recent retrospective case control study showed no increase in arthropathy (arthritis and arthralgia) in women immunised post-partum compared with their immune (unimmunised) controls

Thrombocytopenia, usually self-limiting, has occasionally been reported after rubella immunisation. Very rarely neurological symptoms have been reported but a causal relationship has not been established.

■ 28.6.2 Serious reactions following rubella immunisation should be reported to the Committee on Safety of Medicines using the yellow card system.

■ 28.7 Contraindications

(i) Rubella vaccine should not be given to a woman known to be pregnant, and pregnancy should be avoided for one month after immunisation.

(ii) Immunisation should be postponed if the patient is suffering from a febrile illness until recovery is complete.

(iii) The vaccine should not be administered to patients receiving high dose corticosteroids or immunosuppressive treatment including general radiation; or to those suffering from malignant conditions of the reticulo-endothelial system such as lymphoma, leukaemia, Hodgkin's disease or where the normal immunological mechanism may be impaired as, for example, in hypogammaglobulinaemia (see 7.3).

(iv) If it is necessary to administer more than one live virus vaccine at the same time, these may be given simultaneously at different sites unless a combined preparation is used. If not given simultaneously they should be separated by an interval of at least three weeks (but see 7.5). A three week interval should be allowed between the administration of rubella vaccine and BCG.

(v) Rubella vaccine should not be given within three months of an injection of immunoglobulin.

(vi) Rubella vaccines contain traces of neomycin and/or polymyxin. Previous anaphylactic reaction to these substances contraindicate rubella immunisation.

■ 28.8   Supplies

Freeze-dried live vaccine manufactured either by Evans or SmithKline Beecham and containing the Wistar RA 27/3 strain, is available from Farillon (Tel 01708 379000) or Scottish Health Care Supplies for use in childhood immunisation programmes and for adult women.

■ 28.9   Human normal immunoglobulin (HNIG)

Post-exposure prophylaxis with immunoglobulin does **not** prevent infection in non-immune contacts and is therefore of little value for protection of pregnant women exposed to rubella. It may however reduce the likelihood of clinical symptoms which may possibly reduce the risk to the fetus. It should only be used if termination for confirmed rubella would be unacceptable when it should be given soon after exposure; serological follow-up of recipients is essential.

Dose: 750mg
For supplies see 19.3.

■ 28.10 Surveillance of CRS and rubella immunisation in pregnancy

■ 28.10.1 Congenital Rubella Syndrome has been included amongst the rare diseases monitored by the British Paediatric Association Surveillance Unit (BPASU) which sends monthly enquiries to paediatricians, who should report CRS on the monthly cards.

■ 28.10.2 Clinicians who do not return information on CRS to BPASU should report any child with congenital rubella defects, or with symptoms suggestive of congenital rubella, or with laboratory evidence of intra-uterine infection without symptoms to the National Congenital Rubella Surveillance Programme:

Ms Pat Tookey
National Congenital Rubella Surveillance Programme
Department of Epidemiology and Biostatistics
Institute of Child Health
30 Guilford Street
London WC1
Tel. 0171-242 9789

This Department is also investigating the effects of rubella immunisation in pregnancy. If a woman is given rubella vaccine in pregnancy, or becomes pregnant within one month of immunisation, the Department should be notified as soon as possible. Arrangements will then be made for the appropriate clinical and virological examination of the new-born infant, and for subsequent follow-up.

■ 28.11 Bibliography

Consequences of confirmed maternal rubella at different stages of pregnancy.
Miller E, Cradock-Watson J E, Pollock T M.
Lancet 1982; ii: 781-4.

Rubella vaccination: persistence of antibodies for up to 16 years.
O'Shea S, et al.
BMJ 1982; 285: 253.

Rubella antibody persistence after immunisation.
Chu S Y, Bernier R H, Stewart J A et al.
JAMA 1988; 259: 3133-6.

Rubella vaccination in pregnancy
Tookey P A, Jones G, Miller B H R & Peckham C S
CDR 1991, 1 R 86-88.

National Congenital Rubella Surveillance Programme 1.7.71-30.6.84.
Smithells R W, Sheppard S, Holzel H, Dickson A.
BMJ 1985: 291; 40-41.

Rational strategy for rubella vaccination.
Hinman A, Orenstein W, Bart K, Preblud S.
Lancet 1983: i; 39-41.

Some current issues relating to rubella vaccine.
Preblud S.
JAMA 1985; 254 (2): 253-6.

Rubella surveillance to December 1990: A joint report from the PHLS and National Congenital Rubella Surveillance Programme
Miller E, Waight P A, Verdien J E et al.
CDR 1991 I: R 33-37.

Congenital rubella in the Asian community in Britain
Miller E, Waight P A, Rousseau S A et al.
Br Med J 1990, 301: 1391.

Outcome of periconceptional maternal rubella.
Enders G, Nickerl-Packer U, Miller E, Cradock-Watson J E.
Lancet 1988; 11: 1445-6.

Rubella surveillance to June 1994: third joint report from the PHLS and
the National Congenital Rubella Surveillance Programme Miller E et al.
CDR Review 1994;4(R12):R146-52.

Absence of an association between rubella vaccination and arthritis in
underimmune postpartum women.
Slater PE et al.
Vaccine 1995;13(16):1529-32.

Rubella

29   Smallpox and vaccinia

■ 29.1   Introduction

In December 1979 the Global Commission for the Certification of Smallpox Eradication declared the world free of smallpox and this declaration was ratified by the World Health Assembly in May 1980.

There is thus no indication for smallpox vaccination for any individual with the exception of some laboratory staff and specific workers at identifiable risk (12.17).

■ 29.2   Recommendations

Workers in laboratories where pox viruses (such as vaccinia) are handled, and others whose work involves an identifiable risk of exposure to pox virus, should be advised of the possible risk and vaccination should be considered. Detailed guidance for laboratory staff has been prepared by the Advisory Committee on Dangerous Pathogens and the Advisory Committee on Genetic Modification (see 29.3). Further advice on the need for vaccination and contraindications should be obtained from the Public Health Laboratory Service Virus Reference Division (Tel 0181 200 4400); if vaccination is considered desirable, vaccine can be obtained through PHLS on this number. In Scotland, advice can be obtained from the Scottish Centre for Infection and Environmental Health (Tel. 0141 946 7120).

■ 29.3   Bibliography

Vaccination of laboratory workers handling vaccinia and related pox viruses infectious for humans. Advisory Committee on Dangerous Pathogens and Advisory Committee on Genetic Modification 1990. HMSO ISBN 0 11 885450.

30　Tetanus

■ 30.1　Introduction

■ 30.1.1　Tetanus is an acute disease characterised by muscular rigidity with superimposed agonising contractions. It is induced by the toxin of tetanus bacilli which grow anaerobically at the site of an injury. The incubation period is between four and 21 days, commonly about ten. Tetanus spores are present in soil and may be introduced into the body during injury, often through a puncture wound, but also through burns or trivial, unnoticed wounds. Neonatal tetanus due to infection of the baby's umbilical stump is an important cause of death in many countries in Asia and Africa. Turkey is the only remaining country reporting cases in the European region. World-wide elimination of neonatal tetanus by the year 1995 was one of the World Health Organisation targets and the number of countries is progressively increasing in which neonatal tetanus no longer occurs. Tetanus can never be eradicated. Tetanus is not spread from person to person.

■ 30.1.2　Effective protection against tetanus is provided by active immunisation which was introduced in some localities as part of the primary immunisation of infants from the mid 1950s and nationally from 1961. Tetanus immunisation was provided by the Armed Forces from 1938. In 1970 it was recommended in the UK that active immunisation should be routinely provided in the treatment of wounds, when immunisation against tetanus should be initiated if appropriate, and subsequently completed.

■ 30.1.3　Between 1984 and 1995 there were 145 cases of tetanus (notifications, deaths and laboratory reports) in England and Wales. 75% occurred in individuals over 45 years and of the remainder, 16% were in individuals from 25 to 44 years. 53% of all cases were in individuals over 65 years, two thirds of them being in women. Thus, the highest risk groups are the elderly with women being at greater risk than men.

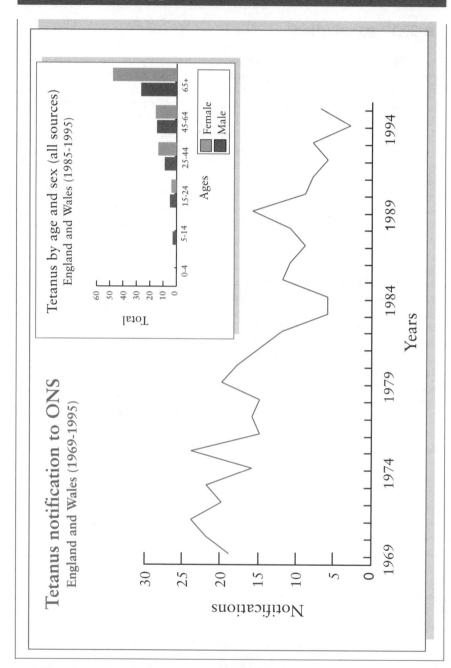

Tetanus notification to ONS
England and Wales (1969-1995)

Tetanus by age and sex (all sources)
England and Wales (1985-1995)

■ 30.2   Tetanus vaccine and adsorbed tetanus vaccine

Immunisation protects by stimulating the production of antitoxin which in turn provides immunity against the effects of the toxin. The immunogen is prepared by treating a cell-free preparation of toxin with formaldehyde and thereby converting it into the innocuous tetanus toxoid. This however is a relatively poor immunogen, and for use as a vaccine it is usually adsorbed onto an adjuvant, either aluminium phosphate or aluminium hydroxide. *Bordetella pertussis* vaccine also acts as an effective adjuvant.

The recommended vaccines for immunisation are:

Adsorbed tetanus (**T**).
Adsorbed diphtheria/tetanus (**DT**).
Adsorbed tetanus /low dose diphtheria vaccine for adults (**Td**).
Adsorbed diphtheria/tetanus/pertussis (**DTP**).

Plain vaccines are no longer supplied as they are less immunogenic and have no advantage in terms of reaction rates.

Vaccines should be stored at 2-8°C. Protect from light. Do not freeze.

Disposal should be by incineration at not less than 1100°C at a registered waste disposal contractor.

The dose is 0.5ml given by intramuscular or deep subcutaneous injection.

■ 30.3   Recommendations

■ 30.3.1   For immunisation of infants and children under ten years.

a. Primary immunisation

Triple vaccine, that is, vaccine containing diphtheria toxoid, tetanus toxoid, and *Bordetella pertussis* (DTP), is recommended for infants from two months of age. Adsorbed DTP vaccine is used as it has been shown to cause fewer reactions than plain vaccine. If the pertussis component is contraindicated, adsorbed diphtheria/tetanus vaccine should be given. **A primary course of immunisation consists of three doses starting at two months with an interval of one month between each dose** (see 11.1). If a course is interrupted it may be resumed; there is no need to start again, whatever the interval. The dose is 0.5ml given by intramuscular or deep subcutaneous injection.

b. Reinforcing doses in children

A booster dose of adsorbed diphtheria/tetanus (DT) should be given at least three years after the final dose of the primary course. If the primary course is only completed at school entry, then the booster dose should be given three years later. A further reinforcing dose of tetanus and low dose diphtheria vaccine (Td) is recommended for those aged 13-18 years or before leaving school. **Teenagers being treated for tetanus prone wounds and who had received their fourth dose of tetanus vaccine approximately ten years earlier, should be given Td vaccine and the school leaving dose omitted.**

■ 30.3.2   Children given DTP at monthly intervals for primary immunisation, without a booster dose at 18 months, have been shown to have adequate antibody levels at school entry. A booster dose at 18 months is therefore not recommended.

■ **30.3.3   For immunisation of adults and children over ten years**

Adults most likely to be susceptible to tetanus are the elderly, especially women and men who have not served in the Armed Forces.

a. For primary immunisation the course consists of three doses of 0.5ml of adsorbed tetanus vaccine (T) by intramuscular or deep subcutaneous injection, with intervals of one month between each dose. If there is no record of diphtheria immunisation either, then three doses of Td vaccine should be given.

b. A reinforcing dose (T or Td) ten years after the primary course and again ten years later maintains satisfactory levels of protection which will probably be life-long.

c. For immunised adults who have received five doses, either in childhood, or as above, booster doses are not recommended, other than at the time of tetanus prone injury, since they have been shown to be unnecessary and can cause considerable local reactions. There are data that show that tetanus has occurred only exceptionally rarely in fully immunised individuals despite the passage of many years since the completing dose of a standard course of immunisation, and without subsequent routine boosting. Cases that have occurred were not fatal. **There is therefore little justification for boosting with tetanus vaccine beyond the recommended 5 dose regimen.**

■ **30.3.4   Treatment of patients with tetanus-prone wounds**
The following are considered tetanus-prone wounds:

a. Any wound or burn sustained more than six hours before surgical treatment of the wound or burn.

b. Any wound or burn at any interval after injury that shows one or more of the following characteristics:

(i)   A significant degree of devitalised tissue.

(ii)   Puncture-type wound.

(iii) Contact with soil or manure likely to harbour tetanus organisms.

(iv) Clinical evidence of sepsis.

Thorough surgical toilet of the wound is essential whatever the tetanus immunisation history of the patient.

Specific anti-tetanus prophylaxis is as follows:

Immunisation status	Type Of Wound	Type of Wound
	Clean	Tetanus Prone
Last of 3 dose course, or reinforcing dose within last 10 years	Nil.	Nil (A dose of human tetanus immunoglobulin may be given if risk of infection is considered especially high, e.g. contamination with stable manure).
Last of 3 dose course or reinforcing dose more than 10 years previously.	A reinforcing dose of adsorbed vaccine.	A reinforcing dose of adsorbed vaccine plus a dose of human tetanus immunoglobulin.
Not immunised or immunisation status not known with certainty.	A full 3 dose course of adsorbed vaccine.	A full 3 dose course of vaccine, plus a dose of tetanus immunoglobulin in a different site.

Dosage human tetanus immunoglobulin	
Prevention 250 iu by intramuscular injection, or 500 iu, if more than 24 hours have elapsed since injury, or there is risk of heavy contamination or following burns. Available in 1ml ampoules containing 250 iu.	Treatment 150 iu/kg given in multiple sites.

■ 30.3.5   Routine tetanus immunisation began in 1961, thus individuals born before that year will not have been immunised in infancy. After a tetanus-prone injury such individuals will therefore require a full course of immunisation unless it has previously been given, as for instance in the armed services.

■ 30.3.6   Immunised individuals respond rapidly to a subsequent single injection of adsorbed tetanus vaccine, even after an interval of years.

■ 30.3.7   For wounds not in the above categories, such as clean cuts, antitetanus immunoglobulin should **not** be given.

■ 30.3.8   Patients with impaired immunity who suffer a tetanus-prone wound may not respond to vaccine and may therefore require antitetanus immunoglobulin (see 7.3 and 30.7) in addition.

■ 30.3.9   HIV positive individuals **should** be immunised against tetanus in the absence of contraindications (see 7.4 and 30.7).

■ 30.4   Adverse reactions

■ 30.4.1   Local reactions, such as pain, redness and swelling round the injection site may occur and persist for several days. General reactions, which are uncommon, include headache, lethargy, malaise, myalgia and pyrexia. Acute anaphylactic reactions and urticaria may occasionally occur and, rarely, peripheral neuropathy. Persistent nodules at the injection site may arise if the injection is not given deeply enough.

■ 30.4.2   Severe or unusual reactions should be reported to the Committee on Safety of Medicines using the yellow card system.

■ 30.5   Contraindications

a. Tetanus vaccine should not be given to an individual suffering from acute febrile illness except in the presence of a tetanus-prone wound. Minor infections without fever or systemic upset are not reasons to postpone immunisation.

Tetanus

b. Immunisation should not proceed in individuals who have had an anaphylactic reaction to a previous dose. A large study of individuals (740) with histories of reactions after tetanus immunisation showed that tetanus immunisation could be completed and none of the patients, when challenged, suffered an adverse reaction. The authors conclude that an adverse reaction to tetanus toxoid does not preclude future immunisation with this same material. If this is to be done in patients with a history of an adverse reaction to a previous dose, then it is best preformed in a setting where there are facilities to deal with any acute allergic reactions.

■ 30.6   Supplies - vaccine

DTP and DT vaccines manufactured by Evans Medical (Tel. 0345 451500 or 01372 364000) and Pasteur Merieux MSD Ltd (Tel 01628 773200) are available from Farillon (Tel. 01708 379000) for use in childhood immunisation programmes. In Scotland, supplies are available from Scottish Health Care Supplies Division of the Common Service Agency.

Low dose diphtheria for adults combined with tetanus vaccine (Td) is available from Pasteur Merieux MSD Ltd (Tel. 01628 773200) or from Farillon (Tel. 01708 379000) for use in childhood immunisation programmes. In Scotland, supplies are available from the Scottish Health Care Supplies Division of the Common Service Agency.

 Adsorbed tetanus vaccine is available from:

Evans Medical (Tel. 0345 451500 or 01372 364000).
Pasteur Merieux MSD Ltd. (Tel. 01628 773200).

■ 30.7   Supplies - antitetanus immunoglobulin

Bio Products Laboratory (Tel. 0181 905 1818).
Regional Blood Transfusion Centres.
Immuno (TETABULIN) (Tel. 01732 458101).

In Northern Ireland, the source of anti-tetanus immunoglobulin is the Northern Ireland Blood Transfusion Services, Lisburn Road, Belfast. Tel. 01232 321414 (issued via hospital pharmacies).

Human tetanus immunoglobulin for intravenous use is available on a named patient basis from the Scottish National Blood Transfusion Service (for telephone numbers see 18.13).

■ 30.8   Bibliography

Prevention of tetanus in the wounded.
Smith J W G, Lawrence D R, Evans D G.
BMJ 1975: (iii) 453-455.

Immunity of children to diphtheria, tetanus and poliomyelitis.
Bainton D, Freeman M, Magrath D I, Sheffield F, Smith J W G.
BMJ 1979 (i) 854-857.

Excessive use of tetanus toxoid boosters.
Edsall G, Elliott M W, Peebles T C, Levine L, Eldred M C.
JAMA 1967 202 (i) 17-19.

Duration of immunity after active immunisation against tetanus.
White W G et al.
Lancet 1969 (ii) 95-96.

Reactions after plain and adsorbed tetanus vaccines.
White W G et al.
Lancet 1980 (i) 42.

To give or not to give; guidelines for tetanus vaccine.
Sheffield F W.
Community View (1985) 33, 8-9.

Durability of immunity to diphtheria, tetanus and poliomyelitis after a three
dose schedule completed in the first eight months of life.
Jones E A, Johns A, Magrath D I, Melville-Smith M, Sheffield F.
Vaccine 1989: 7; 300-2.

Adverse Reactions to Tetanus Toxoid
Jacobs R L, Lowe R S, Lahier B Q
JAMA 1992; 247: 40-4.

Tetanus

■ 31.1   Introduction

Tick-borne encephalitis is a meningoencephalitis caused by a flavivirus transmitted to man by the bite of an infected tick (or, less commonly, by ingestion of unpasteurised milk from infected animals, especially goats). In Sweden, 10-15% of adults with the illness are reported to develop paresis during the acute phase and recovery may be slow. The case fatality is around 1%. The disease is endemic in forested parts of Europe and Scandinavia, especially where there is heavy undergrowth, the greatest risk being in late spring and summer when ticks are active. The virus is maintained in nature in small mammals, domestic livestock and certain species of birds.

■ 31.2   Vaccine

■ 31.2.1   An unlicensed vaccine is available on a named patient basis. It is an inactivated whole cell virus vaccine containing a suspension of purified TBE virus grown in chick embryo cells and inactivated with formalin. It contains thiomersal as preservative. The vaccine should be stored between 2°C and 8°C. Freezing or storage at a higher temperature must be avoided.

■ 31.2.2   An immunoglobulin preparation is also available for post-exposure prophylaxis.

■ 31.3   Recommendations

■ 31.3.1   The vaccine is recommended for travellers who are to walk, camp or work in late spring and summer in warm heavily forested parts of Central and Eastern Europe and Scandinavia, especially if there is heavy undergrowth.

■ 31.3.2   Protection is also afforded by covering arms, legs and ankles and using insect repellents on socks and outer clothes. These measures are advised whether or not vaccine is given.

■ 31.4   Route of administration and dosage

■ 31.4.1   Two doses of 0.5ml (irrespective of age) given 4-12 weeks apart will give protection for one year. The injections must be given intramuscularly.

■ 31.4.2   A third dose 9-12 months after the second gives three years protection. A further booster dose can be given up to six years later for longer protection.

■ 31.4.3   Booster doses are recommended at 3 yearly intervals for those at continued risk.

■ 31.5   Adverse reactions

■ 31.5.1   Reported reactions to tick-borne encephalitis vaccine are very rare. Local reactions at the immunisation site and some local lymphadenopathy may occur. Febrile reactions in children are described after the first dose.

■ 31.5.2   General reactions such as fatigue, limb pain, fever, nausea and headache lasting up to 24 hours may occur occasionally and a transient pruritic rash may rarely occur.

■ 31.5.3   Neurological symptoms have occurred on rare occasions following administration of the vaccine.

■ 31.6   Contraindications

Allergy to the preservative thiomersal and to egg protein are contraindications.

■ 31.7   Supplies

Both the vaccine and the immunoglobulin preparation are available from Immuno Limited (Telephone 01732-458101). The vaccine is supplied in pre-loaded syringes, each syringe containing a single dose of 0.5ml. The immunoglobulin is supplied in single vials of 1, 2 and 5ml.

■ 31.8   Bibliography

Tick-borne encephalitis
WHO Weekly Epidemiol Rec 1995; 70: 120-2

Tick-borne encephalitis in southern Germany
Kaiser R
Lancet 1995; 345: 463

Prevalence of antibodies against tick-borne encephalitis among residents of north-eastern Poland
Prokopowicz D, Bobrowska E, Bobrowski M, Grzeszczuk A
Scand J Infect Dis 1995; 27: 15-16

Immunogenicity and reactogenicity of a highly purified vaccine against tick-borne encephalitis
Kunz C et al
J Med Virol 1980; 6: 103-9

Tick-borne encephalitis despite specific immunoglobulin prophylaxis
Kluger G, Schottler A, Waldvogel K et al
Lancet 1995; 346: 1502

31   Tick borne encephalitis

■ 32   TUBERCULOSIS: BCG IMMUNISATION

Please note that this chapter is arranged differently from other chapters in this book. For ease of reference, it is divided into three sections:

  i.   BCG immunisation policy (paragraphs 32.1 to 32.4)

  ii. The tuberculin skin test (paragraphs 32.5 to 32.17)

  iii. BCG immunisation   (paragraphs 32.18 to 32.28)

BCG IMMUNISATION POLICY

■ 32.1   Introduction

■ 32.1.1   Human tuberculosis is caused by infection with *Mycobacterium tuberculosis, M. bovis* or *M. africanum* and may affect any part of the body. In the UK, about 75% of new cases involve the respiratory system; non-respiratory forms are more common in immigrant ethnic groups and in those with impaired immunity. Tuberculosis is most commonly acquired by aerosol spread; such transmission is only likely when the index case is sputum smear-positive for the bacillus, and after prolonged close contact.

■ 32.1.2 Notifications of tuberculosis in the UK declined tenfold between 1948 and 1987, although high immigration levels, particularly from the Indian subcontinent (ISC), slowed the decline in the late 1960s. The decline stopped in 1987, and in recent years small year on year increases have occurred to 6,528 in 1993 (the provisional total for 1994 is 6229, and for 1995, 6249). The incidence varies widely between areas and between ethnic groups, but is generally higher in inner city areas and in groups of the population originating from high risk areas or situations (eg ISC, Africa, refugees). HIV infection, although undoubtedly a risk factor for tuberculosis, is not thought to have contributed significantly to the recent increases in notifications in the UK. Mortality from tuberculosis decreased rapidly after the introduction of effective chemotherapy. In recent years about 400 deaths a year have been attributed to tuberculosis in England and Wales. Drug resistant tuberculosis is uncommon in the UK, but has increased slightly in recent years.

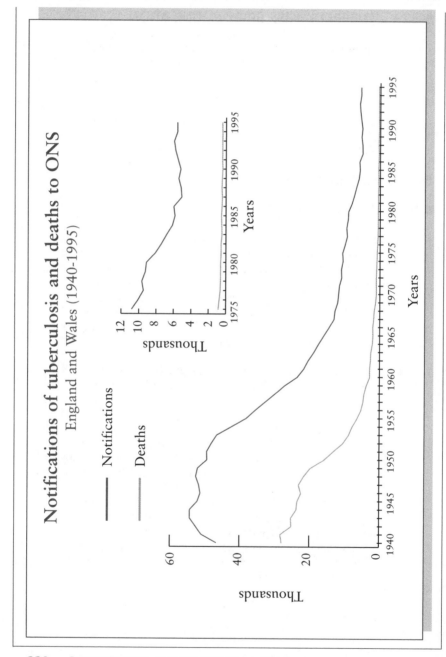

Notifications of tuberculosis and deaths to ONS
England and Wales (1940-1995)

Notifications
Deaths

■ 32.2   Bacillus Calmette-Guérin (BCG) vaccine

■ 32.2.1   BCG vaccine contains a live attenuated strain derived from *Mycobacterium bovis*. Two preparations are available: one for intradermal administration, containing 8-26 million colony forming units per 10 dose vial, and one for percutaneous use containing 50-250 million colony forming units per vial. **The latter is for use only in infants when using the multiple puncture technique.** Both preparations are available freeze-dried in rubber-capped vials with diluent in a separate ampoule.

■ 32.2.2   The vaccine has been shown to have an efficacy in protecting against tuberculosis of 70-80% when given to British schoolchildren, protection lasting at least 15 years.

■ 32.2.3   BCG vaccine was introduced for general use in the UK in 1953. A national immunisation programme was then started with the aim of immunising all children at age 13 before they left school. By 1958, 35% of children in this age cohort had been immunised and by 1962, 60%. In recent years about 70% of the target group have been immunised each year. National returns suggest about a further 8% were exempt from immunisation as they were tuberculin positive. Up to 50,000 neonates are also now immunised each year in selective neonatal immunisation programmes.

■ 32.2.4   Adverse reactions to BCG vaccine are rare if attention is paid to proper selection of subjects and to the techniques for both tuberculin testing and BCG immunisation. All personnel performing these tests must be properly instructed and observed to be using the correct techniques. A Department of Health video, for use in teaching sessions, demonstrates the techniques. Copies have been sent to all District Immunisation Coordinators in England and Northern Ireland, and are also available on free loan (England only) or to buy from the address at the end of this chapter.

■ 32.3   Recommendations for immunisation

■ 32.3.1   The following groups are recommended for immunisation with BCG provided:

a. BCG immunisation, as evidenced by the presence of a characteristic scar (see 32.3.4), has not previously been carried out,

b. the tuberculin skin test is negative as defined in paragraph 32.16.3 (although babies up to three months of age may be immunised without prior skin testing), and

c. there are no other contraindications (see 32.4).

■ 32.3.2   All those at **higher risk of tuberculosis:**

a. **Health service staff** who may have contact with infectious patients or their specimens. These comprise doctors, nurses, physiotherapists, radiographers, occupational therapists, technical staff in microbiology and pathology departments including attendants in autopsy rooms, students in all these disciplines, and any others considered to be at high risk. It is particularly important to test and immunise staff working in maternity and paediatric departments, and departments in which the patients are likely to be immunocompromised, eg transplant, oncology and HIV units.

b. **Veterinary and other staff** who handle animal species known to be susceptible to tuberculosis eg simians.

c. **Staff of prisons**, old people's homes, refugee hostels and hostels for the homeless.

d. **Contacts** of cases known to be suffering from active pulmonary tuberculosis.

Contacts of a sputum smear positive index case may have a negative tuberculin skin test when first seen but be in the early stages of infection before tuberculin sensitivity has developed. A further skin test should be performed six weeks later and immunisation only carried out if this second test is negative. (If the second skin test is positive, the patient has converted and must be referred for consideration of chemoprophylaxis.) However, if for some reason a further test is impossible, vaccine may be given after the first test.

All HIV positive contacts of a smear positive case should be referred for consideration of chemoprophylaxis.

Infants and children who are contacts of a smear positive case:
Children under two years of age who have not previously received BCG should be given chemoprophylaxis even if the skin test is negative and

then, if appropriate, immunised with BCG on completion of the course. Newly born babies should be given prophylactic isoniazid chemotherapy and tuberculin tested after 3-6 months. If the skin test is positive, chemotherapy is continued; if negative, BCG vaccine is given provided the infant is no longer in contact with infectious tuberculosis. It is not necessary to use isoniazid resistant BCG.

Newly born contacts of other cases should be immunised immediately.

e. **Immigrants from countries with a high prevalence of tuberculosis, their children and infants wherever born.**

New entrants to the UK, including students, from countries with a high prevalence of tuberculosis (eg the Indian Subcontinent, Africa), and all refugees and asylum seekers, should be tuberculin skin tested as part of the initial screening procedure unless there is **definite** evidence of a BCG scar. Those with positive reactions should be referred for investigation as they may require chemoprophylaxis or treatment. BCG immunisation should be offered immediately to those who are tuberculin negative.

Infants born subsequently in this country should be immunised within a few days of birth. If this is not done, BCG can conveniently be given at two months of age at the same time as the first dose of the routine childhood vaccines.

f. **Those intending to stay in Asia, Africa, Central or South America for more than a month.**

■ 32.3.3   In addition, the following who are at '**normal**' risk of developing tuberculosis:

a. **School children** between the ages of 10 and 14 years.

b. **Newly-born babies, children or adults** where the parents or the individuals themselves request BCG immunisation.

■ 32.3.4   **Re-immunisation:**
BCG immunisation results in a characteristic pale, flat, circular scar (this will usually be on the upper arm or lateral aspect of the thigh). Subjects who give a history of previous BCG immunisation should only be re-immunised if there is no characteristic scar **and** they are tuberculin negative.

■ 32.4   Contraindications

■ 32.4.1   BCG vaccine should **NOT** be given to:

a. Patients receiving corticosteroid or other immunosuppressive treatment, including general radiation (see 7.3). Inhaled steroids are not a contraindication.

b. Those suffering from a malignant condition such as lymphoma, leukaemia, Hodgkin's disease or other tumour of the reticuloendothelial system.

c. Those in whom the normal immunological mechanism may be impaired, as in hypogammaglobulinaemia.

d. HIV positive individuals (see 7.4). BCG is absolutely contraindicated in symptomatic HIV positive individuals. In countries such as the UK where the risk of tuberculosis is low, it is recommended that BCG is withheld from **all** subjects known or suspected to be HIV positive, including infants born to HIV positive mothers. There is no need to screen mothers for HIV before giving BCG as part of a selective neonatal immunisation programme (see 32.3.2(e)).

e. Pregnant women. Although no harmful effects on the fetus have been observed from BCG immunisation during pregnancy, it is wise to avoid immunisation in the early stages and if possible to delay until after delivery.

f. Individuals with positive sensitivity skin tests to tuberculin protein.

g. Individuals who are febrile.

h. Individuals with generalised septic skin conditions (if eczema exists, an immunisation site should be chosen that is free from skin lesions).

■ 32.4.2   BCG vaccine may be given concurrently with another live vaccine. If they are not given at the same time, an interval of at least three weeks is normally recommended between two live vaccines (based on experience with live viral vaccines). However, BCG need not delay primary childhood immunisations even though they include live polio vaccine.

■ 32.4.3   Neonatal BCG, if indicated, is usually given at birth, but may be given at two months at the same time as other childhood immunisations, or at any time up to the age of three months, without prior tuberculin testing.

■ 32.4.4   No further immunisation should be given for at least three months in the arm used for BCG immunisation because of the risk of regional lymphadenitis

THE TUBERCULIN SKIN TEST

■ 32.5   Introduction

A tuberculin skin test must be carried out before BCG immunisation. The only exception to this rule is infants up to three months old who may be immunised without a prior test providing they have had no known recent contact with tuberculosis. The test assesses the individual's sensitivity to tuberculin protein: the greater the strength of the tuberculin reaction the more likely an individual is to have active disease. People with a positive test should not be given BCG - it is unnecessary and may cause a larger reaction. Those with strongly positive tests need to be referred to a chest clinic for assessment of the need for further investigation and treatment.

■ 32.6   Tuberculin testing techniques

■ 32.6.1   There are several techniques for tuberculin skin testing. All the common ones have been considered for their reliability, ease of use and safety and only two are recommended for general use: the Heaf test and the Mantoux test. It is strongly recommended that one of these two techniques is used.

■ 32.6.2   The techniques described should be closely adhered to, to minimise variability in the tests. Even so, some tester and reader variation can be expected.

■ 32.6.3   Both these tests use Purified Protein Derivative (PPD) which users can obtain either from their Health Authority/Health Board free of charge (see 32.25) or direct from Farillon (tel 01708 379000). The various preparations of PPD are described in paragraph 32.7. **Care must be taken to ensure that the dilution of PPD used is that specified for the particular technique.**

■ 32.6.4 Careful attention must also be given to the precautions described for each test to prevent any risk of cross-infection.

■ 32.7 Purified protein derivative

■ 32.7.1 Tuberculin Purified Protein Derivative is a sterile preparation made from the heat-treated products of growth and lysis of the mycobacterium. Several strengths of PPD are available and it is very important that the correct solution is used (see table).

■ 32.7.2 All tuberculin PPD must be stored between 2°C and 8°C (never frozen) and protected from light. Once an ampoule is opened, its contents should be used within four hours and not retained beyond that session. PPD tends to adsorb onto syringe surfaces and should therefore be used within 30 minutes after the syringe is filled. Note that PPD may persist on the surface of any non-disposable syringe and on the endplate and needles of the standard Heaf gun, both of which need careful cleaning after use.

Strength units/ml	Dilution of PPD	Units in dose of 0.1 ml	Use
100,000	—	10,000	Heaf (multiple puncture) test ONLY
1,000	1 in 100	100	Mantoux test (special)*
100	1 in 1,000	10	Mantoux test (routine)
10	1 in 10,000	1	Mantoux test (special)*

* For special diagnostic purposes only

■ 32.8   The multiple puncture test (Heaf test)

■ 32.8.1   This test was conventionally performed with a reusable Heaf multiple puncture apparatus (commonly known as a Heaf gun) which requires disinfection between subjects. Concern that blood borne infections such as hepatitis B and HIV might be transferred via this apparatus should the recommended disinfection procedure not be strictly adhered to, led to the development of disposable devices. Two are now available: an apparatus in which disposable heads attach to a reusable handle (Bignall 2000, Bignall Surgical Instruments) and a self contained single use device (UniHeaf, Owen Mumford). These are now recommended as the preferred methods for Heaf testing. They avoid the disinfection, cleansing and maintenance required for the standard Heaf apparatus, eliminate the risk of cross infection between subjects and also avoid the possibility of needles becoming blunt and tuberculin building up on needles which are reused. They are particularly suitable for the schools BCG programme in which multiple tests are performed in one session.

■ 32.8.2   Concentrated PPD 100,000 units/ml is used for the Heaf test. This strength is used only for Heaf testing. It is supplied in packs of five ampoules of 1.0ml, each ampoule normally being sufficient for up to about 20 tests.

■ 32.9   The disposable head apparatus

■ 32.9.1   The disposable head attaches by a magnet to a simplified handle. Six standard steel needles are retained in a plastic base which is enclosed in an outer plastic case with holes corresponding to the needles. The needles protrude only after activation and then remain protruding so that it is easy to detect and discard ones which have been fired. The heads are prepacked and sterile.

■ 32.9.2   There are three versions of the disposable head:

i.   **White** - which is the standard version for tuberculin testing in adults and children aged two years and over. The needles protrude 2mm on firing.

ii.   **Blue** - for tuberculin testing in children under two years. The needles protrude 1mm on firing.

iii. **Red** - this version contains 18 needles for administering BCG by the percutaneous multiple puncture technique and **must never be used for Heaf testing.**

■ 32.10 The self-contained single use multiple puncture device for Heaf testing:

This consists of a sterile single use unit containing six needles which protrude 0.6mm intradermally when the device is activated. The needles permanently retract after use so that it cannot be reused. It is **not** suitable for use in children under two years of age.

■ 32.11 The standard reusable Heaf gun

■ 32.11.1 The apparatus consists of a needle block of six needles attached to a firing mechanism and handle. The six needles are fired through corresponding holes in the end plate.

■ 32.11.2 The puncture depth of the needles is adjustable and should be set to 2mm for adults and children aged two years or more, and 1mm for children under two years.

■ 32.12 Disinfection of the Heaf gun

■ 32.12.1 The gun must be disinfected before every test and at the end of a testing session and it is essential that the user personally observes this being done. If a sufficient number of spare heads is available, the use of a replacement autoclaved head for each patient is a satisfactory alternative.

■ 32.12.2 The disinfection procedure recommended below is virucidal as long as it is strictly followed. It uses highly flammable spirit and proper precautions are needed to prevent fire hazard. The disinfection procedure requires an interval of three minutes or more between consecutive tests with any one instrument. Therefore for immunisation sessions at least three guns should be available for each team and they should be disinfected and used in rotation. This will sustain a testing rate of 60 subjects an hour with the required interval for disinfection and cooling.

■ 32.12.3 Disinfection is a three stage process:

a. Soaking in spirit. The end of the instrument is immersed in Industrial Methylated Spirit BP to a depth that totally covers the end plate and the needles but does not wet the body of the gun (about 1cm). This should be done in a substantial heavy vessel which will support the gun and ensure immersion at the correct depth for at least two minutes. Industrial methylated spirit is a colourless preparation containing 95% ethyl alcohol adulterated with wood naphtha which will burn readily. Note that this is a volatile liquid that may create a highly flammable vapour. It should not be left in an open vessel near a naked flame. Mineralised methylated spirits (the violet preparation sold retail for general use) and Surgical Spirit BP contain only 90% alcohol and other adulterant substances that may inhibit flammability. They are not suitable.

b. Flaming. The gun is withdrawn from the spirit and held at an angle of 45° to the vertical with the end plate directed upwards. The spirit is set alight by momentary contact with a flame from which the gun is removed on ignition. The spirit is allowed to burn until the flame goes out.

c. Cooling. It is essential to allow adequate time - a minimum of 30 seconds - for the gun to cool, while ensuring that the needles do not become contaminated prior to use.

■ 32.13 Maintenance of the Heaf gun

The apparatus requires thorough cleaning after each session. The needles should be scrubbed with a stiff brush using a hot soap or detergent solution and rinsed with distilled water. The needles must be checked to see whether they are becoming blunt or slipping in the retaining plate. It is good practice to replace needles every six months if the gun is in regular use. Periodic servicing by the manufacturer is also recommended.

■ 32.14 Performing the Heaf test

■ 32.14.1 The recommended site for testing is on the flexor surface of the left forearm at the junction of the upper third with the lower two thirds, avoiding any eczematous areas. Cleansing the skin is only necessary if it is visibly dirty, in which case spirit should be used but must be allowed to dry completely before the test.

■ 32.14.2 Tuberculin 100,000 units/ml should be withdrawn from the ampoule by needle and syringe and after detaching the needle a small quantity of solution should be dropped directly from the syringe onto the skin at the standard test site. Sufficient tuberculin should be used to disperse over an area of skin just greater than the diameter of the perforated head of the unit. (Note that the head of the disposable head is wider than the standard gun). The head of the apparatus should be used to disperse the tuberculin.

■ 32.14.3 **If using the disposable head apparatus, check that the correct head is being used.** Apply the apparatus firmly and evenly to the tuberculin covered skin and press on the handle until a click occurs, indicating that the needles have been fired. Do not press further after this, but remove the apparatus from the skin, remove the disposable head from the handle by holding the outer rim and discard the head into a 'sharps' bin. **If using the single use device,** press firmly on the top (purple) firing arm. After firing, an audible click is heard as the needles retract. **If using the conventional gun,** check that the gun is at the correct needle setting. The end plate should then be applied firmly and evenly to the area of skin covered by the tuberculin and pressure applied to the handle until the clicking firing mechanism operates. Do not apply further pressure after this, and withdraw the apparatus.

■ 32.14.4 Wipe off any excess tuberculin from the skin and observe the presence of **six** puncture marks. If these are not present the test has not been adequately applied. Advise the subject that the arm may become wetted and washed normally but perfumes and other cosmetics should not be applied. Instructions should be given to the subject to return to have the test read. Ideally this should be at seven days but the test can be read between three and 10 days.

■ 32.15 The Mantoux test

■ 32.15.1 The PPD preparation for routine use in the Mantoux test contains 100 units/ml and is supplied in 1.0ml ampoules. The contents of an ampoule will therefore be sufficient for five or six tests. For tests in patients in whom tuberculosis is suspected, or who are known to be hypersensitive to tuberculin, the preparation containing 10 units/ml should be used.

■ 32.15.2 The Mantoux test is performed using a 1ml syringe and a short bevel 25 gauge (0.5 x 10mm) or 26 gauge (0.45 x 10mm) needle. A separate syringe and needle must be used for each subject to prevent cross-infection.

■ 32.15.3 As for the Heaf test, the test is normally performed on the flexor surface of the left forearm at the junction of the upper third with the lower two thirds. The site is cleaned if visibly dirty with spirit and allowed to dry. 0.1ml of the appropriate tuberculin PPD dilution (see 32.15.1) is injected **intradermally** so that a bleb (peau d'orange) is produced typically of 7mm diameter. The results should be read 48 to 72 hours later, but a valid reading can usually be obtained up to 96 hours. A positive result consists of induration with a transverse diameter of at least 5mm following injection of 0.1ml PPD 100 units/ml. The area of flare is irrelevant.

■ 32.16 Interpretation of the Heaf and Mantoux tests

■ 32.16.1 There is some variability in the time at which a test develops its maximum response. For a given test the majority of subjects will be positive at a given time. A few however may have their maximum response just before or after the standard time.

■ 32.16.2 The Heaf reaction is graded 0-4 according to the degree of induration produced (erythema alone should be ignored). The results should be recorded as a number and not merely as positive or negative.

Grade 0 -   no induration at the puncture sites.
Grade 1 -   discrete induration at 4 or more needle sites.
Grade 2 -   induration around each needle site merging with the next, forming a ring of induration but with a clear centre.
Grade 3 -   the centre of the reaction becomes filled with induration to form one uniform disc of induration 5-10mm wide.
Grade 4 -   solid induration over 10mm wide. Vesiculation or ulceration may also occur.

Please refer to inside back cover for examples of Heaf test responses.

■ 32.16.3 Heaf grades 0 and 1 or a Mantoux response of 0-4mm induration are regarded as negative. Individuals who have not previously received BCG immunisation may be offered immunisation in the absence of contraindications. However, those who give a history of previous BCG should only be re-immunised if there is no evidence of a character-istic scar and they are tuberculin negative (see 32.3.4).

■ 32.16.4 Those with a grade 2 reaction (or a Mantoux response of induration of diameter 5-14mm following injection of 0.1ml PPD 100 units/ml) are positive. They are hypersensitive to tuberculin protein and should not be given BCG vaccine. When the immunisation is performed as part of a routine health promotion programme such as the schools programme, no further action is required. In other circumstances (eg new immigrants under 16 years, contacts of tuberculosis), subjects with a grade 2 reaction who have not previously had a BCG immunisation should be referred to a chest clinic.

■ 32.16.5 Contacts of tuberculosis, children in the schools immunisation programme and new immigrants who show a strongly positive reaction to tuberculin (grade 3 or 4 or a Mantoux response with induration of at least 15mm diameter following 0.1ml PPD 100 units/ml) should be referred for further investigation and supervision (which may include prophylactic chemotherapy).

■ 32.17 Factors affecting the tuberculin test

■ 32.17.1 The reaction to tuberculin protein may be suppressed by the following:

a. infectious mononucleosis
b. viral infections in general, including those of the upper respiratory tract
c. live viral vaccines. Tuberculin testing should not be carried out within three weeks of receiving a live viral vaccine: immunisation programmes should be arranged so that tuberculin testing is carried out before live viral vaccines are given.
d. Hodgkin's disease
e. sarcoidosis
f. corticosteroid therapy
g. immunosuppressing treatment or diseases, including HIV

■ 32.17.2 Subjects who have a negative test but who may have had an upper respiratory tract or other viral infection at the time of testing or at the time of reading should be retested 2-3 weeks after clinical recovery before being given BCG. If a second tuberculin test is necessary it should be carried out on the other arm: repeat testing at one site may alter the reactivity either by hypo- or more often hypersensitising the skin and a changed response may reflect local changes in sensitivity only.

BCG IMMUNISATION

■ 32.18 Introduction

It is recommended that BCG vaccine be administered intradermally using a separate tuberculin syringe and needle for each subject. **Jet injectors should not be used.** In neonates, infants and very young children (up to five years of age) **only**, administration of BCG by the percutaneous route using a multiple puncture technique is an acceptable alternative to the intradermal method. **It is not recommended for older children, teenagers and adults.** 18-20 needles are required and BCG vaccine prepared specifically for percutaneous use (see 32.21.2).

■ 32.19 BCG vaccine

■ 32.19.1 Freeze-dried vaccine is supplied to NHS users in England without charge by either Health Authorities or Farillon. The arrangements for Scotland, Wales and Northern Ireland are described in paragraph 32.25. **Users should specify clearly whether they require the preparation for intradermal or percutaneous (multiple puncture) immunisation and the package label should be checked before use.**

■ 32.19.2 The freeze-dried vaccine should be protected from light, stored between 2° and 8°C and never frozen. It has a shelf life of 12-18 months and should not be used after the expiry date stated on the label.

■ 32.19.3 The multidose vial of vaccine should be diluted as instructed on the package insert using aseptic precautions, a syringe and suitable large needle. The needle may be left in situ for subsequent withdrawal of vaccine. Do not shake it to mix. Once made up the vaccine should be used within two hours. Any unused reconstituted vaccine should be discarded at the end of the session.

■ 32.20 Standard immunisation technique

■ 32.20.1 The recommended site for giving the vaccine is at the insertion of the deltoid muscle near the middle of the left upper arm. Sites higher on the arm are more likely to lead to keloid formation, the tip of the shoulder particularly. For cosmetic reasons, a scar on the upper and lateral surface of the thigh may be preferred and this is an alternative site.

■ 32.20.2 The vaccine must be given strictly intradermally with a fresh needle and syringe for each subject. The dose is 0.1ml (0.05ml for infants under three months). This should be drawn into a tuberculin syringe and a 3/8" 25g (0.5 x 10mm) or 26g (0.45 x 10mm) short bevelled needle attached to give the injection. The needle must be attached firmly with the bevel uppermost.

■ 32.20.3 The upper arm must be approximately 45° to the body. This can be achieved if the hand is placed on the hip with the arm abducted from the body.

■ 32.20.4 If the skin is visibly dirty it should be swabbed with spirit and allowed to dry. The operator stretches the skin between the thumb and forefinger of one hand and with the other slowly inserts the needle, with the bevel upwards, for about 2mm into the superficial layers of the dermis almost parallel with the surface. The needle can usually be seen through the epidermis. A correctly given intradermal injection results in a tense blanched raised bleb (peau d'orange) and considerable resistance is felt when the fluid is being injected. A bleb typically of 7mm diameter follows a 0.1ml injection. If little resistance is felt when injecting and a diffuse swelling occurs as opposed to a tense blanched bleb, the needle is too deep. The needle should be withdrawn and reinserted intradermally before more vaccine is given.

■ 32.20.5 The subject must always be advised of the normal reaction to the injection.

The site and technique for BCG immunisation

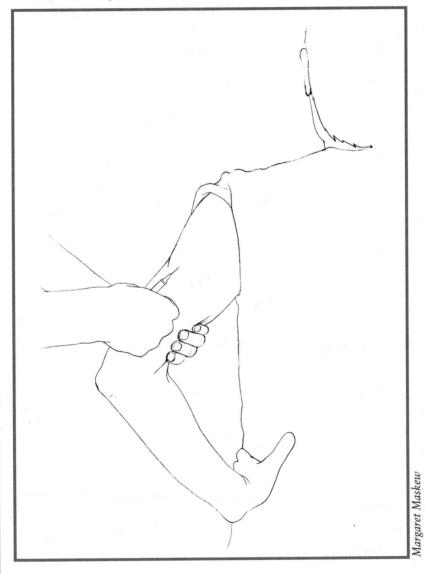

Margaret Maskew

■ 32.21 Percutaneous BCG immunisation by the multiple puncture technique (for infants and very young children only)

■ 32.21.1 BCG immunisation as described above by intradermal injection, using a separate needle and syringe for every subject, is the only recommended method for older children, teenagers and adults. However, this technique can be difficult in infants and very young children. In these latter groups only, percutaneous BCG immunisation by multiple puncture technique is an acceptable alternative.

■ 32.21.2 Only percutaneous BCG vaccine, which has 50-250 million colony forming units/vial (approximately 10 times the strength of intradermal BCG), should be used. Users can obtain this from Farillon or their Health Authority or Health Board free of charge (see 32.25). The preparation required should be clearly stated and checked before use.

■ 32.21.3 The site of injection is over the insertion of the deltoid muscle as previously described. 18-20 needle punctures, with 2mm skin penetration at a pressure of 5-7lb, are required. The technique is as described for Heaf testing (32.14).

■ 32.22 Immunisation reaction and care of the immunisation site

■ 32.22.1 Following intradermal administration of BCG, normally a local reaction develops at the immunisation site within two to six weeks, beginning as a small papule which increases in size for a few weeks widening into a circular area up to 7mm in diameter with scaling, crusting and occasional bruising. Occasionally a shallow ulcer up to 10mm in diameter develops. It is not necessary to protect the site from becoming wet during washing and bathing, but should any oozing occur, a temporary dry dressing may be used until a scab forms. It is essential that air is not excluded. If absolutely essential an impervious dressing may be applied but only for a short period (for example, to permit swimming) as it may delay healing and cause a larger scar. The lesion slowly subsides over several months and eventually heals leaving only a small, flat scar.

■ 32.22.2 Following percutaneous administration of BCG in neonates, a small amount of erythema occurs. However this and the 18 point marks fade quickly so that by 8 weeks (a little longer in pigmented skins) there is little to see. A visible long term scar is unlikely.

■ 32.22.3 After immunisation with BCG vaccine there is a high tuberculin conversion rate and routine further observation of those at normal risk is not necessary, nor is further tuberculin testing recommended. However, in large immunisation programmes, some check should be made of the severity of the reactions six weeks or so later, possibly on a sample basis, as part of monitoring the programme.

■ 32.22.4 **In health-care staff and others at occupational risk,** the site of immunisation should be inspected six weeks later to confirm that a satisfactory reaction has occurred. Reactions should be recorded by measuring the transverse diameter in mm. Only those who show no reaction to BCG require a post-BCG tuberculin test, after which anyone at occupational risk who is still tuberculin negative should be re-immunised. If after reimmunisation there is still no evidence of a satisfactory reaction or of conversion to a positive tuberculin test, the individual should be told the result and consideration given to moving to work not involving exposure to patients with tuberculosis or with tuberculous material.

■ 32.23 Adverse reactions to BCG

■ 32.23.1 Vertigo and dizziness have occasionally been reported following BCG immunisation, and, rarely, immediate allergic type or anaphylactic reactions.

■ 32.23.2 Severe injection site reactions, large ulcers and abscesses are most commonly caused by faulty injection technique where part or all of the dose is administered too deeply (subcutaneously instead of intradermally). The immunisation of individuals who are tuberculin positive may also give rise to such reactions. To avoid these, doctors and nurses who carry out tuberculin skin tests and administer BCG vaccine must be trained in the interpretation of the results of tuberculin tests as well as in the technique of intradermal injection with syringe and needle.

■ 32.23.3 Keloid formation at the injection site is an uncommon and largely avoidable, complication of BCG immunisation. Some sites are more prone to keloid formation than others and those immunising should adhere to the two sites recommended in this chapter (the mid-upper arm or the thigh). Most experience has been gained in the use of the upper arm and it is known that the risk of keloid formation is increased manyfold when the injection is given at a site higher than the **insertion of the deltoid muscle near the middle of the upper arm (see 32.20.1 and figure on page 235).**

■ 32.23.4 Apart from these injection site reactions, other complications following BCG immunisation are rare and mostly consist of adenitis with or without suppuration and discharge. A minor degree of adenitis may occur in the weeks following immunisation and should not be regarded as a complication. Very rarely a lupoid type of local lesion has been reported. A few cases of widespread dissemination of the injected organisms have been reported.

■ 32.23.5 It is important that all complications are recorded and reported to a chest physician. Serious or unusual complications (including abscess and keloid scarring) should be reported to the Committee on Safety of Medicines using the yellow card system, and techniques reviewed. Every effort should be made to recover and identify the causative organism from any lesion constituting a serious complication.

■ 32.24 Record keeping and monitoring

■ 32.24.1 It is important that records are maintained to show the result of tuberculin skin testing, whether the subject had previously received BCG, and whether or not BCG was subsequently given. These records should show who administered the skin test or vaccine, the batch number of the vaccine, and who recorded the result or lesion. Particular attention should be paid to unusual or severe reactions. Such records should be kept for at least 10 years.

■ 32.24.2 The results of tuberculin skin tests and of BCG immunisation of hospital staff (including students) should be recorded on appropriate records. If staff or students move to another hospital or training school, the record cards should be transferred to the occupational health unit. Individual record cards may be carried by members of staff.

■ 32.24.3 For monitoring selective neonatal and schools BCG programmes, records will need to be kept of numbers in the target groups, the number skin tested and the number found to be negative (for the schools programme), and the number given BCG.

■ 32.25 Supplies of BCG vaccine and PPD

■ 32.25.1 BCG vaccines and PPD: are manufactured by Evans Medical Tel 0345 451500 (local rate) or 01372 364000.

■ 32.25.2 In England, supplies of freeze-dried BCG vaccine (intradermal and percutaneous) and tuberculin PPD are distributed at no charge to the user by Farillon (tel 01708 379000) either to Health Authorities or direct to users.

■ 32.25.3 In Scotland, the Health Boards order BCG vaccine and Tuberculin PPD direct from AAH or Unichem Ltd as and when required.

■ 32.25.4 In Wales, orders for both BCG vaccine and PPD should be sent monthly by health authorities to Farillon (tel 01708 379000).

■ 32.25.5 In Northern Ireland, BCG vaccine and PPD are provided through the Hospital Pharmaceutical Service. Enquiries about supplies should be directed to the Regional Pharmacist Procurement Co-ordinator, Eastern Health and Social Services Board, 12-21 Linenhall Street, Belfast (Tel. 01232 321313).

■ 32.26 Supplies of devices for Heaf testing and percutaneous administration of BCG

■ 32.26.1 The disposable head Bignell 2000 multiple puncture apparatus for tuberculin skin testing by the Heaf method (re-usable handle and disposable heads) is available from: Bignell Surgical Instruments Ltd, 18 River Road, Littlehampton, West Sussex BN17 5BN, tel 01903 715751, fax 01903 731242. An 18 needle disposable head is available for use with this apparatus for BCG immunisation using the percutaneous (multiple puncture) technique.

■ 32.26.2 The UniHeaf single use multiple puncture device for Heaf testing is available from Owen Mumford Ltd, Brook Hill, Woodstock, Oxford OX20 1TU, tel 01993 812021, fax 01993 813466.

■ 32.26.3 The 20 needle modified Heaf gun for percutaneous (multiple puncture) administration of BCG (previously supplied by East Healthcare Ltd) is no longer available; East Healthcare do not have supplies of spare parts.

■ 32.27 The Department of Health Video

The Department of Health's video 'Heaf Testing and BCG Vaccination: A Practical Guide' (UK 6257) is available to Nursing and Medical Professionals on free loan for five days (in England only) and to purchase for £19.90 inc VAT from CFL Vision, PO Box 35, Wetherby, Yorkshire LS23 7EX, Telephone number 01937 541010 (cheques payable to CFL Vision).

■ 32.28 Bibliography

Tuberculosis in England and Wales 1982-1993.
Hayward AC, Watson JM.
Comm Dis Rep 1995; 5: R29-33

Tuberculosis in 1993: preliminary results of national survey
Comm Dis Rep 1994; 4: 235

Recommendations for the prevention and control of tuberculosis at local level.
The Interdepartmental Working Group on Tuberculosis. Department of Health and The Welsh Office, 1996.

Control and prevention of tuberculosis in the United Kingdom: an updated Code of Practice.

Joint Tuberculosis Committee of the British Thoracic Society.
Thorax 1994; 49: 1193-1200

Modern vaccines: Mycobacterial vaccines.
Fine PEM, Rodrigues LC.
Lancet 1990; 335: 1016-20

Effectiveness of BCG vaccination in England and Wales in 1983.
Sutherland I and Springett V H.
Tubercle 1987; 68; 81-92

BCG vaccination in the first year of life protects children of Indian subcontinent ethnic origin against tuberculosis in England.
Rodriguez LC, Gill ON, Smith PG.
J Epidemiol Community Health 1991; 45: 78-80

Multiple puncture vaccination in the new born with freeze dried BCG vaccine
BMJ Griffiths MI 1960, ii: 1116-9

BCG immunisation of infants by percutaneous multiple puncture
BMJ Cundall DB, Ashelford DJ, Pearson SB. BMJ 1988, 297: 1173-4

Efficacy of Bacillus Calmette-Guérin and isoniazid-resistant Bacillus Calmette-
Guérin with and without isoniazid chemoprophylaxis from day of vaccination.
II. Field trial in man.
Vandiviere HM, Dworski M, Melvin IG et al.
Amer Rev Resp Dis 1973; 108: 301-13

Practical problems of the tuberculin test.
Davies P D O, Leitch A G
in Clinical Tuberculosis Ed P D O Davies p345-9. 1994 Chapman and Hall,
London.

The prevalence of keloid formation in BCG scars.
Lunn J A and Robson D C.
Personal communication.

HIV and routine childhood immunisation
WHO Wkly Epidem Rec 1987; 62: 297-9.

Bacillus Calmette-Guérin complications in children born to HIV-1-infected
women with a review of the literature.
O'Brien K L, Ruff A J, Louis M A et al
Pediatrics 1995;95: 414-418

33 Typhoid

■ 33.1 Introduction

■ 33.1.1 Typhoid fever is a systemic infection caused by the Gram negative bacillus *Salmonella typhi*. Most of the nearly 2000 serotypes in the genus *Salmonella* cause only local infection of the gastro-intestinal tract (gastro-enteritis or 'food poisoning'). *S. typhi, S. paratyphi* A, B and C and occasionally other salmonella species may invade systemically to produce a serious illness with prolonged pyrexia and prostration. The incubation period varies from one to three weeks depending on the infecting dose. All patients with typhoid and paratyphoid excrete the organisms at some stage during their illness. About 10% of patients with typhoid fever excrete the organism for three months following the acute illness and 2-5% become permanent carriers. The likelihood of becoming a chronic carrier increases with age, especially in females.

■ 33.1.2 Typhoid fever is spread by the faecal-oral route, usually through food or drink that has been contaminated with the excreta of a human case or carrier. It is therefore predominantly a disease of countries with poor sanitation and poor standards of personal and food hygiene. Outbreaks of infection have been caused by corned beef (Aberdeen 1964), water supplies (Zermatt 1963) and shellfish contaminated by infected water or sewage. Around 200 cases of typhoid fever are notified in England and Wales each year; over 80% of these have been acquired abroad, principally in the Indian Sub-continent.

■ 33.2 Vaccine

■ 33.2.1 Three typhoid vaccines are available.

■ 33.2.2 *Monovalent whole cell typhoid vaccine* contains not less than 1000 million heat-killed, phenol-preserved *S. typhi* organisms per ml. One 0.5ml injection confers around 70-80% protection which fades after one year. Two doses, four to six weeks apart, give protection for three years or more.

■ 33.2.3 *Typhoid Vi polysaccharide antigen vaccine* is a parenteral vaccine containing Vi antigen from the capsule of the organism, preserved with phenol. Each 0.5ml dose contains 25mcg of antigen. A single dose gives 70-80% protection for at least three years.

■ 33.2.4 *Oral typhoid vaccine* contains a live attenuated *Salmonella typhi* strain (Ty 21a) in an enteric-coated capsule. One capsule taken on alternate days for three doses appears to produce similar efficacy to parenteral vaccines, although the length of protection may be less: in those not repeatedly or constantly exposed to *S. typhi* it is recommended the full course is repeated after one year. The vaccine is unstable at normal room temperatures.

■ 33.2.5 The efficacy of typhoid vaccines is partly related to the size of any infecting dose encountered after immunisation. The vaccines are not 100% effective and the importance in preventing infection of scrupulous attention to personal, food and water hygiene must still be emphasised for those travelling to endemic areas.

■ 33.2.6 Typhoid vaccines for injection should be stored at 2-8°C and not frozen. Any partly used multidose containers should be discarded at the end of the immunisation session.

■ 33.2.7 Oral typhoid vaccine is not stable at normal room temperature. It is essential to replace unused vaccine in the refrigerator between doses. The package should be kept dry and out of the light.

■ 33.3 Recommendations

■ 33.3.1 Typhoid immunisation is advised for:

(a) Laboratory workers handling specimens which may contain typhoid organisms (see 12.20).

(b) Travellers to countries in Africa, Asia, Central and South America and the Caribbean where sanitation and hygiene may be poor and for some countries in Eastern Europe, although immunisation against typhoid may be less important for short stays in good accommodation (see Health Information for Overseas Travel for more details).

■ 33.3.2 Typhoid immunisation is **not** recommended for contacts of a known typhoid carrier or for controlling common-source outbreaks.

■ 33.4   Route of administration and dosage

Adults

■ 33.4.1 **Whole cell vaccine:** a primary course of two doses four to six weeks apart. A reinforcing dose every three years for those at continued or repeated risk. (A single primary injection will give short-term immunity; a reinforcing dose will then be needed after one year).

■ 33.4.2 The first dose of the primary course must be given by intramuscular or deep subcutaneous injection for a reliable antigenic response. Subsequent doses may be given by intradermal injection, which may reduce the severity of adverse reactions.

■ 33.4.3 **Vi polysaccharide vaccine:** a single dose by intramuscular or deep subcutaneous injection. Re-immunisation with a single dose every three years for those who remain at risk of infection.

■ 33.4.4 **Oral Ty 21a vaccine:** one capsule on alternate days for three doses. It should be taken on an empty stomach with a cool drink. Those taking the vaccine home must be instructed to keep it in the refrigerator between doses.

Children

■ 33.4.5 Immunisation against typhoid is not recommended for children under one year of age: the risk of infection is low and none of the vaccines is suitable for use in this age group. Children under 18 months may show a suboptimal response to polysaccharide antigen vaccines; use of this vaccine in this age group should be governed by the likely risk of exposure to infection.

■ 33.4.6 Oral typhoid vaccine is not suitable for children under six years of age.

■ 33.4.7 Parenteral typhoid vaccines do not contain live organisms and **may** therefore be given to HIV positive individuals in the absence of contraindications. The oral vaccine contains live organisms and is contraindicated.

■ 33.4.8   Dose

Vaccine	Primary Course	Boosters
Whole cell vaccine **Adults**	0.5ml im or deep sc **then** 0.5ml im or deep sc or 0.1ml id 4-6 weeks later	0.5ml im or sc or 0.1ml id every three years
Children aged 1-10 years	0.25ml im or deep sc then 0.25ml im or deep sc or 0.1ml id 4-6 weeks later	0.25ml im or deep sc or 0.1ml id every 3 years
under one year	not recommended	
Vi polysaccharide antigen vaccine Adults and children > 18 months	0.5ml im or deep sc	0.5ml im or deep sc every 3 years
Children < 18 months	see 33.4.5	
Oral Ty 21a vaccine Adults and children > 6 years	1 capsule on alternate days x 3 doses	For residents of non- -endemic areas 3 dose course annually
under 6 years	not recommended	

■ 33.5 Adverse reactions

■ 33.5.1   Whole cell typhoid vaccine commonly produces local reactions such as redness, swelling, pain and tenderness which may persist for a few days. Systemic reactions include malaise, nausea, headache and pyrexia. They usually resolve within 36 hours. Neurological complications have been described but are rare. Reactions are especially common after repeated injections and are often more marked in people over 35 years. They may be reduced by giving the second and subsequent injections intradermally.

Typhoid

■ 33.5.2   Local reactions to Vi polysaccharide vaccine are mild and transient and systemic reactions less common than with whole cell vaccine.

■ 33.5.3   Oral Ty 21a vaccine may cause transient mild nausea, vomiting, abdominal cramps, diarrhoea and urticarial rash.

■ 33.5.4   All severe reactions should be reported to the Committee on Safety of Medicines using the yellow card system.

■ 33.6   Contraindications

■ 33.6.1   The following contraindications should be observed:

a)   Acute febrile illness.

b)   Severe reaction to a previous dose of the same type of vaccine.

c)   Pregnancy: as with other vaccines, typhoid vaccine should only be given if a clear indication exists.

d)   Oral Ty 21a vaccine should not be given to those taking an antimicrobial agent, and if mefloquine is being taken for malaria chemoprophylaxis the vaccine should be taken at least 12 hours before or after the mefloquine.

e)   Oral Ty 21a vaccine should not be taken during persistent diarrhoea or vomiting.

f)   Oral typhoid vaccine is contraindicated in those with immunosuppression due to disease or treatment.

■ 33.6.2   Oral typhoid vaccine and oral polio vaccine should be given at least three weeks apart on the theoretical grounds of possible interference of the immune response in the gut.

■ 33.6.3   Typhoid vaccine is not recommended during an outbreak of typhoid fever in the UK. It affords no immediate protection, it may temporarily increase susceptibility to infection and, by stimulating antibody production, it makes interpretation of diagnostic serological tests more difficult.

Typhoid

■ 33.7   Management of outbreaks

■ 33.7.1   The Consultant in Communicable Disease Control (CCDC) or in Scotland, the Chief Administrative Medical Officer (CAMO) should be informed immediately whenever a patient is suspected of having typhoid fever without waiting for laboratory confirmation. Early identification of the source of infection is vital in containing this disease.

■ 33.7.2   Household or other close contacts of cases should be excluded from work if they are involved in food handling, until at least two, and in some cases three, negative faecal cultures have been obtained. The need for strict personal hygiene should be stressed.

■ 33.8   Supplies

■ 33.8.1   Whole cell typhoid vaccine is available in 1.5 ml vials from Evans Medical Ltd, Tel. 0345 451500 (local rate) or 01372 364000 (this vaccine is not available at the time of going to press.)

■ 33.8.2   Vi polysaccharide antigen vaccine is available from Pasteur Merieux MSD Ltd (Tel 01628 773200)

■ 33.8.3   Oral Ty 21a vaccine is available from Evans Medical Ltd, Tel. 0345 451500 (local rate) or 01372 364000

■ 33.9   Bibliography

The changing pattern of food borne disease in England and Wales
Galbraith NS , Barrett NJ, Sockett PN
Public Health 1987; 101: 319-328

Enteric fever in Scotland 1975-1990
Braddick MR, Sharp JCM
Public Health 1993; 107: 193-8

Vaccination against typhoid: present status
Ivanoff B, Levine MM, Lambert PH
Bull WHO, 1994; 72: 957-71

Typhoid

Typhoid vaccination: weighing the options
Editorial
Lancet 1992; 340: 341-2
Intradermal versus subcutaneous immunisation with typhoid vaccine
Iwarson S, Larrson P
J Hyg, Camb 1980; 84: 11-16

Protective activity of Vi capsular polysaccharide vaccine against typhoid fever
Klugman KP, Gilbertson IT, Koornhof HJ et al
Lancet 1987; 330: 1165-9

Persistence of antibody titres three years after vaccination with Vi
polysaccharide vaccine against typhoid fever
Tacket CO, Levine MM, Robbins JB
Vaccine 1988; 6: 307-8

Clinical and serological responses following primary and booster immunisation
with Salmonella typhi Vi capsular polysaccharide vaccines
Keitel W, Bond N L, Zahradnik J M, Cramton T A, Robbins J B
Vaccine 1994; 12: 195-9

Oral immunisation against typhoid fever in Indonesia with Ty21a vaccine
Simanjuntak CH, Paleologo FP, Punjabi NH et al
Lancet 1991; 338: 1055-59

Precautions with oral live typhoid (Ty21a) vaccine
Wolfe MS (letter)
Lancet 1990; 336: 631-2

Inhibition of the Salmonella typhi oral vaccine strain, Ty21a, by mefloquine
and chloroquine
Horowitz H, Carbonaro CA
J Infect Dis 1992; 166: 1462-4

Typhoid

34   Varicella

■ 34.1   Introduction

■ 34.1.1   Varicella (chickenpox) is an acute highly infectious disease which is transmitted directly by personal contact or droplet spread, and indirectly via fomites. In the home the secondary infection rate from a case of chickenpox can be as high as 90%. It is most common in children below the age of ten in whom it is usually mild. Since chickenpox is so common in childhood, 90% of adults are immune.

■ 34.1.2   The incidence of varicella is seasonal and reaches a peak from March to May. The incubation period is between two and three weeks.

■ 34.1.3   Vesicles appear without prodromal illness on the face and scalp, spreading to the trunk and abdomen and eventually to the limbs; after three or four days they dry with a granular scab and are usually followed by further crops. Vesicles may be so few as to be missed or so numerous that they become confluent, covering most of the body. Virus is plentiful in the naso-pharynx in the first few days and in the vesicles before they dry up; the infectious period is therefore from one to two days before the rash appears until the vesicles are dry. This may be prolonged in immunosuppressed patients.

■ 34.1.4   The disease can be more serious in adults, particularly pregnant women and those who smoke, as they are at risk of fulminating varicella pneumonia. For neonates and immunosuppressed individuals, the risk is greatly increased for disseminated or haemorrhagic varicella.

■ 34.1.5   Herpes zoster is caused by the reactivation of the patient's varicella virus. It is transmissible to susceptible individuals as chickenpox but there is very little evidence that it can be acquired from another individual with chickenpox. Although more common in the elderly, it can occur in children and especially in immunosuppressed individuals. Vesicles appear in the dermatome representing cranial or spinal ganglia where the virus has been dormant. The affected area may be intensely painful with associated paraesthesiae.

Varicella

■ 34.1.6   Risks to the fetus and neonate from maternal chickenpox are related to the time of infection in the mother:

a. **In the first 20 weeks of pregnancy.** Congenital (fetal) varicella syndrome which includes limb hypoplasia, microcephaly, cataracts, growth retardation and skin scarring. The mortality rate is high. From the largest available prospective study, the incidence has been estimated to be less than 1% in the first 12 weeks and around 2% between 13 and 20 weeks of pregnancy.

b. **In the 2nd and 3rd trimesters of pregnancy.** Herpes zoster in an otherwise healthy infant.

c. **A week before, to a week after delivery.** Severe and even fatal disease in the neonate. Before the introduction of VZIG in the UK, half the deaths in infants under one year occurred in those aged less than 3 weeks in whom infection would have been contracted before, during birth or during the first week of life.

■ 34.2   Varicella vaccine

Live attenuated varicella vaccine has recently been licensed in some countries, but currently no vaccine is licensed for use in the UK. It is available on a named patient basis from SmithKline Beecham and Pasteur Merieux MSD Ltd for immunocompromised individuals, particularly children with leukaemia or solid organ transplants.

■ 34.3   Human Varicella-Zoster Immunoglobulin (VZIG)

■ 34.3.1   Two licensed VZIG preparations are available in the UK. VZIG distributed in England and Wales is made by the Bio Products Laboratory (BPL), Elstree; and in Scotland and Northern Ireland it is provided by the Protein Fractionation Centre (PFC), Edinburgh. VZIG is prepared from pooled plasma of UK blood donors with a history of recent chickenpox or herpes zoster, or from those who on screening are found to have suitably high titres of V-Z antibody. The supply of VZIG is limited by the availability of suitable donors and its use is therefore restricted to those at greatest risk and for whom there is evidence that it is likely to be effective.

Varicella

■ 34.3.2 VZIG is a clear, pale yellow fluid or light brown solution dispensed in vials containing 250 mg protein in a nominal 1.7ml of fluid (minimum potency 100 iu of VZ antibody per ml) with added thiomersal and sodium chloride. On keeping, a slight turbidity or occasional particles may appear.

■ 34.3.3 VZIG should be stored in a refrigerator between 2-8°C. Under these conditions it has a nominal shelf life of three years. It can be stored for short periods at room temperature and is sufficiently heat stable to be despatched by post. VZIG must NOT be frozen.

■ 34.3.4 All immunoglobulins are prepared from HIV, hepatitis B and hepatitis C negative donors.

■ 34.4   Recommendations

VZIG prophylaxis is recommended for individuals who fulfil all of the following three criteria:

(a) a clinical condition which increases the risk of severe varicella; this includes immunosuppressed patients (see 34.5), neonates (see 34.6) and pregnant women (see 34.7).

(b) no antibodies to varicella-zoster (VZ) virus (see 34.8).

(c) significant exposure to chickenpox or herpes zoster (see 34.9).

Antiviral chemotherapy may be used for patients with other clinical conditions in whom attenuation of an attack of chickenpox would be desirable.

Varicella

■ 34.5 Immunosuppressed patients

These are defined in Chapter 7 and include the following:

(a) patients currently being treated with chemotherapy or generalised radiotherapy, or within 6 months of terminating such treatment;

(b) patients who have received an organ transplant and are currently on immunosuppressive treatment;

(c) patients who within the previous 6 months have received a bone marrow transplant;

(d) children who within the previous 3 months have received prednisolone, orally or rectally, at a daily dose (or its equivalent) of 2 mg/kg/day for at least one week, or 1 mg/kg/day for one month. For adults, an equivalent dose is harder to define but immunosuppression should be considered in those who have received a dose of around 40 mg prednisolone per day for more than one week in the previous 3 months;

(e) patients on lower doses of steroids, given in combination with cytotoxic drugs (including anti-thymic globulin or other immunosuppressants);

(f) patients with evidence of impaired cell mediated immunity, for example severe combined immune deficiency syndromes, Di George syndrome and other combined immunodeficiency syndromes;

(g) patients with symptomatic HIV infection. VZIG is not indicated for asymptomatic HIV positive patients with normal CD4 counts as there is no evidence of increased risk of severe varicella in these individuals;

(h) patients with gammaglobulin deficiencies who are receiving replacement therapy with intravenous normal immunoglobulin, do not require VZIG (see 7.3.7).

■ Note:

For immunosuppressed patients with bleeding disorders in whom intramuscular injections are contraindicated, see 34.10.

Severe or fatal varicella can occur despite VZIG prophylaxis; varicella immunisation should therefore be considered for susceptible immunosuppressed patients at long term risk (see 34.2). About half of susceptible immunosuppressed home contacts will develop clinical chickenpox despite VZIG prophylaxis and a further 15% will be infected subclinically. There is no difference in outcome whether VZIG is given within 3 days or 4-7 days after exposure.

■ 34.6   Neonates

VZIG is recommended for the following:

(a) Infants whose mothers develop chickenpox (but not herpes zoster) in the period 7 days before to 28 days after delivery.

(b) VZ antibody negative infants exposed to chickenpox or herpes zoster in the first 28 days of life. If supplies of VZIG are short, issues to infants with post-natal exposure may be restricted to those in contact during the first 7 days of life.

The following infants do not require VZIG since maternal antibody will be present:

Infants born **more than** seven days after the onset of maternal chickenpox.

Infants whose mothers have a positive history of chickenpox and/or a positive VZ antibody result.

Infants whose mothers develop zoster before or after delivery.

■ Note:

About half of neonates exposed to maternal varicella will become infected despite VZIG prophylaxis. In up to two thirds of these infants infection is mild or asymptomatic, but rare fatal cases have been reported despite VZIG prophylaxis in those with onset of maternal chickenpox in the period 4 days before to 2 days after delivery. Early treatment with intravenous acyclovir is recommended for infants in this exposure category who develop varicella despite VZIG prophylaxis.

Varicella

■ 34.7   Pregnant women

VZIG is recommended for VZ antibody negative pregnant contacts exposed at any stage of pregnancy. However, when supplies of VZIG are short, issues to pregnant women may be restricted to those exposed during the first 20 weeks of pregnancy or near term (within 21 days of the estimated date of delivery).

■ Note:

VZIG does not prevent infection even when given within 72 hours of exposure. However it may attenuate disease if given up to ten days after exposure. Severe maternal varicella may still occur despite VZIG prophylaxis. There is some evidence that the likelihood of fetal infection during the first 20 weeks of gestation is reduced in women who develop chickenpox under cover of VZIG.

■ 34.8   Determination of VZ immune status

■ 34.8.1   The majority of adults and a substantial proportion of children without a definite history of chickenpox will be VZ antibody positive. One UK study found that 11% of children aged 1 to 5 years, 37% aged 6 to 16 years and 89% of adults given VZIG on the basis of a negative history of chickenpox were VZ antibody positive. To prevent wastage of VZIG, all individuals being considered for VZIG should have a serum sample tested for VZ antibody; **only those without antibody require VZIG.** In an emergency, antibody can be estimated within 24 hours; VZIG can be ordered (see 34.12) and should be returned if the test is positive. Advice on testing for VZ antibody should be obtained from the local Public Health or Hospital Laboratory.

■ 34.8.2   VZ antibody detected in patients who have been transfused or who have received intravenous immunoglobulin in the previous 3 months may have been passively acquired. Although VZIG is not indicated if antibody from other blood products is detectable, re-testing in the event of a subsequent exposure will be required as the patient may have become antibody negative.

■ 34.8.3   About 15% of patients given VZIG who remain symptom free after a home contact will have had a subclinical infection. Patients who have received VZIG in the past, following a close exposure, should therefore be re-tested in the event of another exposure, to identify those who have seroconverted asymptomatically and are antibody positive.

■ 34.8.4   The value of a clinical history of chickenpox in determining immune status varies with patient group:

(a) **Immunosuppressed contacts:** Whenever possible, contacts with a positive history of chickenpox should be tested to confirm the presence of VZ antibody. Those with a positive history in whom VZ antibody is not detected by a sensitive assay should be given VZIG.

VZIG is not indicated in immunosuppressed contacts with detectable antibody as the amount of antibody provided by VZIG will not significantly increase VZ antibody titres in those who are already positive. Second attacks of chickenpox can occasionally occur in immunosuppressed VZ antibody positive patients, but these appear be related to defects in cell-mediated immunity.

While it is recommended that immunosuppressed patients without a history of chickenpox should be tested for VZ antibody, VZIG administration should not be delayed past 7 days after initial contact while an antibody test is done. Under these circumstances VZIG should be given on the basis of a negative history of chickenpox.

(b) **Neonates:** Infants whose mothers develop chickenpox less than 8 days before delivery, or after birth, can be presumed to be VZ antibody negative. The VZ antibody status of infants whose mothers have a negative history should determined by testing a maternal blood sample before VZIG is given.

A small proportion of premature infants who are born before 28 weeks of gestation or with a birth weight less than 1000 gms may not possess maternal antibody despite a positive history in the mother.

(c) **Pregnant women:** Those with a positive history of chickenpox do not require VZIG. Those with a negative history must be tested for VZ antibody before VZIG is given. The outcome in pregnant women is not adversely affected if administration of VZIG is delayed up to 10 days after initial contact while a VZ antibody test is done.

Varicella

■ 34.9   Definition of a significant exposure to varicella-zoster virus

Three aspects of the exposure are relevant:

(a) **Type of varicella-zoster infection in index case:** The risk of acquiring infection from an immunocompetant individual with non-exposed zoster lesions (e.g. thoraco-lumbar) is remote. The issue of VZIG should therefore be restricted to those in contact with chickenpox, or the following: disseminated zoster, immunocompetent individuals with exposed lesions (e.g. ophthalmic zoster) or immunosuppressed patients with localised zoster on any part of the body (in whom viral shedding may be greater).

(b) **The timing of the exposure in relation to onset of rash in index case:** VZIG should normally be restricted to patients exposed to a case of chickenpox or disseminated zoster between 48 hours before onset of rash until cropping has ceased and crusting of all lesions, or day of onset of rash until crusting for those exposed to localised zoster.

(c) **Closeness and duration of contact:** The following should be used as a guide to the type of exposure, other than maternal/neonatal and continuous home contact, that requires VZIG prophylaxis:

Contact in the same room (e.g. in a house or classroom or a 2-4 bed hospital bay) for a significant period of time (15 minutes or more).

Face-to-face contact, for example while having a conversation.

In the case of large open wards, where air-borne transmission at a distance has occasionally been reported, the necessity of giving VZIG to all susceptible high risk contacts should be considered, particularly in paediatric wards where the degree of contact may be difficult to define.

■ 34.10 Dose of VZIG for prophylaxis

The dosage for both the BPL and PFC products are as follows:

0 - 5 years	250 mg (1 vial)
6 - 10 years	500 mg (2 vials)
11 - 14 years	750 mg (3 vials)
15 years and over	1000 mg (4 vials)

VZIG is given by **intramuscular** injection as soon as possible and not later than ten days after exposure. It must **not** be given intravenously.

If a second exposure occurs after three weeks, a further dose is required.

Contacts with bleeding disorders who cannot be given an intramuscular injection should be given intravenous normal immunoglobulin at a dose of 0.2g per kg body weight (ie. 4 mls/kg for a 5% solution) instead. This will produce serum VZ antibody levels equivalent to those achieved with VZIG.

■ 34.11 Treatment

There is no evidence that VZIG is effective in the treatment of severe disease. Since antibody production can be delayed in immunosuppressed individuals, intravenous commercial preparations of normal human immunoglobulin may be used to provide an immediate source of antibody.

■ 34.12 Supplies

England and Wales: Available from Public Health Laboratories and the Communicable Disease Surveillance Centre (CDSC) (Tel. 0181 200 6868).

Northern Ireland: Available from the Public Health Laboratory, Belfast City Hospital, Lisburn Road, Belfast Tel. 01232 329241.

Scotland: Available from Regional Transfusion Centres

VZIG is issued free of charge to patients who meet the criteria given in 34.4. No other licensed VZIG preparations apart from the BPL and PFC products are available in the UK.

Varicella

■ 34.13 Safety

■ 34.13.1   VZIG is well tolerated. Very rarely anaphylactoid reactions occur in individuals with hypogammaglobulinaemia who have IgA antibodies, or those who have had an atypical reaction to blood transfusion

■ 34.13.2   Severe reactions should be reported to the Committee on Safety of Medicines using the yellow card system.

■ 34.13.3   No cases of blood borne infection acquired through immunoglobulin preparations designed for intramuscular use have been documented in any country.

■ 34.14 Management of hospital outbreaks

■ 34.17.1   Susceptible staff with a significant exposure to VZ virus (see 34.9) including those dressing localised zoster lesions on non-exposed areas of the body, should whenever possible be excluded from contact with high risk patients from eight to 21 days after exposure.

■ 34.17.2   To simplify procedures after the admission or recognition of a case, it is recommended that hospital staff without a definite history of chickenpox should be routinely screened for V-Z antibody so that those susceptible are already identified. This is particularly important for staff in contact with high risk groups such as pregnant women and immunosuppressed patients.

■ 34.15 Bibliography

Evans EB, Pollock TM, Cradock-Watson JE, Ridehalgh MK. Human anti-chickenpox immunoglobulin in the prevention of chickenpox. Lancet 1980: i:354-356

Miller E, Cradock-Watson JE, Ridehalgh MKS. Outcome in newborn babies given anti-varicella zoster immunoglobulin after perinatal infection with varicella-zoster virus. Lancet 1990;ii:371-373.

Patou G, Midgely P, Meurisse EV, Feldman RG. Immunoglobulin prophylaxis for infants exposed to varicella in a neonatal unit. J Infection 1990;29:207-213.

Miller E, Marshall R, Vurdien JE. Epidemiology, outcome and control of varicella-zoster infection. Rev Med Microbiol 1993:4:222-230.

Enders G, Miller E, Cradock-Watson JE, Bolley I, Ridehalgh M. The consequences of chickenpox and herpes zoster in pregnancy; a prospective study of 1739 cases. Lancet 1994; 343: 1548-1551.

Parayani SG, Arvin AM, Koropchak CM, Dobkin MB, Wiitek AE, Amylon MD, Budinger MD. Comparison of varicella-zoster antibody titres in patients given intravenous immune globulin or varicella-zoster immune globulin. J Pediatrics 1984:105:200-205.

Varicella

35   Yellow Fever

■ 35.1 Introduction

■ 35.1.1 Yellow fever is an acute flavivirus infection spread by the bite of an infected mosquito and occurring in tropical Africa and South America (it has never been seen in Asia). It ranges in severity from non-specific symptoms to an illness of sudden onset with fever, vomiting and prostration which may progress to haemorrhage and jaundice. In indigenous populations in endemic areas fatality is about 5%; in non-indigenous individuals and during epidemics, the case fatality rate for unimmunised adults can exceed 50%. The incubation period is generally 3-6 days but may be longer. Death usually occurs 7-10 days after the onset of illness. There is no specific treatment for yellow fever.

■ 35.1.2 Two epidemiological forms of yellow fever are recognised although they are clinically and aetiologically identical. In *urban* yellow fever, the host is man and the disease is spread by the mosquito *Aedes aegypti* which lives and breeds in close association with man. *Jungle* yellow fever is transmitted among non-human hosts (mainly monkeys) by forest mosquitoes which may also bite and infect humans. These may, if subsequently bitten by *Aedes aegypti*, become the source of outbreaks of the urban form of the disease. The virus can reappear after long intervals, and outbreaks and severe epidemics continue to occur from time to time in Africa. Rural populations are at greatest risk.

■ 35.1.3 Preventative measures against urban yellow fever include eradication of *Aedes* mosquitoes, protection from mosquito bites, and immunisation. Jungle yellow fever can only be prevented by immunisation.

■ 35.1.4 There is no risk of transmission in the UK from imported cases since the mosquito vector does not occur in the UK.

■ 35.1.5 Immunisation against yellow fever, documented by a valid International Certification of Vaccination, is compulsory for entry into some countries either for all travellers or for those arriving from infected areas. Requirements are published annually by the World Health Organisation in the publication 'International Travel and Health' and are included in 'Health Information for Overseas Travel', but should also be checked at the relevant Embassy before travel.

Yellow Fever

■ 35.2 Vaccine

■ 35.2.1 Yellow fever vaccine is a live attenuated freeze-dried preparation of the 17D strain of yellow fever virus grown in leucosis-free chick embryos. Each 0.5ml dose contains not less than 1000 mouse LD50 units. The vaccine contains no more than 2 iu of neomycin and 5 iu of polymyxin per dose.

■ 35.2.2 The vaccine should be stored at 2-8°C and protected from light. The diluent supplied for use with the vaccine should be stored below 25°C but not frozen. After reconstitution, the vaccine should be kept cool, protected from light and used within one hour. Any unused vaccine should be destroyed at the end of the immunisation session by incineration at a temperature of not less than 1100°C by a registered waste disposal contractor, or by disinfection.

■ 35.2.3 A single dose correctly given confers immunity in nearly 100% of recipients; immunity persists for at least ten years and probably for life, although re-immunisation is currently recommended after ten years.

■ 35.2.4 Yellow fever vaccine is given only at designated centres (these are listed in the UK Health Departments' book 'Health Information for Overseas Travel') and costs are passed on to the vaccinee.

■ 35.3 Recommendations

■ 35.3.1 The following should be immunised:

a. Laboratory workers handling infected material.

b. Persons aged nine months and over travelling through or living in infected areas and those travelling outside urban areas of countries in the yellow fever endemic zone (see maps in 'Health Information for Overseas Travel'), even if these countries have not officially reported the disease and do not require evidence of immunisation on entry. Immunisation under nine months is not recommended but may be performed if exposure to the risk of infection cannot be avoided.

c. Travellers requiring an International Certificate of Vaccination for entry into a country.

Further details about the recommendations for travellers are contained in the UK Health Departments' book 'Health Information for Overseas Travel'.

■ 35.3.2 The dose is 0.5ml by deep subcutaneous injection irrespective of age but see 35.5.2.

■ 35.3.3 Re-immunisation every ten years is recommended for those at risk.

■ 35.3.4 The International Certificate is valid for ten years from the tenth day after primary immunisation and immediately after re-immunisation.

■ 35.4 Adverse reactions

■ 35.4.1 5-10% of recipients have mild headache, myalgia, low-grade fever or soreness at the injection site 5-10 days after immunisation. Immediate allergic type reactions such as urticaria and, rarely, anaphylaxis have also been reported.

■ 35.4.2 Rarely, encephalitis has been described following the 17D tissue culture vaccine in young infants, all but one of whom have recovered without sequelae.

■ 35.4.3 Severe reactions should be reported to the Committee on Safety of Medicines using the yellow card system.

■ 35.5 Contraindications

■ 35.5.1 The usual contraindications to a live virus vaccine should be observed (see 7.3). Yellow fever vaccine should not be given to:

a. Persons suffering from febrile illness.

b. Patients receiving high-dose corticosteroid or immuno-suppressive treatment, including radiation.

c. Patients suffering from malignant conditions such as lymphoma, leukaemia, Hodgkin's disease or other tumours of the reticulo-endothelial system, or where the immunological mechanism may be impaired as in hypogammaglobulinaemia.

Yellow Fever

d. Pregnant women, because of the theoretical risk of fetal infection. However if a pregnant woman must travel to a high-risk area, she should be immunised since the risk from yellow fever outweighs that of immunisation.

e. Persons known to be hypersensitive to neomycin or polymyxin or to have had an anaphylactic reaction to egg. A letter stating that immunisation is contraindicated on these grounds may be acceptable in some countries. Advice should be sought from the appropriate Embassy.

f. HIV positive individuals, whether symptomatic or asymtpomatic, since there is as yet insufficient evidence as to the safety of its use. Travellers should be told of this uncertainty and advised not to be immunised unless there are compelling reasons (see 7.4.4).

■ 35.5.2 Infants under nine months should only be immunised if the risk of yellow fever is unavoidable as there is a very small risk of encephalitis (35.4.2).

■ 35.5.3 If travellers in whom the vaccine is contraindicated still intend to visit countries where a yellow fever certificate is required for entry, then they should obtain a letter of exemption from a medical practitioner.

■ 35.5.4 If more than one live vaccine is required, they should either be given at the same time in different sites or with an interval of three weeks between them.

■ 35.5.5 Normal human immunoglobulin obtained in the UK is unlikely to contain antibody to the yellow fever virus; travellers may therefore be given the vaccine at the same time as an injection of immunoglobulin.

■ 35.6 Supplies

The vaccine is manufactured and supplied in 1 dose vials (5 per pack) and in 5 dose vials (5 per pack) to designated centres only by Evans Medical Ltd Tel. 0345 451500 (local rate) or 01372 364000

■ 35.7   Yellow fever vaccination centres

■ 35.7.1   Designated yellow fever vaccination centres are listed in the UK Health Departments' book 'Health Information for Overseas Travel'.

■ 35.7.2   Practitioners in England wishing to apply for designation as an approved yellow fever vaccination centre should apply to:

> Mrs Sue Doran
> Department of Health
> Room 601A, Skipton House
> 80 London Road
> LONDON SE1 6LW

■ 35.7.3   Practitioners in Wales should apply to:

> Mrs Catherine Pyman
> Public Health Division 3
> Welsh Office
> Cathays Park
> CARDIFF
> CF1 3NQ

■ 35.7.4   Practitioners in Scotland should apply to:

> Mr Charles Hodgson
> Scottish Office
> Department of Health
> Public Health Policy Unit
> Room 14
> St Andrew's House
> EDINBURGH
> EH1 3DE

■ 35.7.5　Practitioners in Northern Ireland should apply to:

Health Protection Branch
Department of Health and Social Services
Annex 4
Castle Buildings
Stormont
BELFAST
BT4　3RA

■ 35.8　Bibliography

Health Information for Overseas Travel.
UK Health Departments and the PHLS Communicable Disease Surveillance
Centre. HMSO, 1995

International Travel and Health: Vaccination requirements and health advice.
World Health Organisation, Geneva　(updated annually).

The duration of immunity following vaccination with the 17D strain of yellow
fever virus.
Fox JP,　Cabral A S.
Am J Hyg 1943; 37: 93-120

Stabilised 17D yellow fever vaccine: dose response studies, clinical reactions
and effects on hepatic function.
Freestone D S et al.
J Biol Stand 1977; 5: 181-6

Neutralising and HAI antibody to yellow fever 17 years after vaccination with
17D vaccine.
Groot H, Ribeivo R B.
Bull WHO 1962; 27: 699-707

Yellow Fever

Northern & Yorkshire

District	BRADFORD
Trust/Locality	AIREDALE
Department	Community Health Offices
	Tel 01756 792233 ex 247 Fax 01756 700485

District	BRADFORD
Trust/Locality	BRADFORD COMMUNITY HEALTH
Department	Child/School Health System Administrator
	Tel 01274 363541 Fax 01274 3633469

District	DURHAM
Trust/Locality	NORTH DURHAM COMMUNITY HEALTH CARE
Department	Admin Support Officer
	Tel 01207 214856 Fax 01207 214888

District	DURHAM
Trust/Locality	SOUTH DURHAM HEALTH CARE
Department	The Health Centre
	Tel 01388 452807 Fax 01388 452806

District	EAST RIDING
Trust/Locality	EAST YORKSHIRE COMMUNITY HEALTHCARE
Department	Admin Manager
	Tel 01482 886600 Fax 01482 886541

District	EAST RIDING
Trust/Locality	HULL AND HOLDERNESS COMMUNITY HEALTH
Department	Child Health and Vaccination Department
	Tel 01482 675857 Fax 01482 229668

District	GRIMSBY AND SCUNTHORPE
Trust/Locality	GRIMSBY HEALTH
Department	Department of Community & Child Health
	Tel 01472-874111 Ext 7004 Fax 01472 875561

District	GRIMSBY AND SCUNTHORPE
Trust/Locality	SCUNTHORPE COMMUNITY HEALTH CARE
Department	Scunthorpe Community Health Care Trust
	Tel 01724 282282 ext 3964 Fax 01724 271016

CHILD HEALTH DEPARTMENT CONTACTS

District	LEEDS
Trust/Locality	LEEDS COMMUNITY AND MENTAL HEALTH
Department	Leeds Community & Mental Health Services
	Tel 0113 2790121 Fax 0113 2319549

District	NEWCASTLE AND NORTH TYNESIDE
Trust/Locality	NEWCASTLE CITY HEALTH
Department	Database Manager
	Tel 0191 273 8811 ex 22504 Fax 0191 273 4872

District	NORTH CUMBRIA
Trust/Locality	NORTH LAKELAND HEALTHCARE
Department	North Lakeland Healthcare
	Tel 01946 695551 Fax 01946 591045

District	NORTH CUMBRIA
Trust/Locality	WEST CUMBRIA
Department	Information Manager
	Tel 01946 693181 Fax 01946 523513

District	NORTH YORKSHIRE
Trust/Locality	AIREDALE
Department	Child Health
	Tel 01756 792233 ex 247 Fax 01756 700485

District	NORTH YORKSHIRE
Trust/Locality	HARROGATE HEALTH CARE
Department	Community Systems Manager
	Tel 01423 889731 ex 3509 Fax 01423 880178

District	NORTH YORKSHIRE
Trust/Locality	NORTHALLERTON HEALTH SERVICES
Department	Office Manager Community Services
	Tel 01609 762045 Fax 01609 777144

District	NORTH YORKSHIRE
Trust/Locality	SCARBOROUGH AND NORTH EAST YORKSHIRE
Department	Administrative Co-ordinator, Child Health
	Tel 01723 363366 Fax 01723 501928

District	NORTH YORKSHIRE
Trust/Locality	YORK HEALTH
Department	Community Health Service
	Tel 01904 630351 Fax 01904 634025

District	NORTHUMBERLAND
Trust/Locality	NORTHUMBERLAND COMMUNITY HEALTH
Department	Northumberland Community NHS Trust
	Tel 01670 517006 Fax 01670 510416

District	SOUTH OF TYNE
Trust/Locality	GATESHEAD HEALTHCARE
Department	Whinney House Resource Centre
	Tel 0191 402 6023 Fax 0191 402 6020

District	SOUTH OF TYNE
Trust/Locality	SOUTH TYNESIDE HEALTH CARE
Department	Child Health Dept
	Tel 0191 456 8821 Fax 0191 427 6009

District	SUNDERLAND
Trust/Locality	CITY HOSPITALS SUNDERLAND
Department	Directorate Manager - Child & Family Health
	Tel 0191 569 9617 Ext 49617 Fax 0191 569 9262

District	TEES
Trust/Locality	HARTLEPOOL COMMUNITY CARE
Department	The Health Centre
	Tel 01429 267 901 ext 4166 Fax 01429 261 744

District	TEES
Trust/Locality	NORTH TEES HEALTH
Department	Information Office Room G7
	Tel 01642 617617 ext 4146 Fax 01642 624089

District	TEES
Trust/Locality	SOUTH TEES COMMUNITY
Department	Child Health
	Tel 01642 813144 ext 275 Fax 01642 822717

District	WAKEFIELD
Trust/Locality	WAKEFIELD AND PONTEFRACT COMMUNITY HEALTH
Department	Childrens Services Manager
	Tel 01977 605517 Fax 01977 605501

District	WEST YORKSHIRE
Trust/Locality	CALDERDALE HEALTHCARE
Department	Child Health System Manager
	Tel 01484 712515 Fax 01484 401348

District	WEST YORKSHIRE
Trust/Locality	Dewsbury Health Care
Department	Child Health Administrator
	Tel 01274 873501 Fax 01274 852198

District	WEST YORKSHIRE
Trust/Locality	HUDDERSFIELD
Department	Princess Royal Community Health Centre
	Tel 01484 545411 Fax 01484 545411

Trent

District	BARNSLEY
Trust/Locality	BARNSLEY COMMUNITY AND PRIORITY SERVICES
Department	Acting Assist Child Health
	Tel 01226 730000 ext 4024 Fax 01226 779120

District	DONCASTER
Trust/Locality	THE DONCASTER ROYAL AND MONTAGU HOSPITAL
Department	Department of Child Health
	Tel 01302 796249 Fax 01302 859496

District	LEICESTERSHIRE
Trust/Locality	LEICESTERSHIRE HEALTH
Department	Immunisation Manager
	Tel 0116 2559600 ex 4163 Fax 0116 2544051

District	LINCOLNSHIRE
Trust/Locality	LINCOLN DISTRICT HEALTHCARE
Department	Child Health Department
	Tel 01522 514814

Annex

District	LINCOLNSHIRE
Trust/Locality	SOUTH LINCOLNSHIRE COMMUNITY AND MENTAL
Department	Child Health Manager
	Tel 01529 416019 Fax 01529 416092

District	NORTH DERBYSHIRE
Trust/Locality	NORTH DERBYSHIRE COMMUNITY HEALTH CARE
Department	Child Health System Manager
	Tel 01246 552956 Ext 4583 Fax 01246 557194

District	NORTH NOTTINGHAMSHIRE
Trust/Locality	BASSETLAW HOSPITAL & COMMUNITY
Department	Child Health Surveillance
	Tel 01777 705261 Fax 01777 710535

District	NORTH NOTTINGHAMSHIRE
Trust/Locality	CENTRAL NOTTINGHAM HEALTHCARE
Department	Acting Manager
	Tel 01623 785176 Fax 01623 424062

District	NOTTINGHAM
Trust/Locality	NOTTINGHAM COMMUNITY HEALTH
Department	Child Health Department
	Tel 0115 9426000 Fax 0115 9428606

District	ROTHERHAM
Trust/Locality	ROTHERHAM PRIORITY HEALTH
Department	Administration Support Manager
	Tel 01709 824863 Fax 01709 824890

District	SHEFFIELD
Trust/Locality	COMMUNITY HEALTH SHEFFIELD
Department	Child Health Services
	Tel 0114 2716600 Fax 0114 2716619

District	SOUTHERN DERBYSHIRE
Trust/Locality	SOUTHERN DERBYSHIRE COMMUNITY HEALTH
Department	Central Support Services Manager
	Tel DERBY 363371 Fax DERBY 341246

CHILD HEALTH DEPARTMENT CONTACTS

Anglia & Oxford

District	BEDFORDSHIRE
Trust/Locality	BEDFORD AND SHIRES HEALTH AND CARE
Department	Directorate Manager - Child Health Services
	Tel 01234 267444 ext 3789 Fax 01234 792309

District	BEDFORDSHIRE
Trust/Locality	SOUTH BEDFORDSHIRE COMMUNITY HEALTH CARE
Department	Senior Information Analyst
	Tel 01582 415381 Fax 01582 484216

District	BERKSHIRE
Trust/Locality	EAST BERKSHIRE COMMUNITY HEALTH
Department	Child Health
	Tel 01753 821441 Fax 01753 635039

District	BERKSHIRE
Trust/Locality	WEST BERKSHIRE PRIORITY CARE SERVICE
Department	Admin Manager - Child Health
	Tel 01734 862277 ext 2220 Fax 01734 750297

District	BUCKINGHAMSHIRE
Trust/Locality	AYLESBURY VALE HEALTHCARE
Department	Child and Family Services
	Tel 01296-89951 Fax 01296 398802

District	BUCKINGHAMSHIRE
Trust/Locality	Milton Keynes Community
Department	Child Health Administrator
	Tel 01908 660033 Fax 01908 694919

District	BUCKINGHAMSHIRE
Trust/Locality	SOUTH BUCKINGHAMSHIRE
Department	Child Health Services Manager
	Tel 01494 526161 EX 6676 Fax 01494 426114

District	CAMBRIDGE
Trust/Locality	LIFESPAN HEALTHCARE
Department	Community Child Health Service
	Tel 01223 884170 Fax 01223 884171

District	EAST NORFOLK
Trust/Locality	East Norfolk Health Commission
Department	Information Manager
	Tel 01603 300600 ext 389 Fax 01603 701380

District	HUNTINGDON
Trust/Locality	HINCHINGBROOKE HEALTH CARE
Department	Admin & Support Manager, Children's Services
	Tel 01480 415200 Fax 01480 415212

District	NORTH WEST ANGLIA
Trust/Locality	N W A (West Norwich & Wisbech)
Department	Pre school Supervisor
	Tel 01733 874907 Fax 01733 318139

District	NORTH WEST ANGLIA
Trust/Locality	N W A (Peterborough)
Department	St James Clinic
	Tel 01553 762911 ex 6379 Fax 01553 774753

District	NORTHAMPTONSHIRE
Trust/Locality	NORTHAMPTON TOWN & SOUTH NORTHAMPTON
Department	Systems Manager - Child Health
	Tel 01604 37221 X 2302 Fax 01604 602413

District	OXFORDSHIRE
Trust/Locality	OXFORDSHIRE COMMUNITY HEALTH
Department	Department of Public Health
	Tel 01865 226860 Fax 01865 226894

District	SUFFOLK
Trust/Locality	ANGLIAN HARBOURS
Department	Information Manager
	Tel 01493 337796 Fax 01493 337809

District	EAST NORFOLK
Trust/Locality	ANGLIAN HARBOURS
Department	Information Manager
	Tel 01493 337796 Fax 01493 337809

District   SUFFOLK
Trust/Locality MID ANGLIA COMMUNITY HEALTH
Department   Child Health Department
                Tel 01284 775066   Fax 01284 750280

North Thames

District   BARKING AND HAVERING
Trust/Locality BHB COMMUNITY HEALTH CARE
Department   Systems Manager, Child Health Department
                Tel 01708 465411   Fax 01708 465496

District   BARNET
Trust/Locality BARNET HEALTHCARE
Department   Operations Manager
                Tel 0181 441 0745 ex 218   Fax 0181 449 1495

District   BRENT AND HARROW
Trust/Locality NORTHWICK PARK HOSPITAL
Department   Child Health Department
                Tel 0181 864 5432 ext 4210   Fax 0181 864 8901

District   BRENT AND HARROW
Trust/Locality PARKSIDE HEALTH
Department   Information Manager
                Tel 0181 451 8165   Fax 0181 451 8236

District   CAMDEN AND ISLINGTON
Trust/Locality CAMDEN AND ISLINGTON COMMUNITY
Department   Child Health Information Manager
                Tel 0171 278 2323 Ex 244   Fax 0171 713 5483

District   CAMDEN AND ISLINGTON
Trust/Locality ROYAL FREE HAMPSTEAD
Department   Department of Child Health
                Tel 0171 794 0500   Fax 0171 830 2003

District   EALING, HAMMERSMITH AND HOUNSLOW
Trust/Locality HOUNSLOW AND SPELTHORNE COMMUNITY
Department   Support Services Manager
                Tel 0181 321 2416/2441   Fax 0181 321 2331

Annex

District	EALING, HAMMERSMITH AND HOUNSLOW
Trust/Locality	RIVERSIDE COMMUNITY HEALTH CARE
Department	Information Manager
	Tel 0181 846 1644 Fax 0181 846 1633

District	EALING, HAMMERSMITH AND HOUNSLOW
Trust/Locality	WEST LONDON HEALTH
Department	West London Healthcare NHS Trust
	Tel 0181 967 5458 Fax 0181967 5002

District	EAST AND NORTH HERTFORDSHIRE
Trust/Locality	EAST HERTFORDSHIRE
Department	Assist to Director of Community
	Tel 01707 328111 Fax 01707 335168

District	EAST AND NORTH HERTFORDSHIRE
Trust/Locality	NORTH HERTS
Department	Systems & Info Manager
	Tel 01462 422444 Fax 01438 181321

District	EAST LONDON AND THE CITY
Trust/Locality	CITY AND HACKNEY COMMUNITY SERVICES
Department	St Leonards Primary Care Centre
	Tel 0171 601 7742 Fax 0171 729 9079

District	EAST LONDON AND THE CITY
Trust/Locality	NEWHAM COMMUNITY HEALTH SERVICES
Department	Information Officer
	Tel 0181 534 7479 Fax 0181 519 8049

District	EAST LONDON AND THE CITY
Trust/Locality	TOWER HAMLETS HEALTHCARE
Department	IM & T
	Tel 0171 377 7000 ext 4207 Fax 0171 377 7825

District	HILLINGDON
Trust/Locality	HARROW AND HILLINGDON HEALTHCARE
Department	Child Health Systems Manager
	Tel 01895 811759 Fax 01895 236018

District	KENSINGTON, CHELSEA AND WESTMINSTER
Trust/Locality	PARKSIDE HEALTH
Department	Information Manager
	Tel 0181 451 8165 Fax 0181 451 8236

District	KENSINGTON, CHELSEA AND WESTMINSTER
Trust/Locality	RIVERSIDE COMMUNITY HEALTH CARE
Department	Information Manager
	Tel 0181 846 1644 Fax 0181 846 1633

District	NEW RIVER
Trust/Locality	ENFIELD COMMUNITY CARE
Department	Child Health Systems Manager
	Tel 0181 370 2500 Ext 3101 Fax 0181 366 4269

District	NEW RIVER
Trust/Locality	HARINGEY HEALTHCARE
Department	RICHS System Manager
	Tel 0181 442 6514 Fax 0181 442 6311

District	NORTH ESSEX
Trust/Locality	ESSEX AND HERTS COMMUNITY
Department	RICHS System Manager
	Tel 01279 827023 Fax 01279 444298

District	NORTH ESSEX
Trust/Locality	ESSEX RIVERS HEALTHCARE
Department	Child Health
	Tel 01206 579411 ext 260 Fax 01206 760518

District	NORTH ESSEX
Trust/Locality	MID ESSEX COMMUNITY AND MENTAL HEALTH
Department	Vacc and Imm and New Births
	Tel 01376 393000 ex 3027 Fax 01376 393001

District	NORTH WEST HERTFORDSHIRE
Trust/Locality	WEST HERTS COMMUNITY
Department	Child Health Manager
	Tel 01727 811888 ex 4716 Fax 01727 857900

District	REDBRIDGE AND WALTHAM FOREST
Trust/Locality	FOREST HEALTHCARE
Department	RICHS System Manager
	Tel 0181 520 8971 Fax 0181 521 4044

District	REDBRIDGE AND WALTHAM FOREST
Trust/Locality	REDBRIDGE HEALTH CARE
Department	Child Health Information Manager
	Tel 0181 970 8298 Fax 0181 970 8268

District	SOUTH ESSEX
Trust/Locality	BHB COMMUNITY HEALTH CARE
Department	Systems Manager, Child Health Department
	Tel 01708 465411 Fax 10708 441915

District	SOUTH ESSEX
Trust/Locality	SOUTHEND COMMUNITY CARE SERVICES
Department	RICHS System Manager
	Tel 01702 546354 ext 358 Fax 01702 546383

District	SOUTH ESSEX
Trust/Locality	Thameside Community Healthcare
Department	Child Health Manager
	Tel 01268 593254 Fax 01268 593756

District	SOUTH WEST HERTFORDSHIRE
Trust/Locality	WEST HERTS COMMUNITY
Department	Watford General Hospital
	Tel 01923 217246

South Thames

District	BEXLEY AND GREENWICH
Trust/Locality	GREENWICH
Department	Child Health Department
	Tel 0181 856 5511 ext 4413 Fax 0181 856 8712

District	BEXLEY AND GREENWICH
Trust/Locality	OXLEAS (BEXLEY)
Department	Child Health Department
	Tel 01322 526282 ext 2344 Fax 01322 336819

District	BROMLEY
Trust/Locality	RAVENSBOURNE
Department	Child Health Department
	Tel 01689 853339 ext 2162 Fax 01689 855662

District	CROYDON
Trust/Locality	Croydon Community Health NHS Trust
Department	Information Manager
	Tel 0181 680 2008 ex 229 Fax 0181 666 0495

District	EAST KENT
Trust/Locality	CANTERBURY AND THANET
Department	Child Health Department
	Tel 01227 459371 ext 2256 Fax 01227 812262

District	EAST KENT
Trust/Locality	SOUTH KENT COMMUNITY
Department	Child Health Department
	Tel 01303 850202 ext 1456 Fax 01303 226903

District	EAST SUSSEX
Trust/Locality	EASTBOURNE AND COUNTY
Department	Child Health Systems Manager
	Tel 01323 440022 ext 3036 Fax 01323 842868

District	EAST SUSSEX
Trust/Locality	HASTINGS AND ROTHER
Department	Child Health Department
	Tel 01424 755255 ext 8453 Fax 01424 758014

District	EAST SUSSEX
Trust/Locality	SOUTH DOWNS HEALTH
Department	Manager, Child Record Unit
	Tel 01273 693600 ext 3821 Fax 01273 623317

District	EASTERN SURREY
Trust/Locality	EAST SURREY HOSPITAL AND COMMUNITY
Department	East Surrey Hospital and Community
	Tel 01737 768511 ex 1381 Fax 01737 782935

Annex

District	KINGSTON AND RICHMOND
Trust/Locality	KINGSTON COMMUNITY HEALTH
Department	Child Health Computer Manager
	Tel 0181 339 0379 ext 225 Fax 0181 398 9835

District	KINGSTON AND RICHMOND
Trust/Locality	RTR HEALTHCARE
Department	Child Health
	Tel 0181 940 0251 Fax 0181 940 2490

District	MERTON, SUTTON AND WANDSWORTH
Trust/Locality	RTR HEALTHCARE
Department	Community Health Services
	Tel 0181 948 0251 Fax 0181 940 2490

District	SOUTH EAST LONDON
Trust/Locality	OPTIMUM HEALTH
Department	Child Health Services Manager
	Tel 0171 635 5555 ex 5200 Fax 0171 7715197

District	SOUTH EAST LONDON
Trust/Locality	WEST LAMBETH
Department	Systems Manager
	Tel 0171 346 5415 Fax 0171 346 5471

District	WEST KENT
Trust/Locality	MID KENT HEALTHCARE
Department	Child Health Department
	Tel 01622 710161 ext 2218 Fax 01622 713115

District	WEST KENT
Trust/Locality	NORTH KENT HEALTHCARE
Department	Child Health Department
	Tel 01634 832160 ext 2543 Fax 01634 840785

District	WEST KENT
Trust/Locality	THAMESLINK HEALTH
Department	Child Health Department
	Tel 01322 292233 ext 217 Fax 01322 292445

District	WEST KENT
Trust/Locality	WEALD OF KENT COMMUNITY
Department	Child Health Department
	Tel 01892 539144 ext 4479 Fax 01892 535522

District	WEST SURREY
Trust/Locality	HOUNSLOW AND SPELTHORNE COMMUNITY
Department	Support Services Manager
	Tel 0181 321 2416/2441 Fax 0181 321 2331

District	WEST SURREY
Trust/Locality	NORTH DOWNS COMMUNITY
Department	Lead Administrator Child Health
	Tel 01483 783126 Fax 01483 783199

District	WEST SUSSEX
Trust/Locality	CHICHESTER
Department	West Sussex NHS Trusts
	Tel 01243 815226 Fax 01243 815225

District	WEST SUSSEX
Trust/Locality	CRAWLEY/HORSHAM
Department	West Sussex NHS Trusts
	Tel 01243 815226 Fax 01243 815225

District	WEST SUSSEX
Trust/Locality	MID SUSSEX
Department	West Sussex NHS Trusts
	Tel 01243 815226 Fax 01243 815225

District	WEST SUSSEX
Trust/Locality	WORTHING
Department	West Sussex NHS Trusts
	Tel 01243 815226 Fax 01243 815225

Annex

South & West

District	BRISTOL
Trust/Locality	AVON HEALTH
Department	Child Health System Manager
	Tel 0117 9766600 Fax 0117 9766601

District	CORNWALL AND ISLES OF SCILLY
Trust/Locality	CORNWALL AND ISLES OF SCILLY
Department	Child Health Directorate
	Tel 01872 254530 Fax 01872 225506

District	DORSET
Trust/Locality	DORSET HEALTHCARE
Department	Child Health Dept
	Tel 01202 303400 Fax 01202 309968

District	DORSET
Trust/Locality	WEST DORSET GENERAL HOSPITALS
Department	Children's Centre
	Tel 01305 251150 Fax 01305 254737

District	EXETER AND NORTH DEVON
Trust./Locality	EXETER AND DISTRICT COMMUNITY TRUST
Department	Exeter & District Community Health Service
	Tel 01392 449700 Fax 01392 445435

District	EXETER AND NORTH DEVON
Trust/Locality	NORTHERN DEVON HEALTHCARE
Department	The Child Health Under 5 records
	Tel 01271 71761 ext 251 Fax 01271 321586

District	GLOUCESTERSHIRE
Trust/Locality	EAST GLOUCESTERSHIRE
Department	Child Health & Comm Nursing Systems Manager
	Tel 01242 516235 Fax 01242 234527

District	GLOUCESTERSHIRE
Trust/Locality	SEVERN
Department	Child Health Systems Manager
	Tel 01452 529421 Fax 01452 383045

Annex

District	ISLE OF WIGHT
Trust/Locality	ST MARY'S HOSPITAL
Department	Child Health Computing System Manager
	Tel 01983 821388 Fax 01983 521561

District	NORTH AND MID HAMPSHIRE
Trust/Locality	LODDON
Department	Child Health Department
	Tel 01256 314767 Fax 01256 314796

District	NORTH AND MID HAMPSHIRE
Trust/Locality	NORTH DOWNS COMMUNITY
Department	Lead Administrator Child Health
	Tel 01483 783126 Fax 01483 783199

District	NORTH AND MID HAMPSHIRE
Trust/Locality	WINCHESTER AND EASTLEIGH HEALTHCARE
Department	Pre-School Immunisation Department
	Tel 01962 863511 ex 368/220 Fax 01962 856726

District	PORTSMOUTH AND SE HAMPSHIRE
Trust/Locality	PORTSMOUTH HEALTHCARE
Department	Information/Logistics Manager
	Tel 01705 822444 ex 4262 Fax 01705 877761

District	SOMERSET
Trust/Locality	SOMERSET HEALTH COMMISSION
Department	Child Health Administrator
	Tel 01823 333491 EXT 4244 Fax 01823 272710

District	SOUTH AND WEST DEVON
Trust/Locality	PLYMOUTH HOSPITALS
Department	Immunisation Administrator
	Tel 01752 763528 Fax 01752 763529

District	SOUTH AND WEST DEVON
Trust/Locality	South Devon Healthcare
Department	Child Health Portacabin
	Tel 01803 655818 Fax 01803 617174

District	SOUTHAMPTON AND SW HAMPSHIRE
Trust/Locality	Southampton Community Health Services
Department	Senior Administrator, Child Health
	Tel 01703 902500 Fax 01703 330329

District	WILTSHIRE
Trust/Locality	Bath and West
Department	Systems Manager
	Tel 01225 313640 Fax 01225 339959

District	WILTSHIRE
Trust/Locality	EAST WILTSHIRE HEALTH CARE
Department	Systems Manager
	Tel 01793 533181 Fax 10793 512973

District	WILTSHIRE
Trust/Locality	SALISBURY HEALTH CARE
Department	Salisbury District Hospital
	Tel 01722 425095 Fax 01722 425284

West Midlands

District	COVENTRY
Trust/Locality	COVENTRY HEALTHCARE
Department	Information Services Manager
	Tel 01203 553344 Fax 01203 526800

District	DUDLEY
Trust/Locality	DUDLEY HEALTH DUDLEY PRIORITY HEALTH
Department	Child Health Manager
	Tel 01384 244303 Fax 01384 400217

District	HEREFORDSHIRE
Trust/Locality	HEREFORDSHIRE COMMUNITY HEALTH
Department	Child Health/Medical Locality
	Tel 01432 344344 ex 3920 Fax 01432 363917

District	NORTH BIRMINGHAM
Trust/Locality	NBC HEALTH
Department	Child Health Manager
	Tel 0121 766 6611 Ext 2893/2898 Fax 0121 321 1299

District	NORTH STAFFORDSHIRE
Trust/Locality	NORTH STAFFORDSHIRE COMBINED HEALTHCARE
Department	Assistant Information Services Manager
	Tel 01782 275027 Fax 01782 213682

District	NORTH WORCESTERSHIRE
Trust/Locality	KIDDERMINSTER
Department	Manager, Child Health
	Tel 01562 820091 Fax 01562 825845

District	NORTH WORCESTERSHIRE
Trust/Locality	N E W Healthcare
Department	Computer Manager
	Tel 01527 60121 Fax 01527 64764

District	SANDWELL
Trust/Locality	SANDWELL HEALTHCARE
Department	Assistant Information Manager
	Tel 0121 553 7676 Fax 0121 607 3579

District	SHROPSHIRE
Trust/Locality	SHROPSHIRE'S COMMUNITY HEALTH SERVICE
Department	Immunisation Section, Children's Directorate
	Tel 01743 761242 Fax 01743 761601

District	SOLIHULL
Trust/Locality	SOLIHULL HEALTHCARE
Department	Manager - Children's Health Department
	Tel 0121 711 7171 Fax 0121 704 0340

District	SOUTH BIRMINGHAM
Trust/Locality	SOUTHERN BIRMINGHAM COMMUNITY HEALTH
Department	Information Manager
	Tel 0121 627 1627 Fax 0121 472 7288

District	SOUTH STAFFORDSHIRE
Trust/Locality	FIRST COMMUNITY HEALTH
Department	Computer Manager
	Tel 01785 222888 Fax 10785 254432

District	WALSALL
Trust/Locality	WALSALL HEALTH
Department	Information Officer Child Health
	Tel 01922 858708 Fax 01922 685868

District	WARWICKSHIRE
Trust/Locality	WARWICKSHIRE
Department	South Warwickshire Child Health Manager
	Tel 01789 269264 Fax 01789 267799

District	WOLVERHAMPTON
Trust/Locality	WOLVERHAMPTON HEALTH CARE
Department	Child Health Records Manager
	Tel 01902 20281/2/3 Fax 01902 713067

District	WORCESTER
Trust/Locality	WORCESTERSHIRE COMMUNITY HEALTHCARE
Department	Information Officer (CHS)
	Tel 01905 681597 Fax 01905 681596

North West

District	BURY AND ROCHDALE
Trust/Locality	BURY HEALTH CARE
Department	Child Health Department
	Tel 0161 705 3013 Fax 0161 705 3052

District	BURY AND ROCHDALE
Trust/Locality	ROCHDALE HEALTHCARE
Department	Support Services Manager
	Tel 01706 755041 Fax 01706 755035

District	EAST LANCASHIRE
Trust/Locality	BURNLEY, PENDLE AND ROSSENDALE
Department	Burnley Healthcare NHS Trust
	Tel 01282 474768 Fax 01282 474827

District	EAST LANCASHIRE
Trust/Locality	COMMUNICARE
Department	Team Leader, Child Health Department
	Tel 01254 695596 Fax 01254 680038

District	LIVERPOOL
Trust/Locality	NORTH MERSEY COMMUNITY
Department	Community Information Manager
	Tel 0151 250 3000 ext 3221 Fax 0151 228 0486

District	MANCHESTER
Trust/Locality	MANCUNIAN COMMUNITY HEALTH
Department	Child Health Department
	Tel 0161 958 4098 Fax 0161 862 9291

District	MORECAMBE BAY
Trust/Locality	LANCASTER PRIORITY SERVICE
Department	Child Health Unit
	Tel 01524 32392 ext 290/217 Fax 01524 844357

District	MORECAMBE BAY
Trust/Locality	SOUTH CUMBRIA
Department	South Cumbria Community & Mental Health NHS Trust
	Tel 01229 836422 Fax 01229 823224

District	NORTH CHESHIRE
Trust/Locality	COUNTESS OF CHESTER (HALTON)
Department	Information Services Manager
	Tel 01244 364837 Fax 01244 364822

District	NORTH CHESHIRE
Trust/Locality	WARRINGTON COMMUNITY
Department	Administrative Manager
	Tel 01925 405724 Fax 01925 405725

District	NORTH WEST LANCASHIRE
Trust/Locality	BLACKPOOL, WYRE AND FYLDE COMMUNITY
Department	Blackpool Wyre & Fydle Community Health Serv
	Tel 01253 306388 Fax 01253 306394

District	NORTH WEST LANCASHIRE
Trust/Locality	GUILD COMMUNITY HEALTHCARE
Department	Information Officer
	Tel 01772 562656 ext 134 Fax 01772 200220

District	SALFORD AND TRAFFORD
Trust/Locality	SALFORD
Department	Salford Community Healthcare NHS Trust
	Tel 0161 789 5135

District	SALFORD AND TRAFFORD
Trust/Locality	TRAFFORD HEALTHCARE
Department	Child Health Department
	Tel 0161 876 7044/5 Fax 0161 862 9165

District	SEFTON
Trust/Locality	SOUTHPORT AND FORMBY
Department	Child Health Manager
	Tel 01704 547471 ext 3048 Fax 01704 530714

District	SOUTH CHESHIRE
Trust/Locality	CHESTER AND HALTON COMMUNITY
Department	Supervisor - Child Health Section
	Tel 01244 364816 Fax 01244 364822

District	SOUTH CHESHIRE
Trust/Locality	EAST CHESHIRE
Department	Family Services Directorate
	Tel 01625 421000 ext 1784 Fax 01625 663055

District	SOUTH CHESHIRE
Trust/Locality	SOUTH CHESHIRE HEALTH
Department	Systems Administrator
	Tel 01270 610000 Fax 01270 627469

District	SOUTH LANCASHIRE
Trust/Locality	CHORLEY AND SOUTH RIBBLE
Department	Child Health Section
	Tel 01257 245405 Fax 01257 245404

District	SOUTH LANCASHIRE
Trust/Locality	WEST LANCASHIRE HEALTH SERVICES
Department	Community Systems Manager
	Tel 01695 585836 Fax 01695 583028

District	ST HELENS AND KNOWSLEY
Trust/Locality	ST HELENS AND KNOWSLEY COMMUNITY HEALTH
Department	Information Systems Manager
	Tel 01744 33722 ext 7205 Fax 01744 453615

District	STOCKPORT
Trust/Locality	STOCKPORT HEALTH COMMISSION
Department	Information Analyst
	Tel 0161 419 4637 Fax 0161 419 4699 or 5416

District	WEST PENNINE
Trust/Locality	OLDHAM
Department	Directorate Services Manager
	Tel 0161 627 8749 Fax 0161 627 8309

District	WEST PENNINE
Trust/Locality	TAMESIDE AND GLOSSOP
Department	Information Systems Officer
	Tel 0161 331 5117/5287/5293 Fax 0161 331 5007

District	WIGAN AND BOLTON
Trust/Locality	COMMUNITY HEALTHCARE BOLTON
Department	Child Health Department
	Tel 01204 377085 Fax 01204 377078

District	WIGAN AND BOLTON
Trust/Locality	WIGAN AND LEIGH HEALTH SERVICES
Department	Computer Section
	Tel 01942 822661 & 822627/8/9 Fax 01942 822630

District	WIRRAL
Trust/Locality	WIRRAL HEALTHCARE
Department	Service Co-ordinator, Child Health Section
	Tel 0151 604 7317 Fax 0151 604 7310